Living as if nature mattered

D0958520

BILL DEVALL

DEEP ECOLOGY

GEORGE SESSIONS

GIBBS SMITH, PUBLISHER
PEREGRINE SMITH BOOKS
SALT LAKE CITY

Copyright © 1985 by Gibbs M. Smith, Inc.

This is a Peregrine Smith Book
Published by Gibbs Smith, Publisher
P.O. Box 667
Layton, Utah 84041

All rights reserved for all countries, including the right
of translation. No part of this book may be used or reproduced
in any manner whatsoever without written
permission from the publisher.

Book design by M. Clane Graves

Manufactured in the United States of America

Library of Congress Cataloging-in-Publication Data
Devall, Bill, 1938—
Deep ecology.
Bibliography: p.
1. Man—Influence on nature. 2. Environmental
protection. 3. Conservation of natural resources. 4. Human
ecology. 5. Environmental policy.
I. Sessions, George, 1938—
II. Title
GV75.D49 1985   333.7′16   84-14044
ISBN 0-87905-247-3
92 91 90 89   9 8 7 6 5

Dedicated to
Arne Naess
mountaineer, deep ecologist,
mentor, activist, philosopher
and
Gary Snyder
poet, mountaineer,
student of Eastern and Native American traditions,
teacher, reinhabitant of the western slope, Sierra Nevada

TABLE OF CONTENTS

PREFACE

The environmental problems of technocratic-industrial societies are beginning to be seen as manifestations of what some individuals are calling "the continuing environmental crisis." This is coming to be understood as a crisis of character and of culture.

The environmental/ecology social movements of the twentieth century have been one response to the continuing crisis. These movements have addressed some of the problems and have tried to reform some of the laws and agencies which manage the land and to change some of the attitudes of people in these societies. But more than just reform is needed. Many philosophers and theologians are calling for a new ecological philosophy for our time.

We believe, however, that we may not need something new, but need to reawaken something very old, to reawaken our understanding of Earth wisdom. In the broadest sense, we need to accept the invitation to the dance — the dance of unity of humans, plants, animals, the Earth. We need to cultivate an ecological consciousness. And we believe that a way out of our present predicament may be simpler than many people realize.

Responding to the environmental crisis, the themes in *Deep Ecology* alternate between personal, individual options and public policy and collective options. On the personal level, we encourage introspection, purification and harmony, and a dancing celebration or affirmation of all being. On the level of intellectual, historical analysis, the book offers an examination of the dominant worldview in our society, which has led directly to the continuing crisis of culture. We then present an ecological, philosophical, spiritual approach for dealing with the crisis.

On the level of public or community policies, we examine various conventional approaches to natural resource management, criticize these approaches and present realistic alternatives. A major thrust of the book is an intellectual examination of the predicament and an attempt to clarify our vital needs as humans.

To readers who feel we live in the best of all possible worlds, with a high standard of living, the book suggests an alternative perspective to consider. To professional philosophers, resource managers and politicians who deal with ideas, abstractions, ethical theory, economics and politics, the book suggests some of the limitations, in our view, of the dominant approach to public policy. To the reader seeking a more authentic existence and integrity of character, the book offers a theory of direct action which can help develop maturity.

In structure, the book begins with a chapter on possible scenarios for the environmental/ecology movement during the next several decades. We suggest an approach based on asking deeper questions and on cultivating ecological consciousness. In chapter two we discuss the minority tradition of culture and community and specific types of direct action which individuals can take to further serve their own vital needs while serving the needs of the larger community of other humans, plants, animals, and the Earth. Chapter three summarizes the dominant worldview and its critics. In chapter four we discuss the reformist response to the dominant worldview, in both philosophy and reform politics.

Chapter five presents the basic intuitions, ultimate norms, and principles of deep ecology. In chapter six, various sources of deep ecological insights and philosophical principles are introduced. Chapter seven discusses the vital need humans have for wilderness and the public policy decisions now affecting the remaining wild places of the Earth.

In chapter eight we confront the real problems of managing natural resources in technocratic-industrial societies and suggest some proposals for management from a deep ecology perspective. The importance of ecotopian visions is presented in chapter nine along with a review of several ecotopian statements by prominent writers.

Chapter ten presents a theory of taking direct action to further the development of maturity based on theories of psycho-social development. The final chapter returns to the theme of direct action, and discusses ecological resisting—the affirmation of life based on deep ecological insights and principles.

Deep Ecology is an invitation to thinking, and presents challenging questions and dilemmas. To help in developing personal insights into deep ecology, brief writings from many authors have been included. These stimulating insights, perceptions, and debates can be read independent of the text. We encourage the reader to read the book creatively by bridging the ideas in the boxed writings and the text.

Taken in its entirety, the increase in mankind's strength has brought about a decisive, many-sided shift in the balance of strength between man and the earth. Nature, once a harsh and feared master, now lies in subjection, and needs protection against man's powers. Yet because man, no matter what intellectual and technical heights he may scale, remains embedded in nature, the balance has shifted against him, too, and the threat that he poses to the earth is a threat to him as well.
—Jonathan Schell, The Fate of the Earth *(1982)*

CANDLES IN BABYLON

Through the midnight streets of Babylon
between the steel towers of their arsenals,
between the torture castles with no windows,
we race by barefoot, holding tight
our candles, trying to shield
the shivering flames, crying
"Sleepers Awake!"
                    hoping
the rhyme's promise was true,
that we may return
from this place of terror
home to a calm dawn and
the work we had just begun.

—*Denise Levertov,* Candles in Babylon

CHAPTER 1

•

NOTHING CAN BE DONE, EVERYTHING IS POSSIBLE

We need nature to be fully alive: air, food, warmth, spiritual. . . . We live as if nature is only needed to provide extras: paper, recreation, specialty foods, a job to provide money.
  —*Susan Griffin,* Women and Nature, *1978*

The major problems in the world are the result of the difference between the way nature works and the way man thinks.
  —*Gregory Bateson, Lindisfarn, Long Island, 1976*

I n this first chapter we assume that the environmental/ecology movement has been a response to the awareness by many people that something is drastically wrong, out of balance in our contemporary culture. In the first section, we present several alternative scenarios for the movement. These scenarios will provide a context in which to understand deep ecology. Some of the major themes of deep ecology and of cultivating ecological consciousness are discussed in the second section of the chapter.

I. SCENARIOS FOR THE ENVIRONMENTAL/ECOLOGY MOVEMENT

1. Reform Environmentalism

Environmentalism is frequently seen as the attempt to work only within the confines of conventional political processes of industrialized nations to alleviate or mitigate some of the worst forms of air and water pollution, destruction of indigenous wildlife, and some of the most short-sighted development schemes.

One scenario for the environmental movement is to continue with attempts at reforming some natural resource policies. For example, ecoactivists can appeal administrative decisions to lease massive areas of public domain lands in the United States for mineral development, or oil and gas development. They can comment on draft Environmental Impact Reports; appeal to politicians to protect the scenic values of the nation; and call attention to the massive problems of toxic wastes, air and water pollution, and soil erosion. These political and educational activities call to the need for healthy ecosystems.

However, environmentalism in this scenario tends to be very technical and oriented only to short-term public policy issues of resource allocation. Attempts are made to reform only some of the worst land use practices without challenging, questioning or changing the basic assumptions of economic growth and development. Environmentalists who follow this scenario will easily be labeled as "just another special issues group." In order to play the game of politics, they will be required to compromise on every piece of legislation in which they are interested. [1]

Generally, this business-as-usual scenario builds on legislative achievements such as the National Environmental Policy Act (NEPA) and the Endangered Species Act in the United States, and reform legislation on pollution and other environmental issues enacted in most industrialized nations.

This work is valuable. The building of proposed dams, for example, can be stopped by using economic arguments to show their economic liabilities. However, this approach has certain costs. One perceptive critic of this approach, Peter Berg, directs an organization seeking decentralist, local approaches to environmental problems. He says this approach "is like running a battlefield aid station in a war against a killing machine that operates beyond reach and that shifts its ground after each seeming defeat."[2] Reformist activists often feel trapped in the very political system they criticize. If they don't use the language of resource economists — language which converts ecology into "input-output models," forests into "commodity production systems," and which uses the metaphor of human economy in referring to Nature — then they are labeled as sentimental, irrational, or unrealistic.

Murray Bookchin, author of *The Ecology of Freedom* (1982) and *Post-Scarcity Anarchism* (1970), says the choice is clear. The environmental/ecology movement can "become institutionalized as an appendage of the very system whose structure and methods it professes to oppose," or it can follow the minority tradition. The minority tradition focuses on personal growth within a small community and selects a path to cultivating ecological consciousness while protecting the ecological integrity of the place.[3]

A critique of reform environmental approaches is presented by Peter Berg:

Classic environmentalism has bred a peculiar negative political malaise among its adherents. Alerted to fresh horrors almost daily, they research the extent of each new life-threatening situation, rush to protest it, and campaign exhaustively to prevent a future occurrence. It's a valuable service, of course, but imagine a hospital that consists only of an emergency room. No maternity care, no pediatric clinic, no promising therapy: just mangled trauma cases. Many of them are lost or drag on in wilting protraction, and if a few are saved there are always more than can be handled jamming through the door. Rescuing the environment has become like running a battlefield aid station in a war against a killing machine that operates just beyond reach, and that shifts its ground after each seeming defeat. No one can doubt the moral basis of environmentalism, but the essentially defensive terms of its endless struggle mitigate against ever stopping the slaughter. Environmentalists

3

have found themselves in the position of knowing how bad things are but are only capable of making a deal.

Why hasn't there been a more positive political approach to valuing the earth and reverencing life? One reason is that shocked bewilderment at the massive failures of Late Industrial society are mounting. Our optimistic attempts to carry out beneficial activities and our deliberate hope for the future seem always subject to instant miniaturization by the next Late Industrial avalanche.

████████████████

Murray Bookchin, in an open letter to the ecology movement published on Earth Day, 1980, was explicitly critical of the move toward professionalizing the environmental movement. Bookchin concludes:

It is necessary, I believe, for everyone in the ecology movement to make a crucial decision; will the eighties retain the visionary concept of an ecological future based on a libertarian (anarchist) commitment to decentralization, alternative technology and a libertarian practice based on affinity groups, direct democracy, and direct action? Or will the decade be marked by a dismal retreat into ideological obscurantism and a "mainstream politics" that acquires "power" and "effectiveness" by following the very "stream" it should be seeking to divert? Will it pursue fictitious "mass constituencies" by imitating the very forms of mass manipulation, mass media, mass culture it is committed to oppose? These two directions cannot be reconciled. Our use of "media," mobilizations, and actions must appeal to mind and to spirit, not to conditioned reflexes and shock tactics that leave no room for reason and humanity. In any case, the choice must be made now before the ecology movement becomes institutionalized into a mere appendage of the very system whose structure and methods it professes to oppose. It must be made consciously and decisively—or the century itself, and not only the decade, will be lost to us forever.

████████████████

2. Tactics of the "New Right" or "Moral Majority"

A second scenario for the environmental movement would be to copy the political tactics of the New Right or Moral Majority. The technology of professionally managed political campaigns, both for issues and candidates for political office, has developed into a sophisticated combination of what twentieth-century British writer George Orwell called "newspeak" and "targeting" segments of the mass public for direct mailing appeals, television and radio advertisements, and promotions playing on the fears, insecurities and the paranoid aspect of the American character. In an anomic society where the only goal is winning, these campaigns can create momentum to gain political power.

Some environmental groups are attempting to form a bloc of environmental voters through political education campaigns. The League of Conservation Voters, the Sierra Club, and the Political Action Committees (PACs) of Friends of the Earth and other groups are explicitly directed to countering the PACs of corporations.

But even though surveys and polls indicate that public opinion in the United States in the 1980s is still strongly in favor of clear air and clean water acts and against opening up wilderness areas for mineral, oil and gas explorations, public opinion is fickle, shallow, and susceptible to manipulation. While deep ecology is explicitly critical of many elements of the modern perspective, some supporters of the movement argue that it is sometimes tactically wise to use the themes of nationalism or energy security to win political campaigns.

However, if the environmental movement moves toward even more professionally run political campaigns and slick advertisements, it could further centralize the leadership of the movement and make it harder for small groups of "radical amateurs" to play meaningful roles in revitalizing the movement or in leading campaigns. Professional leadership in centralized organizations could cut at the roots of volunteerism and could reinforce the trend toward ruling organizations by experts and bureaucracy, and the trend to mass politics.

3. New Age/Aquarian Conspiracy

A third scenario would be that the environmental/ecology movement would be coopted and incorporated into the New Age/Aquarian Conspiracy, which views the Earth as primarily a resource for human use. The popularity of Jesuit scholar Pierre Teilhard de Chardin and technologist R. Buckminster Fuller is testimony to the continuing appeal of anthropocentrism (human-centeredness) and to a teleological vision of humans as God's chosen instruments of progress and evolution.

Teilhard is criticized in our discussion of the management of natural resources, but he is an inspiration for many people in industries such as genetic engineering, computer technology, and mass media. California's famed Silicon Valley south of San Francisco has thousands of liberal, articulate, upscale, youngish professionals who are "turned on" by high technology, visions of human colonies on Mars, space travel, and humans as copilots of "spaceship Earth."

5

Ecologist James Lovelock, in *Gaia: A New Look at Life on Earth,* states the New Age vision: "In a Gaian world our species with its technology is simply an inevitable part of the natural scene. Yet our relationship with our technology releases ever-increasing amounts of energy and provides us with a similarly increasing capacity to channel and process information. Cybernetics tells us that we might safely pass through these turbulent times if our skills in handling information develop faster than our capacity to produce more energy. In other words, if we can always control the genie we have let out of the bottle."[4]

Many New Age thinkers conclude that humans' role as partner with Earth's natural processes "need not be vile" but coequal.[5] The ultimate New Age fantasy is the metaphor of the spaceship Earth. Humans from spaceship Earth will move to totally man-made and manipulated spaceships carrying colonies of humans to Mars, and the expert—the technologist—will be the hero.

4. Revised Libertarian

A fourth scenario for the environmental/ecology movement would be a libertarian approach. Resource economist John Baden and biologist Garrett Hardin have worked for some years defining what they call a "rational foundation" for conservation. For them, this means clarifying property "rights" to overcome the "tragedy of the commons." The carrying capacity of a parcel of land is the amount of crops, sheep, timber, etc., that can be grown on an area for many generations without diminishing the capacity of the area to yield more natural resources. When people hold land in common, each seeks to maximize short-term gain at the expense of the commons.

If environmental groups, such as the Sierra Club, Audubon Society, and Nature Conservancy, want to hold lands as property and use those parcels for preservation of biological diversity, then that is their choice. They will undoubtedly forego developing the lands for increased income, such as building shopping centers. But they would be legitimate property owners making "rational decisions" based on their subjective value preferences.

As an example of this strategy, Baden frequently cites the Audubon Society, which owns lands in several areas of the United States as "wildlife sanctuaries," but allows oil and gas extraction and cattle grazing on some of the lands in order to generate income for the organization.

In preserving wilderness on public lands, Baden asserts "the self-interest of wilderness advocates imposes a cost on the rest of society.

On the other hand, if miners prevail, they frequently destroy wilderness values, again without compensation to the rest of society." Baden continues: "What we propose is that lands presently included in the wilderness system be put into the hands of qualified environmental groups such as the Sierra Club, the Audubon Society, and the Wilderness Society in exchange for (1) their agreement that in the future no wilderness areas be established by political fiat and (2) either their development of the acquired land (according to their own rules) or their clean-up of an environmentally degraded area be equal in size to the wilderness area acquired. The result would be that these areas, vast portions of which are currently closed to all mining activity, would be managed by groups with the expertise to weigh potential damage to the ecology against potential profits."[6]

The strategy is appealing to the environmental movement during an era of renewed devotion in America to the free enterprise system and an era in which government regulations are criticized as interfering with private property rights. The danger for environmental groups in accepting Baden's proposal is that the larger issues of deep ecology are not addressed. The Revisionist Libertarian approach would tie environmental groups more firmly to the existing version of what we call the Resource Conservation and Development ideology, which is human-centered.

II. DEEP ECOLOGY AND CULTIVATING ECOLOGICAL CONSCIOUSNESS

In contrast to the preceding scenarios, deep ecology presents a powerful alternative.

Deep ecology is emerging as a way of developing a new balance and harmony between individuals, communities and all of Nature. It can potentially satisfy our deepest yearnings: faith and trust in our most basic intuitions; courage to take direct action; joyous confidence to dance with the sensuous harmonies discovered through spontaneous, playful intercourse with the rhythms of our bodies, the rhythms of flowing water, changes in the weather and seasons, and the overall processes of life on Earth. We invite you to explore the vision that deep ecology offers.

The deep ecology movement involves working on ourselves, what poet-philosopher Gary Snyder calls "the real work," the work of really looking at ourselves, of becoming more real.

This is the work we call cultivating ecological consciousness. This process involves becoming more aware of the actuality of rocks, wolves, trees, and rivers — the cultivation of the insight that everything is connected. Cultivating ecological consciousness is a process of learning to appreciate silence and solitude and rediscovering how to listen. It is learning how to be more receptive, trusting, holistic in perception, and is grounded in a vision of nonexploitive science and technology.

This process involves being honest with ourselves and seeking clarity in our intuitions, then acting from clear principles. It results in taking charge of our actions, taking responsibility, practicing self-discipline and working honestly within our community. It is simple but not easy work. Henry David Thoreau, nineteenth-century naturalist and writer, admonishes us, "Let your life be a friction against the machine."

Cultivating ecological consciousness is correlated with the cultivation of conscience. Cultural historian Theodore Roszak suggests in *Person/Planet* (1978), "Conscience and consciousness, how instructive the overlapping similarity of those two words is. From the new consciousness we are gaining of ourselves as persons perhaps we will yet create a new conscience, one whose ethical sensitivity is at least tuned to a significant good, a significant evil."[7]

We believe that humans have a vital need to cultivate ecological consciousness and that this need is related to the needs of the planet. At the same time, humans need direct contact with untrammeled wilderness, places undomesticated for narrow human purposes.

Many people sense the needs of the planet and the need for wilderness preservation. But they often feel depressed or angry, impotent and under stress. They feel they must rely on "the other guy," the "experts." Even in the environmental movement, many people feel that only the professional staff of these organizations can make decisions because they are experts on some technical scientific matters or experts on the complex, convoluted political process. But we need not be technical experts in order to cultivate ecological consciousness. Cultivating ecological consciousness, as Thoreau said, requires that "we front up to the facts and determine to live our lives deliberately, or not at all." We believe that people can clarify their own intuitions, and act from deep principles.

Deep ecology is a process of ever-deeper questioning of ourselves, the assumptions of the dominant worldview in our culture, and the meaning and truth of our reality. We cannot change consciousness by only listening to others, we must involve ourselves. We must take direct action.

Organizations which work only in a conventional way on political issues and only in conventional politics will more or less unavoidably neglect the deepest philosophical-spiritual issues. But late industrial society is at a turning point, and the social and personal changes which are necessary may be aided by the flow of history.

One hopeful political movement with deep ecology as a base is the West German Green political party. They have as their slogan, "We are neither left nor right, we are in front." Green politics in West Germany, and to some extent in Great Britain, Belgium and Australia in the 1980s, goes beyond the conventional, liberal definition of a party, combining personal work (that is, work on clarifying one's own character) and political activism. In West Germany, especially, the Green party has sought a coalition with antinuclear weapons protesters, feminists, human rights advocates and environmentalists concerned with acid rain and other pollution in Europe.[8] Ecology is the first pillar of the German Greens' platform.

In Australia, the Greens are the most important political movement in the nation. In national and state elections in the early 1980s they were a deciding factor in electing Labor Party governments dedicated to some of the planks of the Green platform, including preserving wilderness national parks and rain forests.

The Greens present a promising political strategy because they encourage the cultivation of personal ecological consciousness as well as address issues of public policy. If the Greens propogate the biocentric perspective — the inherent worth of other species besides humans — then they can help change the current view which says we should use Nature only to serve narrow human interests. (The Green political platform is presented in more detail in chapter two.)

Alan Watts, who worked diligently to bring Eastern traditions to Western minds, used a very ancient image for this process, "invitation to the dance," and suggests that "the ways of liberation make it very clear that life is not going anywhere, because it is already *there*. In other words, it is playing, and those who do not play with it, have simply missed the point."[9]

Watts draws upon the Taoist sages, Sufi stories, zen, and the psychology of Carl Jung to demonstrate the process of spontaneous understanding. It is recognized, however, that to say "you must be spontaneous" is to continue the massive double-bind that grips consciousness in the modern ethos.

9

The trick is to trick ourselves into reenchantment. As Watts says, "In the life of spontaneity, human consciousness shifts from the attitude of strained, willful attention to *koan*, the attitude of open attention or contemplation." This is a key element in developing ecological consciousness. This attitude forms the basis of a more "feminine" and receptive approach to love, an attitude which for that very reason is more considerate of women. [10]

In some Eastern traditions, the student is presented with a *koan*, a simple story or statement which may sound paradoxical or nonsensical on the surface but as the student turns and turns it in his or her mind, authentic understanding emerges. This direct action of turning and turning, seeing from different perspectives and from different depths, is required for the cultivation of consciousness. The *koan*-like phrase for deep ecology, suggested by prominent Norwegian philosopher Arne Naess, is: "simple in means, rich in ends."

Cultivating ecological consciousness based on this phrase requires the interior work of which we have been speaking, but also a radically different tempo of external actions, at least radically different from that experienced by millions and millions of people living "life in the fast lane" in contemporary metropolises. As Theodore Roszak concludes, "Things move slower; they stabilize at a simpler level. But none of this is experienced as a loss or a sacrifice. Instead, it is seen as a liberation from waste and busywork, from excessive appetite and anxious competition that allows one to get on with the essential business of life, which is to work out one's salvation with diligence." [11]

But I believe nevertheless that you will not have to remain without a solution if you will hold to objects that are similar to those from which my eyes now draw refreshment. If you will cling to Nature, to the simple in Nature, to the little things that hardly anyone sees, and that can so unexpectedly become big and beyond measuring; if you have this love of inconsiderable things and seek quite simply, as one who serves, to win the confidence of what seems poor: then everything will become easier, more coherent and somehow more conciliatory for you, not in your intellect, perhaps, which lags marveling behind, but in your inmost consciousness, waking and cognizance. . . . Be patient toward all that is unsolved in your heart and to try to love the *questions themselves* like locked rooms and like books that are written in a very foreign tongue. Do not now seek the answers, which cannot be given you because you would not be able to live them. And the point is, to live everything. *Live*

the questions now. Perhaps you will then gradually, without noticing it, live along some distant day into the answer.
   — Rainer Maria Rilke, *Letters to a Young Poet* (1963)

Quiet people, those working on the "real work," quite literally turn down the volume of noise in their lives. Gary Snyder suggests that, "The real work is what we really do. And what our lives are. And if we can live the work we have to do, knowing that we are real, and that the world is real, then it becomes right. And that's the real work: to make the world as real as it is and to find ourselves as real as we are within it."[12]

Engaging in this process, Arne Naess concludes, people ". . . will necessarily come to the conclusion that it is not lack of energy consumption that makes them unhappy."[13]

One metaphor for what we are talking about is found in the Eastern Taoist image, the *organic self.* Taoism tells us there is a way of unfolding which is inherent in all things. In the natural social order, people refrain from dominating others. Indeed, the ironic truth is that the more one attempts to control other people and control nonhuman Nature, the more disorder results, and the greater the degree of chaos. For the Taoist, spontaneity is not the opposite of order but identical with it because it flows from the unfolding of the inherent order. Life is not narrow, mean, brutish and destructive. People do not engage in the seemingly inevitable conflict over scarce material goods. People have fewer desires and simple pleasures. In Taoism, the law is not required for justice; rather, the community of persons working for universal self-realization follows the flow of energy.[14]

> *To study the Way is to study the self.*
> *To study the self is to forget the self.*
> *To forget the self is to be enlightened*
> *by all things.*
> *To be enlightened by all*
> *things is to remove the*
> *barriers between one's self*
> *and others.*
>   *— Dōgen*

As with many other Eastern traditions, the Taoist way of life is based on compassion, respect, and love for all things. This compassion arises from self-love, but self as part of the larger *Self,* not egotistical self-love.

11

SONG OF THE TASTE

Eating the living germs of grasses
Eating the ova of large birds

   the fleshy sweetness packed
   around the sperm of swaying trees

The muscles of the flanks and thighs of
       soft-voiced cows
   the bounce in the lamb's leap
   the swish in the ox's tail

Eating roots grown swoll
      inside the soil

Drawing on life of living
   clustered points of light spun
      out of space
hidden in the grape.

Eating each other's seed
      eating
ah, each other.

Kissing the lover in the mouth of bread:
   lip to lip.

     — Gary Snyder in Regarding Wave (1970)

████████████

ON "SONG OF THE TASTE"

The primary ethical teaching of all times and places is "cause no unnecessary harm." The Hindus, Jains, and Buddhists use the Sanskrit term *"ahimsa,"* "non-harming." They commonly interpret this to mean "don't take life" with varying degrees of latitude allowed for special situations. In the Eastern traditions "cause no unnecessary harm" is the precept behind vegetarianism.

Non-vegetarians too try to understand and practice the teaching of "non-harming." People who live entirely by hunting, such as the Eskimo, know that taking life is an act requiring a spirit of gratitude and care, and rigorous mindfulness. They say "all our food is souls." Plants are alive, too. All of nature is a gift-exchange, a potluck banquet, and there is no death that is not somebody's food, no life that is not somebody's death.

Is this a flaw in the universe? A sign of a sullied condition of being? "Nature red in tooth and claw?" Some people read it this way, leading to a disgust with self, with humanity, and with life itself. They are on the wrong fork of the path. Otherworldly philosophies end up doing more damage to the planet (and human psyches) than the existential conditions they seek to transcend.

So again to the beginning. We all take life to live. Weston LaBarre says, "The first religion is to kill god and eat him" or her. The shimmering food-chain, food-web, is the scary, beautiful condition of the biosphere. Non-harming must be understood as an approach to all of living and being, not just a one-dimensional moral injunction. Eating is truly a sacrament.

How to accomplish this? We can start by saying Grace. Grace is the first and last poem, the few words we say to clear our hearts and teach the children and welcome the guest, all at the same time. To say a good grace you must be conscious of what you're doing, not guilt-ridden and evasive. So we look at the nature of eggs, apples, and oxtail ragoût. What we see is plenitude, even excess, a great sexual exuberance. Millions of grains of grass-seed to become flour, millions of codfish fry that will never—and *must* never—grow to maturity: sacrifices to the food-chain. And if we eat meat it is the life, the bounce, the swish, that we eat, let us not deceive ourselves. Americans should know that cows stand up to their hocks in feed-lot manure, waiting to be transported to their table, that virgin forests in the Amazon are clear-cut to make pasture to raise beef for the American market. Even a root in the ground is a marvel of living chemistry, making sugars and flavors from earth, air, water.

Looking closer at this world of one-ness, we see all these beings as of our own flesh, as our children, our lovers. We see ourselves too as an offering to the continuation of life.

This is strong stuff. Such truth is not easy. But hang on: if we eat each other, is it not a giant act of love we live within? Christ's blood and body becomes clear: The bread blesses you, as you bless it.

So at our house we say a Buddhist verse of Grace:

"We venerate the Three Treasures"
(Buddha, Dharma, Sangha)
"And are thankful for this meal
The work of many people
And the sharing of other forms of life."

Anyone can use a grace from their tradition, if they have one, and infuse it with deeper feeling and understanding, or make up their own, from the heart. But saying Grace is not fashionable in much of America now, and often even when said is mechanical and flat, with no sense of the deep chasm that lies under the dining table. My poem "Song of the

13

Taste" is a grace for graces, a model for anyone's thought, verse, song, on "the meal" that the fortunate ones on earth partake of three times a day.
—Gary Snyder (Unpublished, 1983)

━━━━━━━━━

Cultivating ecological consciousness in contemporary societies, however, is a two-edged sword. We must not be misled by our zeal for change so that we are concerned only with the narrow self or ego. If we seek only personal redemption we could become solitary ecological saints among the masses of those we might classify as "sinners" who continue to pollute. Change in persons requires a change in culture and vice versa. We cannot ignore the personal arena nor the social, for our project is to enhance harmony with each other, the planet and ourselves.

The type of community most conducive to this cultivation of ecological consciousness is what we call in this book the minority tradition. In the next chapter we outline some of the major aspects of this tradition.

RECOVERING OUR ROOTS
From Tao Te Ching

Reach for the higher
Desert places of your self
All calm and clear

And see
Now all things rise
To flourish and return,
Each creature coming home
To recover its roots.

Recovering the root
Means just this:
The dynamics of peace—
Being recalled to our common fate
In the kinship of all creation.

Knowing this eternal truth
One sees all things with
Extraordinary clarity —
Eternity's radiant light.

Blind to this truth
Leaders sow the seeds of
Reckless deed and their
Evil fruits.

But when rulers plant
By this constant star
They embrace the world
And serve it fairly,
Guiding the world
On the celestial path,
And pass death's gate
On the everlasting way.

—Translated by Tom Early

CHAPTER 2

•

THE MINORITY TRADITION AND DIRECT ACTION

The notion that man is destined to dominate nature is by no means a universal feature of human culture. If anything, this notion is almost completely alien to the outlook of so-called primitive or preliterate communities. I cannot emphasize too strongly that the concept emerged very gradually from a broader social development: the increasing domination of human by human. Perhaps only by examining the attitudes of certain preliterate peoples can we gauge the extent to which domination shapes the most intimate thoughts and the most minute actions of the individual today.

—*Murray Bookchin,* The Ecology of Freedom (1982)[1]

The ideally nonviolent state will be an ordered anarchy.

—*Gandhi*

The type of community most compatible, in our estimation, with engaging in the "real work" of cultivating ecological consciousness is found in the minority tradition. There is a minority, but persistent tradition in Western politics and social philosophy. It is also a tradition found in many other cultures and historical eras, including Native American cultures, and Eastern traditions including Taoism and some Buddhist communities. In the West, it is found in numerous revolts of people seeking local autonomy from centralized state authority. In the nineteenth and twentieth centuries this tradition erupted in such events as the Paris Commune of 1871 and the numerous utopian communities founded in the United States. In the twentieth century it is seen in the persistence of New England town meeting traditions, in older communities in New York and Chicago and among the anarchists in Spain during the 1930s.

Leading theorists of this tradition in Western thought include Peter Kropotkin *(Mutual Aid)* in the nineteenth century and Murray Bookchin *(Post-Scarcity Anarchism* and *The Ecology of Freedom)* from 1950 on.

In some forms, this tradition is expressed by such diverse individuals as Thomas Jefferson, Henry Thoreau, Walt Whitman, Woody Guthrie and Carl Sandburg, as well as Paul Goodman, and in the novels of Ursula LeGuin and many others.

The central elements of this tradition as contrasted with the elements of the dominant form of community in technocratic-industrial societies are summarized in figure 2-1.

Figure 2-1

Dominant Position	Minority Tradition
Centralized authority	Decentralized; nonhierarchical; democratic
Bureaucratized	Small-scale community
Police	Local autonomy
Individualism (radical subjectivism or "deluxe nihilism")	Self-responsibility
Leadership by holding instruments of violence (such as police)	Leadership by example ("not leading")
Competitive	Helping others; mutual aid; communalism

18

Frequent encouragement to "produce more, consume more"	Simplicity of "wants"
More government regulation	Self-regulation; nonviolent in a "professional" way
Secular authority	Respect spiritual-religious mentors
Churches monopolize religious ritual	Community fully participates in rituals
Tends toward monoply of ideology whether religious or secular	Tolerance of variety of approaches to being (religious experiences)
Nature perceived as "data" or as "natural resources"	More open communication with Nature
Narrow definition of citizenship; all other inhabitants of place are slaves or disenfranchised	Broader definition of community (including animals, plants); intuition of organic wholeness

The minority tradition, as defined in this book, should not be confused with the advocacy of chaos or unrestrained individualism. It does not mean a lack of authority, but a lack of centralized authority relying on large forces of police or military to keep power over restless local communities. Nor does the minority tradition as used in this book mean a lack of control by individuals or a lack of clear thinking. It is not radical subjectivism whereby people claim "that's only your opinion."

The essence of the minority tradition is a self-regulating community. Anthropology provides abundant evidence from primal societies that authority need not be hierarchical and centralized. The "chief" was frequently noncoercive, primarily a ritual ruler and specific in dealing with members of the community.

Pierre Clastres concludes in *Society Against the State* that: "One is confronted, then, by a vast constellation of societies in which the holders of what elsewhere would be called power are actually without power; where the political is determined by a domain beyond coercion and violence, beyond hierarchical subordination; where, in a word, no relation of command-obedience is in force."[2]

Theodore Roszak in *Person/Planet* points to many examples of this persistent tradition in the United States. One is the revival of the household economy with groups of people (not always related by kinship or marriage) engaging in the process of raising some of their own food, practicing some spiritual tradition together, and working on projects such as energy self-reliance and conservation.

Other examples include the existence of trade and bargain, small communal farms, monistic groups, and the continuing attempts to scale down the size of institutions, organizations and industries.

Primal societies (usually called *preliterate* or *primitive* by anthropologists) provide numerous examples of what we call the minority tradition. Stanley Diamond, in his review of the crisis of the Western world in contrast to the balance of primal societies, concluded that small-scale, local communities provided both for the vital needs of the individual and the vital need to sustain the community of humans in Nature.[3]

———

Jack Forbes, using northern California tribes as his reference, points out the critical difference between white invaders and Native Americans:

Native Californians . . . felt themselves to be something other than independent, autonomous individuals. They perceived themselves as being deeply bound together with other people (and with the surrounding non-human forms of life) in a complex interconnected web of life, that is to say, a true community. All creatures and things were . . . brothers and sisters. From this idea came the basic principle of non-exploitation, of respect and reverence for all creatures, a principle extremely hostile to the kind of economic development typical of modern society and destructive of human morals. It is this principle, I suspect, which more than anything else preserved California in its *natural* state for 15,000 years, and it is the steady violation of this principle which, in a century and a half, has brought California to the verge of destruction.[4]

———

Stanley Diamond in *In Search of the Primitive* suggests that primal societies are characterized by individuation, personalism, nominalism, and existentialism. These continuously reinforce each other and they are fully consonant with the social structure.

1. Existentialism is evident in 1) ritual expression of primary needs of the person in nature and society, 2) emphasis on existence rather than essence, 3) the responsibility of the individual to self and society, and 4) the lack of concern for analytic modes of thought.

2. Personalism is revealed in 1) the web of kinship, 2) organic community, and 3) apprehension of consciousness THROUGHOUT SOCIETY AND NATURE.

3. Nominalism is focused in 1) emphasis on concrete particulars and contexts, 2) naming of existents in nature and society, in dream and reality, 3) in the fact that ideas were not typically reified.

4. Individuation is nurtured by 1) full and manifold participation of individuals IN NATURE AND SOCIETY, 2) the intensely personal socialization process through which individual qualities are delineated, and 3) the expression of society in person and person in society.

[In contemporary cultures, Diamond says] Our pathology consists in our dedication to abstractions, to our collectivism, pseudo-individualism, and lack of institutional means for the expression and transcendence of human ambivalence. . . . Our illness springs from the very center of civilization, not from too much knowledge, but from too little wisdom. . . .

In machine-based societies, the machine has incorporated the demands of the civil power or of the market, and the whole life of society, of all classes and grades, must adjust to its rhythms. Time becomes lineal, secularized, "precious," it is reduced to an extensior in space that must be filled up, and sacred time disappears. . . .

Primitive society may be regarded as a system in equilibrium, spinning kaleidoscopically on its axis but at a relatively fixed point. Civilization may be regarded as a system in internal disequilibrium; technology or ideology or social organization are always out of joint with each other — that is what propels the system along a given track. Our sense of movement, of incompleteness, contributes to the idea of progress. Hence, the idea of progress is generic to civilization. And our idea of primitive society as existing in a state of dynamic equilibrium and as expressive of human and natural rhythms is a logical projection of civilized societies and is in opposition to civilization's actual state. . . . The longing for a primitive mode of existence is no mere fantasy or sentimental whim, it is consonant with fundamental human needs.

I. A NATURAL WAY TO ORGANIZE: BIOREGION

In an age in which government agencies and some economists talk of the "world system of economy" and military uses of outer space, it is deeply conservative to turn attention to our bioregions. Our bioregion is the best place to begin cultivating ecological consciousness.

The notion of bioregion is hardly new. Jim Dodge, a sheep rancher living in Western Sonoma County, California, says, "It has been the animating cultural principle through ninety-nine percent of human history and is at least as old as consciousness."[5]

Dodge states that the central element of bioregion is the importance given to natural systems "both as the source of physical nutrition and as the body of metaphors from which our spirits draw sustenance. To understand natural systems is to begin an understanding of the self."

21

A second element of bioregion is self-regulation. As Dodge says, "anarchy doesn't mean out of control; it means out of their control." Local communities inspired by a shared concern for the bioregion, for "letting be" the plants and native animals of that place, can make decisions concerning individual and communal actions which respect the integrity of natural processes in that place. Caring for a place means avoiding exploitation.

"A third element composing the bioregional notion is spirit," Dodge explains. There is no single religious practice for this sense of bioregional spirit. It can be Christian, Buddhist, Native American or others; based on deep ecological insights, it can be expressed in numerous ways.

Jim Dodge and his associates have developed a questionnaire in figure 2-2, "Where You At?"[6] Answering these questions is an excellent way to begin cultivating a sense of place and ecological consciousness.

Figure 2-2

WHERE YOU AT?

What follows is a self-scoring test on basic environmental perception of place. Scoring is done on the honor system, so if you fudge, cheat, or elude, you also get an idea of where you're at. The quiz is culture bound, favoring those people who live in the country over city dwellers, and scores can be adjusted accordingly. Most of the questions, however, are of such a basic nature that undue allowances are not necessary. This test was adapted from the version appearing in *CoEvolution*, no. 23 (Winter, 1981).

1. Trace the water you drink from precipitation to tap.

2. How many days until the moon is full (plus or minus a couple of days)?

3. Describe the soil around your home.

4. What were the primary subsistence techniques of the culture(s) that lived in your area before you?

5. Name five native edible plants in your bioregion and their season(s) of availability.

6. From what direction do winter storms generally come in your region?

7. Where does your garbage go?

8. How long is the growing season where you live?

9. On what day of the year are the shadows the shortest where you live?

10. Name five trees in your area. Are any of them native? If you can't name names, describe them.

22

11. Name five resident and any migratory birds in your area.

12. What is the land use history by humans in your bioregion during the past century?

13. What primary geological event/process influenced the land form where you live?

14. What species have become extinct in your area?

15. What are the major plant associations in your region?

16. From where you are reading this, point north.

17. What spring wildflower is consistently among the first to bloom where you live?

18. What kinds of rocks and minerals are found in your bioregion?

19. Were the stars out last night?

20. Name some beings (nonhuman) which share your place.

21. Do you celebrate the turning of the summer and winter solstice? If so, how do you celebrate?

22. How many people live next door to you? What are their names?

23. How much gasoline do you use a week, on the average?

24. What energy costs you the most money? What kind of energy is it?

25. What developed and potential energy resources are in your area?

26. What plans are there for massive development of energy or mineral resources in your bioregion?

27. What is the largest wilderness area in your bioregion?

In California, the people of the Shasta Nation, Turtle Island, have developed some criteria for practicing bioregional politics. The Shasta Nation is a bioregion encompassing all of northern California and part of southern Oregon from Big Sur on the south to the Rogue River on the north. Their suggestions are presented in figure 2-3.

Figure 2-3

Some Criteria for the Consciousness and Practice of Bioregional Politics

1. What is your definition of the region? Watershed, biotic province, geological history, land-form characteristics, climate zone. Original and potential vegetation, fauna, soils?

2. Who are indigenous peoples, early settlers, their unique inhabitory skills and understandings? What is their present situation in the region?

3. What is the present condition of nature in the region: what has been

destroyed, or lost? Build an inventory of priorities in rebuilding soils and reestablishing certain flora and fauna, in consultation where possible with both scientists and indigenous teachers.

4. What are necessary long-range economics of the area in terms of a high-cost energy future? What would be a sustainable economic base? What sort and how much trade could be done with neighboring areas? What is the probable human carrying capacity of the region?

5. As a new "bioregional nation," what would the probable boundaries be? What sort of government would be wanted, instructed by biotic and local sociological consideration? What steps must be taken to correct injustices to indigenous people and early settlers and to guarantee their proper political and economic role in the nation?

6. What role would this bioregional nation play in relation to its nearest neighbors in culture, politics, trade? What on a planetary scale?

7. What spiritual and social disciplines are required for continued habitation of the region: How must people adapt to live well but also in the company of all other beings who are part of that zone? Lessons from biology and ecology. Lessons from the nature-sensitive philosophies of Hinduism, Buddhism, and Taoism. Lessons especially from the mythologies, songs, stories, and teachings of the indigenous peoples.

———

Even in large cities, a sense of place can be recultivated. For example, Nancy Morita's project in San Francisco, "Wild in the City," sponsored by Planet Drum, is attempting to uncover information on the geology, native plants, animals and land forms buried under the mass of concrete that forms the modern image of the city. And Malcolm Margolin's *The Ohlone Way: Indian Life in the San Francisco-Monterey Bay Area* (1978) has helped thousands of readers see the complex ecosystem of San Francisco Bay in the new, but very old, way of hunter-gatherers.

Local bioregional magazines are now published in many parts of North America, but better still, you can start your own magazine by drawing from your knowledge and the wisdom of "old timers" in your bioregion.

II. SUGGESTIONS FOR PERSONAL DIRECT ACTION

In the concluding section of this chapter we suggest some specific types of direct action. Some are directed to the process of cultivating ecological consciousness, others are actions within the political arena,

24

working in organizations promoting wise use of natural resources or preservation of habitat for plants and animals.

Byron Kennard, whose book on the zen of social activism, *Nothing Can Be Done, Everything Is Possible* (1982), inspired the title of chapter one, suggests that many of our actions can be celebrations and affirmations. Earth Day 1970, for example, was a "happening, that even many politicians felt obligated to engage in their busy schedules."[7] Earth Day brought together in many cities over 100,000 people to affirm their hope for the maintenance of Earth's integrity.

A simple celebration is to express oneself artistically through painting, writing poems, etc., in a relatively untrammeled landscape or by a stream (perhaps polluted but still flowing) in one's neighborhood. Reading the poetry of some of the poets of place, including Gary Snyder and Robinson Jeffers, to a group of friends can revive the oral tradition.

Certain forms of yoga and breathing exercises, nonegotistical mountain climbing, and other integrative activities are also aspects of direct action.

SMOKEY THE BEAR SUTRA

Once in the Jurassic, about 150 million years ago, the Great Sun Buddha in this corner of the Infinite Void gave a great Discourse to all the assembled elements and energies: to the standing beings, the walking beings, the flying beings, and the sitting beings — even grasses, to the number of thirteen billion, each one born from a seed, were assembled there: a Discourse concerning Enlightenment on the planet Earth.

"In some future time, there will be a continent called America. It will have great centers of power called such as Pyramid Lake, Walden Pond, Mt. Rainier, Big Sur, Everglades, and so forth; and powerful nerves and channels such as Columbia River, Mississippi River, and Grand Canyon. The human race in that era will get into troubles all over its head, and practically wreck everything in spite of its own strong intelligent Buddha-nature."

"The twisting strata of the great mountains and the pulsings of great volcanoes are my love burning deep in the earth. My obstinate compassion is schist and basalt and granite, to be mountains, to bring down the rain. In that future American Era I shall enter a new form: to cure the world of loveless knowledge that seeks with blind hunger; and mindless rage eating food that will not fill it."

And he showed himself in his true form of
SMOKEY THE BEAR.

A handsome smokey-colored brown bear standing on his hind legs, showing that he is aroused and watchful.

25

Bearing in his right paw the Shovel that digs to the truth beneath appearances; cuts the roots of useless attachments, and flings damp sand on the fires of greed and war;

His left paw in the Mudra of Comradely Display—indicating that all creatures have the full right to live to their limits and that deer, rabbits, chipmunks, snakes, dandelions, and lizards all grow in the realm of the Dharma;

Wearing the blue work overalls symbolic of slaves and laborers, the countless men oppressed by a civilization that claims to save but only destroys;

Wearing the broad-brimmed hat of the West, symbolic of the forces that guard the Wilderness, which is the Natural State of the Dharma and the True Path of man on earth; all true paths lead through mountains—

With a halo of smoke and flame behind, the forest fires of the kali-yuga, fires caused by the stupidity of those who think things can be gained and lost whereas in truth all is contained vast and free in the Blue Sky and Green Earth of One Mind;

Round-bellied to show his kind nature and that the great earth has food enough for everyone who loves her and trusts her;

Trampling underfoot wasteful freeways and needless suburbs; smashing the worms of capitalism and totalitarianism;

Indicating the Task: his followers, becoming free of cars, houses, canned food, universities, and shoes, master the Three Mysteries of their own Body, Speech and Mind; and fearlessly chop down the rotten trees and prune out the sick limbs of this country America and then burn the leftover trash.

Wrathful but Calm, Austere but Comic, Smokey the Bear will Illuminate those who would help him; but for those who would hinder or slander him,

HE WILL PUT THEM OUT.

Thus his great Mantra:

Namah samanta vajranam chanda maharoshana

Sphataya hum traka ham mam

"I DEDICATE MYSELF TO THE UNIVERSAL DIAMOND BE THIS RAGING FURY DESTROYED"

And he will protect those who love woods and rivers, Gods and animals, hobos and madmen, prisoners and sick people, musicians, playful women, and hopeful children;

And if anyone is threatened by advertising, air pollution, or the police, they should chant SMOKEY THE BEAR'S WAR SPELL:

DROWN THEIR BUTTS

CRUSH THEIR BUTTS

DROWN THEIR BUTTS

CRUSH THEIR BUTTS

And SMOKEY THE BEAR will surely appear to put the enemy out with his vajra-shovel.

Now those who recite this Sutra and then try to put it in practice will accumulate merit as countless as the sands of Arizona and Nevada,

Will help save the planet Earth from total oil slick,
Will enter the age of harmony of man and nature,
Will win the tender love and caresses of men, women, and
beasts
Will always have ripe blackberries to eat and a sunny spot
under a pine tree to sit at,
AND IN THE END WILL WIN HIGHEST PERFECT
ENLIGHTENMENT.
thus have we heard.
—Gary Snyder (1969)

A deeply conservative approach to direct action is the revival of Earth-bonding rituals, celebrating specific places. One function of ritual is to release energy, which we see in contemporary culture in such events as football games and rock music concerts. But these events are not harnessed to the other functions of ritual. On making a commitment to a ritual, a participant is enabled to *purify* in the oldest sense of the word, of clearing away anger and focusing on action.

Dolores LaChapelle, author of "Ritual Is Essential" (in appendix F of this book), *Earth Wisdom* (1978) and *Earth Festivals* (1976), provides an example of this type of direct action, which she uses at her Way of the Mountain Center at Silverton, Colorado (figure 2-4). This example is derived from the Taoist tradition, but such Earth rituals could be revived or derived from Christian and other traditions.

Figure 2-4

AUTUMN EQUINOX TAOIST CELEBRATION

Way of the Mountain Center, Silverton, Colorado

We learn from the inter-relationships of sky/rock/water/trees in the same manner as the ancient Taoist masters learned. Taoism is not a religion but a "way of looking" which allows us to step back into the flow of the universe. Taoism developed out of the Warring States period in China when certain "intellectuals" chose not to stay at the courts of the warring feudal lords but to withdraw into the mountains to meditate on the Order of Nature. They felt that human nature could never be brought into order until there was some understanding of the way of Nature because human society was only a small pattern within the whole of Nature.

We, too, can make the same discovery as the Taoist master:

"I did not *find* but suddenly realised that I had never lost the Way. Those crimson dawn clouds, that shining noonday light, the procession of the seasons, the waxing and waning of the moon—these are not majestic functions or auspicious symbols of what lies behind. They *are* the Tao."

We do as traditional peoples the world over have always done— ritually circle our sacred mountain. Each day we go out to view the sacred mountain from a different aspect, thus experiencing the yin and yang of the universe.

First day

* From a sunny south (yang) setting we become acquainted with the north (yin) face of our sacred mountain.

* We begin learning a short form of Tai Chi.

* Full moon autumn equinox ceremony.

Second day

"Who can break the snares of the world
And sit with me among the white clouds?"

* Hike up our "dragon mountain" to view natural bonsai trees and a hanging waterfall.

* Tai Chi on the "dragon mountain" while viewing the western face of the sacred mountain.

* Setting sun ceremony.

Third day

"The morning sun pops from the jaws of blue peaks;
Bright clouds are washed in green pond.
Who ever thought I would leave the dust world
And come bounding up the southern slope of Cold Mt."

* Hike up the third waterfall—site of a tea ceremony with the waterfall as "honored guest."

* View the sacred mountain's southern (yang) side from our northerly (yin) valley.

* Tai Chi.

Fourth day

* All day in the shimmering, golden aspen, followed by a ritual meal.

Some lifestyles contribute more to cultivating ecological conscious-ness than do others. *Voluntary simplicity* is a label for lifestyles that promote personhood and self-realization. Duane Elgin, in *Voluntary Simplicity,* provides many practical examples of outward simplicity and

inward richness. He shows how we can distinguish between *wants* —
encouraged by mass-media advertising and the demands of our society that we "consume more" in order to keep the economy growing —
and real, vital *needs*. [8] At an elementary level, he suggests criteria that
touch on the issue of balanced consumption:

1. Does what I own or buy promote activity, self-reliance, and
involvement, or does it induce passivity and dependence?

2. Are my consumption patterns basically satisfying or do I buy
much that serves no real need?

3. How tied is my present job and lifestyle to installment payments,
maintenance and repair costs, and the expectations of others?

4. Do I consider the impact of my consumption patterns on other
people and on the Earth?

Another example of personal direct action is aikido, a practice
developed in Japan by Morihei Uyeshiba, which helps integrate body
and mind. *Ai* means harmony or coordination; *ki,* spirit or energy;
do, the way or process of practicing. The authors of a major book
on aikido conclude that all people, of whatever religious or philosophical belief, can benefit from practicing aikido: "The improved physi-
cal/mental health, the deeper understanding and awareness of the
problems facing every person, the essential unity and identification
of all persons, their integration with and necessity to one another, as
well as a sense of 'belonging' to their times and their world — this is
the potential that the theory and practice of the art of aikido can offer
all persons, wherever they may be." [9]

III. DIRECT ACTION IN POLITICAL CONTEXTS

Besides personal actions, working in our own households, on wilderness trips with fellow seekers, and in our own lifestyles, many people
work through and with reformist environmental organizations. We can
change the conventional political process by using it for deeper
purposes.

Advocates of deep ecology can work on large wilderness proposals,
wilderness preservation on private lands, and public policy on pollution and land use. The best environmental reform can be encouraged
by acting from the deep ecology principles discussed in chapter five.

1. Reform Legislation

In the United States, the National Environmental Policy Act of 1969
and various state acts, such as the California Environmental Quality

Act of 1970, provide requirements for legal environmental assessment. The Wilderness Act of 1964 provides a framework for legally designated wilderness. Environmental Impact Statements are available to the public for review and comment.

Many environmental groups have worked diligently to expose the hazards of nuclear wastes, pesticides, herbicides, and a variety of toxic wastes and have worked to implement regulations for forest practices, water and air quality, and range management.

Supporters of the deep ecology movement can strongly support enforcement of existing reform legislation and use of criminal sanctions against polluters. In Los Angeles, for example, an assistant attorney asked for jail sentences for corporate executives of polluting firms. Ira Reiner, commenting on his decision to bring criminal charges against corporate executives of polluting firms, said, "A burglar goes to jail, and if he only does ninety to a hundred days, that's a vacation for him. But the top executive officer of a business doesn't expect to go to the slammer. It puts the fear of God in them."[10]

Traffickers in prohibited importation of wildlife, poachers, and eagle killers have been successfully prosecuted. More will be prosecuted if citizens demand law and order for reform environmental laws as much as they do for crimes against persons.

Supporting large wilderness proposals is one of the most vital activities for interim protection of the biosphere. The tropical rain forests of Africa, Asia, Central and South America, Australia, and Oceania are threatened by social and economic factors. We strongly urge zoning the remaining world rain forests as wilderness where only small populations of humans can live engaged in nonexploitive ways, and where large-scale clear-cutting for timber, oil and mineral development, and conversion of forests to grazing lands is forbidden.

The entire continent of Antarctica should be zoned as wilderness. In the United States, tens of millions of acres should be zoned wilderness with rigid restrictions on industrial developments. In the United States, as well as in Africa, park police guard national parks and reserves from poachers, timber fellers, and vandals. Local populations can protect local wilderness areas with the same sense of caring as they protect public buildings and monuments. Earth First!, a movement developed in 1981 to defend wilderness and biological diversity, has presented feasible and defensible proposals for U.S. Forest Service and Bureau of Land Management areas in Oregon, California, and elsewhere.

Some environmental groups have started "adopt a wilderness or roadless area" programs whereby members visit an area frequently, get to know it intimately, and defend the area before legislative committees and public lands agencies who want to intensively manage the area. Many people cultivate a *sense of place*. For example, Gray Brechin, in the epilogue to the *Mono Lake Handbook,* speaks eloquently of the *spirit* of Mono Lake. The lake is connected to the migrations and reproduction of seagulls and other bird populations, but also to the vast urbanization of southern California through a series of dams and aqueducts. It is connected through time to the Pleistocene Ice Ages, and to the ever-increasing human population and per-capita consumption of natural resources in California. But it is also connected to the ecological consciousness of those who defend its integrity. There are many other places, such as the Colorado Plateau and Maine's Mt. Katahdin, which can bring about a sense of place.

───────

If there are place spirits, Mono has one of the strongest I have ever encountered. It's easy to personify the lake; I sometimes wonder what it thinks as its millions of years of existence come to an abrupt end. I have thought of Mono as an old friend for so many years that it now looks to me like a prone patient being bled to death on an operating table, and I wonder if that great reservoir of experience dreams back to the ground-breakings and upthrust of the Sierra which gave it birth, to the icebergs and volcanic formations which have reflected on its surface in the recent past. Morbidly I wonder if it will stink when its prodigious life finally expires on the bone-white lakebed.

Whether Mono Lake has a consciousness will remain one of its mysteries. But Mono endows its friends with awareness, for we have all had to learn from it. Mono has taught us to see the world anew, to accept and perceive beauties we had been unaware of, and to ask questions whose answers may be far from simple or comfortable. On the solitude of its beaches, at dawn and at dusk, we have learned to listen and to watch and to live quietly with ourselves. But mostly, we have learned to live with other beings which we cannot use but whose mere presence enhances our daily existence.

Mono doesn't ask simple questions. It demands an examination of the inner and outer worlds which constitute human awareness. And that is why it is the best kind of friend, and that is why we cannot let it die.

— Gray Brechin, *The Mono Lake Handbook*

───────

31

2. Coalitions

Forming coalitions is another form of direct action. The peace movement and environmental/ecology movement share common concerns for public policy on weapons research and the threat of nuclear holocaust. Leaders of the peace movement have faced the psychological problem of nuclear threat and provided constructive suggestions, many of which are summarized in Joanna Rogers Macy's book, *Despair and Personal Power in the Nuclear Age* (1983). Workshops on empowering the individual, and direct action on specific issues can be jointly sponsored by peace groups, women's groups and environmental groups.

The peace movement and antinuclear movement provide excellent examples of engaging in the political process creatively. Use of affinity groups, decision-making by consensus and decentralized authority as exemplified by the Greens in West Germany illustrate that even within contemporary societies there are opportunities for direct action within the minority tradition.

3. Protests

People can engage in direct, nonviolent action in the form of protest. Protesters at the Livermore Atomic Laboratory and Diablo Canyon nuclear reactor, both in California, and the well-documented actions in Tasmania in the early 1980s to blockade the building of a dam provide examples of such creative action.

Other examples of direct action in defense of wilderness are provided by Earth First! In one creative action, Earth Firsters "cracked" the dam at Glen Canyon on the Colorado River as part of a traditional Fourth of July celebration of American wilderness. After a patriotic rally for the American heritage of wilderness, they unrolled a huge black plastic "crack" down the face of the dam in front of a horde of TV cameras.

In other actions, Earth First! blockaded the construction of a road contracted by the U.S. Forest Service to be built on the borders of a major wilderness area in southwestern Oregon. After weeks of blockade, the courts ordered a halt to construction, stating that the U.S. Forest Service had violated the law in attempting to build the road.

In March 1984, Earth First! sponsored a speaking tour in North America by Australian ecoactivist John Seed, who has done much to alert us to the damage currently being done to the world's remaining rain forests by multinational corporations and government agencies. In April 1984, Earth First! coordinated a nationwide day of protest at a leading fast food chain, protesting the importation of beef from Central America raised on lands cleared of rain forest and converted into grasslands.

4. Women's Movement

In some aspects of the women's movement we are taught that social action is not abstract ideological sloganizing and posturing. Social action is personal, caring, individual action in the context of small groups.

The values that have been labeled "feminine" — love, compassion, receptivity, caring, cooperation, listening, patience, nurturing, deep feeling, affirmation, quiet statement — can guide us in our practice of creative direct action.

5. Working in the Christian Tradition

Some Christian groups in Norway encourage priests and ministers to address ecological issues or environmental controversies. Other Christians now recognize the need for a new natural theology for Christianity.

Those Christians who agree with the platform of deep ecology as stated in chapter five can do much to develop ideas within a Christian context, to justify preserving ecological diversity, designating large wilderness areas, limiting the growth of human populations, preserving the world's rain forests, and criticizing the destructive aspects of technology.

In America we still see many preachers arguing that the American government must develop a huge military to "fight godless Communism," but few preachers express deep ecology principles.

John Carmody, a Christian teacher and scholar, in *Ecology and Religion: Toward a New Christian Theology of Nature,* sketches some themes that might be incorporated into such a theology. These, he says, are signposts to a complete theology, but any such formal philosophy begins from "foundational attitudes proper to a converted Christian consciousness aware of today's ecological issues," and the biblical doctrines germane to a contemporary theology of Nature. [11]

Carmody has set the agenda for Christian scholars, theologians, preachers, and laypersons engaged in ecological social action. It is hoped that preachers in all Christian churches will rise to the crisis not with sermons on "the end of the world," but with sermons on the glorious fecundity of God's creation and our responsibility to

33

restrain human population growth, protect wild areas, and develop new bioregional ways of life.

━━━━━━━━

In the face of the spiritual-ecological crisis, some Christians propose an Eleventh Commandment expressed in the spirit of the Scriptures which should be preached in every church of the land:

THE EARTH IS THE LORD'S AND THE FULLNESS THEREOF: THOU SHALL NOT DESPOIL THE EARTH, NOR DESTROY THE LIFE THEREON.

Vincent Rossi, leader of the Eleventh Commandment Fellowship, suggests in this essay some of the personal actions which Christians who accept the Eleventh Commandment might find important for their own lives: [12]

1. Make the Eleventh Commandment the foundation of your personal ethic of the environment.

2. Learn all you can about the ecological crisis so you will be able to make informed choices.

3. Become familiar with the many ecologically appropriate techniques, practices and devices that are being developed. Find ways to use them in your own life.

4. Examine your life. Begin to eliminate habits or activities that are destructive to the environment, no matter how slight. Begin to incorporate in your life activities and practices that are supportive to the environment, no matter how insignificant these may appear.

5. Know that what is healthy for the environment is healthy for you. What is not healthy for the environment, no matter what the short term gains may be, will ultimately threaten your own personal health, and the health of your children.

6. Study the lives and works of great naturalists, such as St. Francis of Assisi, Henry David Thoreau, and John Muir, to begin to appreciate the joy and spiritual fulfillment to be found in attuning yourself with nature.

7. Form environmental action associations, or the like, in order to raise the collective consciousness about the environment and to promote positive environmental action with a spiritual foundation.

Healing the environment must begin in our own personal lives. We must examine our own choices and actions. Do the choices we make each day support the forces that are destructive to the environment? If so, we must commit ourselves to changing our choices, our habits, one by one. Nothing is too small to be overlooked. Everything we do counts, as far as its effect on the environment is concerned. What we eat, what we wear, what we buy, what we do for work or pleasure, everything must be weighed in the environmental balance.

━━━━━━━━

6. Questioning Technology

Questioning technology is a process of direct action that anyone can develop, as a consumer, participating in public meetings, commenting on Environmental Impact Reports, in classrooms, with friends, and in religious groups. It is one of the most serious actions that can be taken in a technocratic society where the assumption that "technology will solve all problems" is so deeply held.

To question technology—as a system or as a specific device such as a certain type of vehicle or a computer—can often arouse hostility, defensiveness, irritation, and resentment in listeners. Anyone who questions technology can be branded a "Luddite" or antimodernist. A person who says "no" to any technological device is often charged as being antiprogressive. Yet it is crucial to question technology, in spite of these criticisms.

We need technology which is compatible with the growth of autonomous, self-determining individuals in nonhierarchical communities. We need principles that will help us escape the trap of technocratic society, where technology is the central institution.

Technology can be criticized and evaluated based on general principles, scale or structure. The following questions can be asked of any technological device or system:

1. Does this technological device serve vital needs?

2. Is this device or system of the sort that can be immediately understood by nonexperts?

3. Does it have a high degree of flexibility and mutability or does it impose a permanent, rigid, irreversible imprint on the lives of citizens?

4. Does this technological device or system foster greater autonomy of local communities or greater dependency on some centralized "authority"?

5. Is this device or system ecologically destructive or conducive to a deep ecology way of life?

6. Does this device or system enhance the individuality of persons or does it lead to bureaucratic hierarchies?

7. Does this device or system encourage people to behave and think like machines?

A fully informed, appropriate technology is a meeting ground of ethics, politics, mechanical understanding and deep ecological consciousness. As Langdon Winner concludes in *Autonomous Technology,* "If one lacks a clear and knowledgeable sense of what means are appropriate to the circumstances at hand, one's choice of means can easily lead to excesses and danger." These means do not involve just narrow utility or efficiency of production or profit in some short-term calculation. Indeed, the narrow emphasis upon efficiency of means drives us away from the larger issues of environmental ethics and individual responsibility for the consequences of our actions. [13]

7. Working in Green Politics

If Green politics is to become a transforming politics, transforming personal consciousness and political systems, it must be something quite different from conventional political parties. Green parties are likely to be based in small affinity groups, with discussions based on platforms focusing on direct action and personal growth.

Two such platforms are presented in figures 2-5 and 2-6. The first is from the Japanese Greens, a group concerned with the task of turning Japanese culture away from the dominant technocratic mode of thinking. The second is from a California-based network of Greens.

Figure 2-5

PLATFORM OF THE JAPANESE GREEN PARTY

It is our opinion that modern civilization has abused the environment beyond the limit of its tolerance and we are facing a disastrous contradiction in all areas of our society, including the political, economic, educational, and scientific.

In order to liberate ourselves from this contradiction, we must harmonize the lives of human beings with the natural environment, and discard materialism, the pursuit of profit, and the idea that human beings are the center of all things.

1. We have seriously reconsidered our present social system, including conventional politics, economics, science, and education, and are determined to work for the establishment of a society based upon new values, in which humans and nature can coexist without the destruction of nature.
2. We will gather people who have realized the same, and establish a new political organization. This organization will not commit the errors of existing systems such as centralization and institutionalism, but will be operated according to democratic principles which are based upon the individual integrity of each member.
3. We will work for the establishment of a naturally governed society which is based upon the principles of the living cosmos, and which transcends anthropocentrism.

—Translated by Rick Davis

Figure 2-6

GREEN POLITICS—POINTS OF UNITY

1. NATURAL PHILOSOPHY. We base our philosophy on a proper understanding of the purposes and workings of nature and do not try to impose an ideology upon it. We seek to transform society based upon this understanding.

2. CONSENSUS DEMOCRACY. We conduct all our meetings according to the principles of consensus democracy, emphasizing unanimous or near-unanimous agreement on all decisions. No representative may make decisions on behalf of the Greens without the approval of the entire membership. We encourage the use of consensus democracy in all social, economic and political institutions.

3. NONVIOLENCE AND FREEDOM. We oppose the threat or use of physical violence to resolve international, civil, political and personal conflicts. We encourage the nonviolent enforcement of all private and public rules and laws. We recognize that a nonviolent society would be a very free society and encourage tolerance of others' views and actions.

4. SOCIAL ECOLOGY. We emphasize the connection of domination and violence toward the environment and toward our fellow humans. We seek a nonviolent society in which the needs of individuals, communities and bioregions are balanced and integrated and in which economic resources are used consciously, democratically and appropriately to further this end.

5. STRATEGY. We will oppose ecologically and socially destructive policies and practices through nonviolent political protest and civil disobedience activities. We will promote alternative projects and institutions consistent with our Green philosophy. We will cooperate in solidarity with all groups in substantial agreement with these points of unity as participants in the international Green movement.

---

8. Global Action

Globally, the *World Conservation Strategy,* written by the International Union for the Conservation of Nature, provides insightful and practical direct action suggestions for conservation of soil, forests, water (both fresh and ocean water), and range lands as well as wildlife habitat of all varieties.

It rests on three major goals:

1. Maintaining essential ecological processes and life-support systems.

37

2. Preserving genetic diversity.

3. Utilizing species and ecosystems sustainably.

The World Charter for Nature, adopted in October 1982 by the United Nations General Assembly, could be used as a framework for constitutional change in nations. Lawyers would have the legal basis upon which to ground cases for habitat preservation if the following General Principles from the World Charter for Nature were included in constitutions:

1. Nature shall be respected and its essential processes shall not be disrupted.

2. The genetic viability on Earth shall not be compromised; the population levels of all life forms, wild and domesticated, must be at least sufficient for their survival, and to this end necessary habitats shall be maintained.

3. All areas, both land and sea, shall be subject to these principles of conservation; special protection shall be given to unique areas, representative samples of all ecosystems and the habitats of rare and endangered species.

4. Ecosystems and organisms, as well as land, marine and atmospheric resources which are utilized by man, shall be managed to achieve and maintain optimum sustainable productivity, but not in such a way as to endanger the integrity of those other ecosystems or species with which they coexist.

5. Nature shall be secured against degradation caused by warfare or other hostile acts.

6. Actions working for nuclear disarmament are essential. [14]

A useful summary of direct action for individuals working within groups is found in G. Tyler Miller's *Living in the Environment* (1982). Miller suggests:

1. You can sensitize yourself to your environment.

2. You can become ecologically informed in all aspects of scientific ecology.

3. You can choose a simpler lifestyle, reducing your energy and matter consumption and waste and pollution production. Recycling is a discipline.

4. You can remember that environment begins in the household economy.

5. You can avoid the extrapolation-to-infinity syndrome as an excuse for not doing anything.

38

6. You can become politically involved on local, regional or national levels in either the best of reform groups or in Green politics.

7. You can do little things: don't litter, be aware of the color of the sky.

8. You can work on the big polluters and big problems through direct action in politics or lobbying, and through environmental education.

9. Don't make people feel guilty. There is plenty to do and no one can do everything.[15]

(In addition, we suggest using the bioregion test.)

We have presented an overview of specific types of direct action which individuals and groups can take to defend ecological diversity and engage in the process of cultivating ecological consciousness. We will present the formal principles of deep ecology after we review the dominant, modern worldview and the reformist response.

> *in the service*
> *of the wilderness*
> *of life*
> *of death*
> *of the Mother's breasts.*
> — Gary Snyder, *from "Tomorrow's*
> *Song" in* Turtle Island *(1974)*

39

CHAPTER 3

·

THE DOMINANT, MODERN WORLDVIEW AND ITS CRITICS

———

(My discoveries) have satisfied me that it is possible to reach knowledge that will be of much utility in this life; and that instead of the speculative philosophy now taught in the schools we can find a practical one, by which, knowing the nature and behavior of fire, water, air, stars, the heavens, and all the other bodies which surround us, as well as we now understand the different skills of our workers, we can employ these entities for all the purposes for which they are suited, and so make ourselves masters and possessors of nature.

—*René Descartes,* Discourse on Method *(1637)*

The awakening of ecological consciousness by increasing numbers of people during the twentieth century gave birth to the reformist political response discussed in the previous chapter and in more detail in chapter four. To more clearly understand the problem, we need to define the dominant worldview, its major assumptions and premises, and then review some of the criticisms which continue to be made of it.

I. THE DOMINANT MODERN WORLDVIEW

A dominant worldview (or social paradigm) is the collection of values, beliefs, habits, and norms which forms the frame of reference for a collectivity of people, such as a nation. According to one writer, "A dominant social paradigm is a mental image of social reality that guides expectations in a society."[1]

A worldview, then, has several elements in thought and action:

1. There are general assumptions about reality, including man's place in Nature.

2. There are general "rules of the game" for approaching problems which are generally agreed upon.

3. Those who subscribe to a given worldview share a definition of the assumptions and goals of their society.

4. There is a definite, underlying confidence among believers in the worldview that solutions to problems exist within the assumptions of the worldview.

5. Practitioners within the worldview present arguments based on the validity of data as rationally explained by experts — be they scientific experts or experts in the philosophy and religious assumptions of the worldview.[2]

There are rarely public debates about the general assumptions of the worldview. Problems that are not soluble are explained away or contradictions are not openly addressed. There may be recurrent attempts to persecute for heresy people who question its basic assumptions. Sometimes the persecution of heretics is quite severe, as illustrated by the thousand-year attempt by the Roman Catholic church to impose its view or orthodoxy on the Christian tradition, as clearly witnessed by the Inquisition.

Drawing from several sources, four basic assumptions of the Western worldview are summarized by sociologists William Catton, Jr. and Riley Dunlap:

1. People are fundamentally different from all other creatures on Earth, over which they have dominion (defined as domination).

2. People are masters of their own destiny; they can choose their goals and learn to do whatever is necessary to achieve them.

3. The world is vast, and thus provides unlimited opportunities for humans.

4. The history of humanity is one of progress; for every problem there is a solution, and thus progress need never cease.[3]

Ecologist David Ehrenfeld provides some corollaries to this last assumption concerning the approach to problems within the worldview:

1. All problems are soluble.

2. All problems are soluble by people.

3. Many problems are soluble by technology.

4. Those problems that are not soluble by technology, or by technology alone, have solutions in the social world (of politics, economics, etc.).

5. When the chips are down, we will apply ourselves and work together for a solution before it is too late.[4]

In this worldview, the Earth is seen primarily, if not exclusively, as a collection of natural resources. Some of these resources are infinite; for those which are limited, substitutes can be created by technological society. There is an overriding faith that human civilization will survive. Humans will continue to dominate Nature because humans are above, superior to or outside the rest of Nature. All of Nature is seen from a human-centered perspective, or anthropocentrism.

In the social sciences, as William Catton demonstrates, this worldview is carried to an extreme position of human-centeredness. Four popular notions dominate the social science perspective:

1. Since humans have a cultural kind of heritage in addition to and distinct from their genetic inheritance, they are quite unlike the earth's other creatures.

2. Culture can vary almost infinitely and can change much more readily than biological traits.

3. Thus, since many human characteristics are socially induced rather than inborn, they can be socially altered, and inconvenient differences can be eliminated.

4. Also, cultural accumulation means that technological and social progress can continue without limit, making all social problems ultimately soluble.[5]

While the dominant worldview has developed in Europe and North America during the past several hundred years, the most articulate expression has been in the United States. Many perceptive commentators have summarized the character and culture of the United States, beginning with Alexis de Tocqueville's classic study in the 1830s, *Democracy in America*. The persistence of many of the aspects of the worldview in America is seen by comparing Tocqueville's assessment with that of social scientist Robin Williams, Jr., published in 1970, the year of Earth Day, when the National Environmental Policy Act became law. [6]

Among the values Williams found as being enduring in this culture was the belief in opportunity for social advancement, a belief that the goal of life was comfort and convenience, a persistent attitude of racism, and a faith in technology and progress. In reviewing the statements of major political leaders, results of public opinion polls and dominant themes in textbooks and other sources, he found no mention of a value in the "quality of the natural environment" nor any statement of the value of maintaining biological diversity or the inherent worth of species other than humans. There was a pervasive sense of individualism and there was little assertion of the value of the community of humans, much less the "land community." He found an overriding value in linking scientific study and technology to exploit and develop some aspect of Nature—energy, minerals, and so forth—to serve the growing economy.

COMPARISON OF WORLDVIEWS

Historian Morris Berman summarizes the worldview of the Middle Ages versus that of the seventeenth century: [7]

Worldview of the Middle Ages

Universe: Geocentric, earth in the center of a series of concentric, crystalline spheres. Universe closed, with God, the Unmoved Mover, as the outermost sphere.

Explanation: In terms of formal and final causes; teleological. Everything but God in process of Becoming; natural place, natural motion.

Motion: Forced or natural, requires a mover.

Matter: Continuous, no vacua.

Time: Cyclical, static.

Nature: Understood via the concrete and the qualitative. Nature is alive, organic; we observe it and make deductions from general principles.

44

Worldview of the Seventeenth Century
Universe: Heliocentric; earth has no special status, planets held in orbit by gravity of the sun. Universe infinite.
Explanation: Strictly in terms of matter and motion, which have no higher purposes. Atomistic in both the material and philosophical sense.
Motion: To be described, not explained, law of inertia.
Matter: Atomic, implying existence of vacua.
Time: Linear, progressive.
Nature: Understood via the abstract and quantitative. Nature is dead, mechanistic, and is known via manipulation (experiment) and mathematical abstraction.

━━━━━━━━━━

There have been extensive attempts by some historians and social scientists to explain the origins and development of the dominant worldview. For some, it derives from Judeo-Christian origins based upon anthropocentric assumptions. For others its driving force is seen in the development of the market economy. Others have explored the impact of the rise of capitalism. There is also a growing body of literature which sees the origins in patriarchical societies based on male-dominated hierarchies. [8]

Sociologist Max Weber described "the disenchantment of the world" as conditioned by the rise of "instrumental rationality." In this perspective, bureaucracy is the social organization most conducive to bringing this instrumental rationality into operation. The primary goal is to use resources efficiently in order to meet planned, purposeful goals.

Our purpose here is not to extensively review the origins and development of the dominant worldview, but to explore, in general, its influence on current societies and on our approach to ultimate reality (metaphysics), to knowledge (epistemology), to being (ontology), to the cosmos (cosmology) and to social organization.

II. THE CONTINUING CRITIQUE OF THE DOMINANT WORLDVIEW

For the last five hundred years, some of the assumptions of the dominant worldview have been questioned and criticized in the West by philosophers, poets, religious spokespeople and others from different philosophical backgrounds. These critics include Thomas Malthus, William Blake, many of the Romantic poets, many in the pastoral-naturalist literary tradition, and thinkers such as seventeenth-century

Dutch philosopher Baruch Spinoza and twentieth-century German philosopher Martin Heidegger. One aspect of this criticism has addressed the prolific use of natural resources by growing human populations.

Malthus, in 1803, presented an argument indicating that human population growth would exponentially outstrip food production, resulting in "general misery," but his warning was ignored by the rising tide of industrial/technological optimism. This warning continues to be articulated in terms of contemporary, sophisticated ecological thinking by William Catton, Jr. Catton applies the ecological concept of *carrying capacity,* the ability of an environment to sustain a given population of a species in the long run, to argue that human population has long ago moved into a dangerous phase of the "boom-bust" cycle of population growth and decline. [9]

American geographer George Perkins Marsh was one of the first Americans to warn that modern man's impact on the environment could result in a rising species extinction rate and possible extinction of humans. The environmental crisis was further articulated by ecologist William Vogt (*Road to Survival,* 1948), anticipating the work of radical ecologists such as Paul Ehrlich in the 1960s.

While the ecologists, geographers and biologists cited above, along with many of their colleagues, focused on the assumptions of progress, other critics focused on the assumption of human domination over Nature. Even in the thirteenth century, Saint Francis of Assisi tried to divert Christianity away from the dominant anthropocentric assumption to an older, more animistic biocentric position. He proposed "a democracy of all God's creatures."

While many modern Western philosophers have been slow in criticizing the dominant modern worldview, one philosopher at the beginning of the twentieth century made a scathing attack on the anthropocentrism of Western philosophy and the dominant version of Christianity. George Santayana's speech, "The Genteel Tradition in American Philosophy," presented at the University of California at Berkeley in 1911, was a historical turning point in the development of the contemporary search for an alternative worldview and an environmental ethic that would not be subjectivist, anthropocentric, and essentially materialistic. [10]

In his speech, Santayana intimated that cultivating ecological consciousness by close, intimate contact with wild Nature would help us discard the baggage of human chauvinistic assumptions:

A Californian whom I had recently the pleasure of meeting observed that if the philosophers had lived among your mountains, their systems would have been different from what they are. Certainly very different from what those systems are which the European genteel tradition has handed down since Socrates; for these systems are egotistical; directly or indirectly they are anthropocentric, and inspired by the conceited notion that man, or human reason, or the human distinction between good and evil, is the center and pivot of the universe. That is what the mountains and the woods should make you at last ashamed to assert.

According to Santayana, while Calvinism saw both man and Nature as sinful and in need of redemption, Transcendentalism, with Ralph Waldo Emerson, saw Nature as "all beauty and commodity." Transcendentalism was a "systematic subjectivism" — a "sham system of Nature." The problem for Santayana was that Western religion and philosophy were failing to provide any restraints on the developing urban-industrial society — the "American Will." If anything, they were providing a justification for the technological domination of Nature. Santayana claimed that only one American writer, Walt Whitman, had fully escaped the genteel tradition and anthropocentrism by extending the democratic principle "to the animals, to inanimate nature, to the cosmos as a whole." Santayana looked forward to a new nonanthropocentric revolution in philosophy — a "noble moral imagination" — of which Whitman was the beginning.

Still alive in California at the time of Santayana's address was the one nonnative American who most fully exemplified this nonanthropocentric "noble moral imagination." John Muir (1838-1914) overcame his Calvinistic upbringing while studying science and Transcendentalism at the University of Wisconsin in the 1860s. Muir walked out of a career as a technological genius as a young man. He developed his nonanthropocentric philosophy while walking one thousand miles from Indiana to the Gulf of Mexico in 1867. For the next ten years, Muir wandered through Yosemite and the High Sierra, studying geology, botany and natural history. He was cultivating his ecological consciousness through direct intuitive *experiencing* of Nature. Muir's development of ecological consciousness has been greatly underrated and misunderstood. Although he has been referred to as mainly a "publicist" for the wilderness preservationist movement, he overcame the subjectivism of Transcendentalism to a much greater extent than did Thoreau. Muir battled against inappropriate water developments and the conversion of forest ecosystems into managed "tree farms."

47

He advocated wilderness protection as a vital necessity for preserving at least some areas where Nature could remain flowing and free.

Technological society not only alienates humans from the rest of Nature but also alienates humans from themselves and from each other. It necessarily promotes destructive values and goals which often destroy the basis for stable viable human communities interacting with the natural world. The technological worldview has as its ultimate vision the total conquest and domination of Nature and spontaneous natural processes — a vision of a "totally artificial environment" remodeled to human specifications and managed by humans *for* humans. Contemporary Christian theologian Harvey Cox spoke for this vision when he looked with approval on the dominance of the city in the future ("the most distinct expression of man's separation from nature") in which "nature in any untrammeled form will exist in sparse lots and only because man allows it."[11] The ultimate value judgment upon which technological society rests — *progress* conceived as the further development and expansion of the artificial environment necessarily at the expense of the natural world — must be looked upon from the ecological perspective as unequivocal *regress*.

In sum, we have provided a sketch of the dominant worldview in the West and some of its critics. Based upon its radical critique of this worldview, the deep ecological perspective leads to an uncompromising stand against the main thrust of modern, technocratic culture.

━━━━━━━

The insight of ecology, to which we return again and again, is the literal *intermingling* of parts in the whole, as biologist Neil Everndon discusses in his essay, "Beyond Ecology":[12]

The really subversive element in Ecology rests not on any of its more sophisticated concepts, but upon its basic premise: interrelatedness. But the genuinely radical nature of that proposition is not generally perceived, even, I think, by ecologists. To the western mind, *interrelatedness* implies a causal connectedness. Things are interrelated if a change in one affects the other. So to say that all things are interrelated simply implies that if we wish to develop our "resources," we must find some technological means to defuse the interaction. The solution to pollution is dilution. But what is actually involved is a genuine *intermingling* of parts of the ecosystem. There are no discrete entities. . . . Ecology undermines not only the growth addict and the chronic developer, but science itself.

━━━━━━━

48

*The heart has its reasons
which reason does not know.*
— *Pascal,* Pensées

CHAPTER 4

•

THE REFORMIST RESPONSE

—————

If we consider all species on Earth, and the rate at which natural environments are being disrupted if not destroyed, it is not unrealistic to suppose that we are losing at least one species per day. By the end of the 1980s we could be losing one species per hour. It is entirely in the cards that by the end of this century, we could lose as many as one million species, and a good many more within the following few decades—until such time as growth in human numbers stabilizes, and until growth in over-consumerist lifestyles changes course.

—Ecologist Norman Myers (1979)

I n the previous chapter we sketched the assumptions of the dominant worldview and some of the challenges from its critics. Now we review some of the reformist responses to these assumptions and the thrust of action which this perspective has generated during the past two hundred years. By *reformist* we mean attempts to address some of the environmental problems in this society without seriously challenging the main contradictions and assumptions of the prevailing worldview.

The first section of this chapter reviews reformist ideas in philosophy. We briefly discuss 1) Resource Conservation and Development; 2) the philosophy of humanism; 3) the animal rights or "animal liberation" movement; and 4) the "limits to growth" response. We suggest that the chief weakness of these positions, from a deep ecology perspective, is that they are ultimately anthropocentric. A more detailed discussion of Resource Conservation and Development ideology is presented in chapter eight.

In the second section of this chapter we briefly review the reformist political response, the gradual awareness, especially in the context of American society during the late nineteenth and twentieth centuries, of the continuing and multiplying problems generated by the dominant worldview. We call this a shift "from conservation to ecology" to indicate a gradual reawakening of ecological consciousness.

I. PHILOSOPHICAL REFORMISM

In these reformist philosophical positions, progress is understood along the lines of the eighteenth- and nineteenth-century Enlightenment thinkers as the cultural development of humans from the primitiveness of gathering/hunting, superstitious religious man, through philosophy and metaphysics, to the scientific-technocratic society considered the zenith of human culture. Philosophy in its traditional Socratic role as a critique of society is no longer thought necessary for the scientific society. There is little awareness of the need for a shift in worldview based upon a metaphysics consistent with ecological interrelatedness.

1. Resource Conservation and Development

A Resource Conservation and Development perspective views Nature as basically a resource for human use and development. The two major contemporary secular theorists for an updated utilitarian conservationist position are John Passmore and Garrett Hardin.

52

Shortly after publishing *Man's Responsibility for Nature,* Passmore dramatically changed his mind and claimed:

We do need a "new metaphysics" which is genuinely not anthropocentric. . . . The working out of such a metaphysics is, in my judgment, the most important task which lies ahead of philosophy . . . the emergence of new moral attitudes to nature is bound up then with the emergence of a more realistic philosophy of nature. This is the only adequate foundation for effective environmental concern. [1]

Garrett Hardin has sophisticated the old conservationist position by calling for more legalistic restraints ("mutual coercion mutually agreed upon") to protect the "commons" from total environmental destruction. And further, as a result of severe overpopulation around the world, he claims that our situation today is similar to that of "lifeboats." To keep the high-consumption energy-intensive urban-industrial system afloat, aid to underdeveloped countries must cease and the people be allowed to starve back to biological carrying capacity while we remain "affluent" by continuing to use their resources on a capitalistic basis. Hardin also argues that there is no alternative to increased management and control of Nature. The great significance of Hardin's writings is that he has carried out to a logical conclusion the inevitable consequences of an anthropocentric, egoistic, exploitive resource approach by humans to the planet and its nonhuman inhabitants. [2]

John Rodman diagnosed the Resource Conservation and Development philosophy as providing a basis for the future generations' argument:

. . . "the criterion of what is best for posterity" became perhaps the major criterion of normative judgment in the Conservationist outlook. Certainly it is with regard to this preoccupation with the good of posterity that the Conservation movement has been most influential; the post-Conservationist forms of ecological consciousness display all the marks of being children of Resource Conservation in this respect. Certainly it is the most powerful of Conservationist appeals." [3]

2. Humanism as a Reformist Perspective

The philosophy of humanism has recently come under sharp attack as promoting an arrogant anthropocentric approach to Nature, and as providing the modern Western secular basis for the vision of a man-controlled artificial environment. Philosopher Pete Gunter claims that:

53

Pragmatism, Marxism, scientific humanism, French positivism, German mechanism: the whole swarm of smug antireligious dogmas emerging in the late eighteenth and nineteenth centuries and by now deeply entrenched in scientific, political, economic, and educational institutions really do not, as they claim, make man a part of nature. *If anything they make nature an extension of and mere raw material for man.*[4]

Theodore Roszak has claimed that, "There are those who believe fervently that the good society may yet be built—if only our humanistic resolve is sufficiently strong. I disagree. Humanism is the finest flower of urban-industrial society; but the odor of alienation yet clings to it and to all culture and public policy that springs from it."[5]

In 1925, George Santayana called John Dewey's pragmatism an extreme subjectivism calculated to justify all the assumptions of American industry and society, and included it within the anthropocentric genteel tradition. Twenty years later, British philosopher Bertrand Russell also pointed to the anthropocentrism of both Dewey and Karl Marx and claimed that their intoxication with the idea of social power over Nature, "however unintentionally, contributes to the increasing danger of vast social disaster."[6]

3. Animal Rights and Animal Liberation

As part of the reformist response, there has recently been a virtual explosion of interest by philosophers in the question of animal rights and animal liberation. Much of this interest was generated by Peter Singer's influential book, *Animal Liberation* (1975), which pointed to the callous way technological society treats nonhumans. Professional philosophers are now actively discussing the moral questions involved in issues such as vegetarianism, vivisection, sport hunting, the inhumane treatment of feed-lot animals, factory hens, confining wild animals in zoos and circuses for the amusement of humans, and the needless and often unspeakable cruelty inflicted on large numbers of animals in the name of science and product-testing.

On the basis of contemporary Western ethical theory, these philosophers argue that other animals besides humans, or at least the more highly evolved conscious ones, have some "rights," or that utilitarianism allows moral significance to those animals capable of suffering or experiencing pain. Deep ecology theorists are also very concerned about many of the issues which the animal liberationists address, but also believe that many of these problems are mainly symptoms of a more deep-seated malaise. Contemporary humanistic ethical theory is ineradicably anthropocentric, designed specifically to deal with the problems of *human* interaction. When the attempt is made to extend this theory to other animals (Moral Extensionism), they are accorded much less moral consideration (less intrinsic worth) than humans.

Under contemporary ethical theory, some beings, thought to have little or no sentience, together with the entire nonliving world, have no moral standing whatsoever. Thus, animal rights theorizing tends to violate the deep ecology insistence on "ecological egalitarianism in principle." As John Rodman remarks, "There is a pecking order in this moral barnyard." Rodman also points out that this theorizing is timid in that no challenge or examination is made of the basic assumptions of the urban/industrial worldview: "The attempt to produce a 'new ethics' by the process of extension perpetuates the basic presuppositions of the conventional modern paradigm; however much it fiddles with the boundaries. . . . [the animal rights movement] while holding out promise of transcending the homocentric perspective of modern culture, subtly fulfills and legitimizes the basic project of modernity—the total conquest of nature by man."[7]

4. The "Limits to Growth" Response

The limits to growth debate is a combination of philosophical and public policy discussion. In philosophy it has focused on debate over the "destiny" of humans. Some argue that more and more humans are desirable on this Earth because humans are the "ultimate resource." More people means more creativity and more opportunity to produce and consume.

The reformist response to the debate has been to amass huge amounts of data on human population, industrialization, resource use interactions and to build models of these interactions. Then, using computer simulation, various scenarios and outcomes of continued human use of resources have been projected.

While Thomas Malthus discussed the consequences of human population growth and food supply in 1803, the most dramatic response to the situation in recent times was the publication of Paul Ehrlich's *The Population Bomb* (1968).

In the early 1970s, the Club of Rome, an organization dedicated to rational planning for the future, publicized Jay Forrester's "world model" and subsequently published several versions.[8] Much of this material was summarized by Gerald Barney in 1980 in *The Global 2000 Report to the President*. Commissioned by President Carter, this book became a best seller in the United States as well as West Germany and Japan.[9] It stimulated debate on the need for much more extensive reforms than environmentalists had envisioned before. In the meantime, numerous voluntary groups have been organized to pursue policy reform, including Zero Population Growth and the "Global 2000 Group."

II. THE REFORMIST POLITICAL RESPONSE

The move to ecological conscience/consciousness has been a slow process for the population as a whole. Until recently, modern people who considered themselves enlightened on the human/Nature relationship have thought of themselves as *conservationists*. Ecologist John Livingston defined conservation as "the care of 'natural resources' and their protection from depletion, waste, and damage, so that they will be readily at hand through perpetuity."[10] John Passmore defined it as the "saving of natural resources for later consumption."[11] Out of the Progressive Movement at the turn of the twentieth century, especially as a result of the influence of politician Gifford Pinchot on Teddy Roosevelt, the modern version of utilitarian Resource Conservation and Development was born. The "wise use" of resources would be achieved through the "rational efficient scientific/technological management" of Nature for the benefit of "the greatest number of humans." Reckless exploitation would cease, and social justice would be achieved.

Pinchot became the first director of the U.S. Forest Service. The rise of the "resource expert" (the scientific manager of Nature) soon followed. Resource management programs were established and expanded rapidly in colleges and universities throughout the world to supply the new demand for scientific foresters, agricultural experts, wildlife experts, range managers, soil scientists, and so on, to industry and to government resource and development agencies. From this point onward most of wild Nature, from forests to wildlife, was to be treated much the same as a domestic field of corn, to be managed and "harvested" by humans.

It is surely no coincidence that humans would also come to be looked upon as a resource to be managed in the best interests of the emerging urban-industrial society. The shift from "people" to "personnel" (and "consumers") to which modern scientific management principles are to be applied for more efficient production of commodities is but the flip side of the mentality and consciousness that sees Nature as but a resource to be managed and manipulated for the benefit of those in power. Indeed, we have programs in our universities to train "leisure management experts" and "wilderness management experts"—experts who are largely in the business of managing people.

The analytical error of contemporary man is that he has not understood in religious terms the meaning of what he has already accomplished scientifically by revealing the world of sensory perceptions. In seeking the ultimate answer to the meaning of existence, that is, reading God's mind, as early scientists considered their work, modern man has foreclosed the possibility of experiencing life in favor of explaining it. Even in explaining the world, however, Western man has misunderstood it.

—Vine Deloria, *God is Red* (1973)[12]

At the same time that resource management ideology was developing as a reformist response to unrestrained and short-sighted treatment of the land, other reformers were focusing on the need to establish institutions which would set aside bits of land and water as recreational space for humans and habitat for other species.

Early in the nineteenth century, some scientists began to understand the connection between urbanization, industrialization, human contamination of air and water and the spread of certain diseases. Physicians and public health professionals agitated for major public investments in water purification systems for cities, protection of the watersheds feeding city water supplies, and for sewage treatment facilities. Debates over proposed technical solutions to perceived public health problems focused on the benefits of clean water and air for human populations.

During the latter half of the nineteenth century, appreciation for scenic, ecological and recreational values of natural landscapes in America had been stimulated by painters, naturalists, biologists and Nature writers. One articulate planner and activist, Frederick Law Olmstead, argued that parks, both in rural areas and very large urban areas, were necessary for the physical and mental health of the masses of citizens. Just as the aristocracy in Europe had their hunting reserves and rural retreats, citizens in a democracy had the right to have access to places for quiet contemplation of the wonders of Nature. Olmstead was instrumental in creating Central Park in New York City before the Civil War and was the first director of what became Yosemite National Park in California in 1864. [13]

In 1872 Congress established the precedent of creating national parks by passing the Yellowstone Park Act. However, Congress failed to resolve what has come to be a most difficult issue: the relation of parks as recreation space for humans and parks as reserves of biological diversity and wild Nature.

The advantage of tourism to economic growth in areas near new parks convinced some railroads and other businesses to support the parks movement. By 1916 when Congress passed the National Parks Act, creating a new agency to manage the parks, the National Park Service, the institution was firmly established. Following 1916, successful campaigns by conservationists led to the creation of many more national parks, including Olympic, Grand Canyon, Grand Teton, Kings Canyon and Redwoods National Park. The Wilderness Act of 1964 further established procedures for setting aside lands in national forests and parks.

The period from 1916 through 1935 was marked especially by reform action to protect wildlife. Professional wildlife experts, hunting groups, gun manufacturers and many conservationists sought the protection of wild animals and the creation of wildlife refuges. Spokespeople for this movement argued that hunting is a great national tradition, that conservation of wildlife can occur side by side with industrial expansion, and that since by common law wildlife was public property, public agencies should be created to compensate private landowners for lands taken for wildlife preserves. Out of this movement most states established Fish and Game (or Wildlife) Commissions and the battles focused over protection of so-called nongame species (those species hunters considered not worth shooting), predator control (particularly wolves and coyotes which were seen to be "interfering" with human uses of the land), and production of game species for hunters. [14]

Most urban centers had municipal water and sewage systems before 1940. However, after 1950 even more serious, possibly insolvable, problems of public health developed into near crisis proportions with the rapid introduction of massive amounts of herbicides, pesticides and many toxic chemicals into the environment. [15] These chemicals were used to increase the efficiency of crop production or were byproducts of industrial processes and the massive consumption of fossil fuels.

During the past five decades, an increasing number of scientists and environmental activists were broadening their concerns to include criticisms of major assumptions of the dominant social worldview and to address social and political factors. And some were following John Muir's lead in articulating the need for a spiritual approach to Nature. Professional ecologists such as Aldo Leopold, Charles Elton, Paul Sears, William Vogt, Eugene Odum, F. Fraser Darling and others were identifying the dangers to humans of environmental degradation and calling for a new *land ethic*. This call for a land ethic and a call that we cultivate ecological consciousness is clearly seen in the work of Rachel Carson, Aldous Huxley, and Leopold, among others.

A turning point in the search for a philosophy of ecology was seen in Stuart Udall's *The Quiet Crisis* (1962). In it he outlined the American conservation crisis and environmental thought from Thomas Jefferson through Pinchot and Muir. A significant issue Udall raised was the difficulty he experienced in writing his history of American conservation. The lack of historical and political scholarship in this area was scandalous. The crucial issue of the human/Nature relationship had largely been ignored by the academic establishment. Tucked away in this ignored issue was the ticking time bomb of the global environmental crisis together with the need to criticize the basic assumption of the Western worldview and to seek a contemporary version of a spiritual approach to Nature, to seek a land wisdom so clearly evidenced in many Native American peoples. [16]

———

History tells us that earlier civilizations have declined because they did not learn to live in harmony with the land. Our successes in space and our triumphs of technology hold a hidden danger: as modern man increasingly arrogates to himself dominion over the physical environment, there is the risk that his false pride will cause him to take the resources of the earth for granted — and to lose all reverence for the land. . . .

[It is ironic that] . . . today the conservation movement finds itself turning back to ancient Indian land ideas, to the Indian understanding that we are not outside of nature, but of it. . . . In recent decades we have slowly come back to some of the truths that the Indian knew from the beginning: that unborn generations have a claim on the land equal to our own; that men need to learn from nature, to keep an ear to the earth, and to replenish their spirits in frequent contacts with animals and wild land. And most important of all, we are recovering a sense of reverence for the land. . . . Within a generation [of White settlement of America] the wildness would begin to convert some of their sons, and

reverence for the natural world and its forces would eventually sound in much of our literature, finding its prophets in Thoreau and Muir.
— Stuart Udall, *The Quiet Crisis* (1962)

From the early 1960s onward, the "quiet crisis" became increasingly visible and discussions over environmental policy became more intense. Smog, urban blight, toxic wastes, loss of productive farmlands due to soil erosion, massive deforestation in some parts of the Earth, all continued to be front page news.

In a wave of reform in the 1960s, concerned citizens sought to change public policy by seeking better government regulation of toxic chemicals. A turning point in this effort was the passage of the National Environmental Policy Act of 1969 and passage of similar legislation in many states. This act (usually referred to as NEPA) created regulatory procedures for air and water polluters and for strip-mining operations. It called for annual reports to citizens on the "State of the Environment," created a new public agency, the Environmental Protection Agency, and mandated that major public projects be considered only after an Environmental Impact Report on the project had been written and considered at public hearings. [17] In 1972 the United Nations sponsored the Stockholm Conference on the Environment, focusing attention to the worldwide dimensions of the crisis.

The reformist political response, generally speaking, has been oriented only toward public policy. It has been based on the liberal democratic assumption that if enough citizens have accurate information on environmental problems, they will assert themselves through voluntary organizations to demand better policies and practices from legislators and regulatory agencies.

Using rational, technical scientific models and data and economic arguments, reformers have altered citizens' perceptions to some degree and have alerted them to the dangerous consequences to human health from many types of pollution. But in the continuing, and at times intense, public debates, more and more people have begun to realize the meaning of the basic ecological principle that everything is connected to everything else.

The reformist response has been extremely valuable. Many parks, nature reserves and forests have been, at least temporarily, "saved." But the integrity of many national parks is threatened by technocratic society. [18] In the 1980s, the massive attack on Nature by the Reagan administration in the United States, combined with the greed of political elites in many Third World nations, and the massive problems of balancing human population growth and increasing per capita consumption of resources with preservation of wilderness, has led many to see the limitations and weaknesses of the reformist response. [19]

While accepting the best of reformist environmentalism, many people have sensed that something is missing. They are asking deeper questions. They understand that the environmental/ecology movement needs an articulate philosophical approach grounded upon assumptions which are different from those of the dominant worldview.

They realize that a perspective is needed that will place the best of the reformist response into a coherent philosophical perspective – a philosophy based on biocentric rather than anthropocentric assumptions. [20] This philosophy should be able to draw on the science of ecology, but should not be constrained by scientism, and by the definition of Nature as just a collection of bits of data to be manipulated by humans.

This philosophy should be both rational and spiritual. It should focus on ways of cultivating ecological consciousness and on principles for public environmental policy. It should be a philosophy that draws from the Earth wisdom of Native Americans and other primal cultures and that makes these approaches to wisdom relevant to contemporary, technocratic-industrial societies.

In 1972, Arne Naess began discussing such a philosophy which he called *deep ecology*. A formal statement of the insights, *ultimate norms* and principles of deep ecology are presented in the next chapter.

Without the energy that lifts mountains,
how am I to live?
      — Mirabai

61

CHAPTER 5

•

DEEP ECOLOGY

———

Then what is the answer?—Not to be deluded by dreams,

To know that great civilizations have broken down into

violence, and their tyrants come, many times before.

When open violence appears, to avoid it with honor or choose

the least ugly faction; the evils are essential.

To keep one's own integrity, be merciful and uncorrupted

and not wish for evil; and not be duped

By dreams of universal justice or happiness. These dreams will

not be fulfilled.

To know this, and know that however ugly the parts appear

the whole remains beautiful. A severed hand

Is an ugly thing, and man dissevered from the earth and stars

and his history . . . for contemplation or in fact . . .

Often appears atrociously ugly. Integrity is wholeness,
the great beauty is
Organic wholeness, the wholeness of life and things, the divine
beauty of the universe. Love that, not man
Apart from that, or else you will share man's pitiful
confusions, or drown in despair when his days darken.

   — *Robinson Jeffers, "The Answer" from* Selected Poetry *(1938)*

The term *deep ecology* was coined by Arne Naess in his 1973 article, "The Shallow and the Deep, Long-Range Ecology Movements."[1] Naess was attempting to describe the deeper, more spiritual approach to Nature exemplified in the writings of Aldo Leopold and Rachel Carson. He thought that this deeper approach resulted from a more sensitive openness to ourselves and nonhuman life around us. The essence of deep ecology is to keep asking more searching questions about human life, society, and Nature as in the Western philosophical tradition of Socrates. As examples of this deep questioning, Naess points out "that we ask why and how, where others do not. For instance, ecology as a science does not ask what kind of a society would be the best for maintaining a particular ecosystem — that is considered a question for value theory, for politics, for ethics." Thus deep ecology goes beyond the so-called factual scientific level to the level of self and Earth wisdom.

Deep ecology goes beyond a limited piecemeal shallow approach to environmental problems and attempts to articulate a comprehensive religious and philosophical worldview. The foundations of deep ecology are the basic intuitions and experiencing of ourselves and Nature which comprise ecological consciousness. Certain outlooks on politics and public policy flow naturally from this consciousness. And in the context of this book, we discuss the minority tradition as the type of community most conducive both to cultivating ecological consciousness and to asking the basic questions of values and ethics addressed in these pages.

Many of these questions are perennial philosophical and religious questions faced by humans in all cultures over the ages. What does it mean to be a unique human individual? How can the individual self maintain and increase its uniqueness while also being an inseparable aspect of the whole system wherein there are no sharp breaks between self and the *other?* An ecological perspective, in this deeper sense, results in what Theodore Roszak calls "an awakening of wholes greater than the sum of their parts. In spirit, the discipline is contemplative and therapeutic."[2]

Ecological consciousness and deep ecology are in sharp contrast with the dominant worldview of technocratic-industrial societies which regards humans as isolated and fundamentally separate from the rest of Nature, as superior to, and in charge of, the rest of creation. But the view of humans as separate and superior to the rest of Nature is only part of larger cultural patterns. For thousands of years, Western culture has become increasingly obsessed with the idea of *dominance:* with dominance of humans over nonhuman Nature, masculine over the feminine, wealthy and powerful over the poor, with the dominance of the West over non-Western cultures. Deep ecological consciousness allows us to see through these erroneous and dangerous illusions.

For deep ecology, the study of our place in the Earth household includes the study of ourselves as part of the organic whole. Going beyond a narrowly materialist scientific understanding of reality, the spiritual and the material aspects of reality fuse together. While the leading intellectuals of the dominant worldview have tended to view religion as "just superstition," and have looked upon ancient spiritual practice and enlightenment, such as found in Zen Buddhism, as essentially subjective, the search for deep ecological consciousness is the search for a more objective consciousness and state of being through an active deep questioning and meditative process and way of life.

Many people have asked these deeper questions and cultivated ecological consciousness within the context of different spiritual traditions — Christianity, Taoism, Buddhism, and Native American rituals, for example. While differing greatly in other regards, many in these traditions agree with the basic principles of deep ecology.

Warwick Fox, an Australian philosopher, has succinctly expressed the central intuition of deep ecology: "It is the idea that we can make no firm ontological divide in the field of existence: That there is no bifurcation in reality between the human and the non-human realms . . . to the extent that we perceive boundaries, we fall short of deep ecological consciousness."[3]

From this most basic insight or characteristic of deep ecological consciousness, Arne Naess has developed two *ultimate norms* or intuitions which are themselves not derivable from other principles or intuitions. They are arrived at by the deep questioning process and reveal the importance of moving to the philosophical and religious level of wisdom. They cannot be validated, of course, by the methodology of modern science based on its usual mechanistic assumptions and its very narrow definition of data. These ultimate norms are *self-realization* and *biocentric equality.*

I. SELF-REALIZATION

In keeping with the spiritual traditions of many of the world's religions, the deep ecology norm of self-realization goes beyond the modern Western *self* which is defined as an isolated ego striving primarily for hedonistic gratification or for a narrow sense of individual salvation in this life or the next. This socially programmed sense of the narrow self or social self dislocates us, and leaves us prey to whatever fad or fashion is prevalent in our society or social reference group. We are thus robbed of beginning the search for our unique spiritual/biological personhood. Spiritual growth, or unfolding, begins when we cease to understand or see ourselves as isolated and narrow competing egos and begin to identify with other humans from our family and friends to, eventually, our species. But the deep ecology sense of self requires a further maturity and growth, an identification which goes beyond humanity to include the nonhuman world. We must see beyond our narrow contemporary cultural assumptions and values, and the conventional wisdom of our time and place, and this is best achieved by the meditative deep questioning process. Only in this way can we hope to attain full mature personhood and uniqueness.

A nurturing nondominating society can help in the "real work" of becoming a whole person. The "real work" can be summarized symbolically as the realization of "self-in-Self" where "Self" stands for organic wholeness. This process of the full unfolding of the self can also be summarized by the phrase, "No one is saved until we are all saved," where the phrase "one" includes not only me, an individual human, but all humans, whales, grizzly bears, whole rain forest ecosystems, mountains and rivers, the tiniest microbes in the soil, and so on.

II. BIOCENTRIC EQUALITY

The intuition of biocentric equality is that all things in the biosphere have an equal right to live and blossom and to reach their own individual forms of unfolding and self-realization within the larger Self-realization. This basic intuition is that all organisms and entities in the ecosphere, as parts of the interrelated whole, are equal in intrinsic worth. Naess suggests that biocentric equality as an intuition is true in principle, although in the process of living, all species use each other as food, shelter, etc. Mutual predation is a biological fact of life, and many of the world's religions have struggled with the spiritual implications of this. Some animal liberationists who attempt to side-step this problem by advocating vegetarianism are forced to say that the entire plant kingdom including rain forests have no right to their own existence. This evasion flies in the face of the basic intuition of equality.[4] Aldo Leopold expressed this intuition when he said humans are "plain citizens" of the biotic community, not lord and master over all other species.

Biocentric equality is intimately related to the all-inclusive Self-realization in the sense that if we harm the rest of Nature then we are harming ourselves. There are no boundaries and everything is interrelated. But insofar as we perceive things as individual organisms or entities, the insight draws us to respect all human and non-human individuals in their own right as parts of the whole without feeling the need to set up hierarchies of species with humans at the top.

The practical implications of this intuition or norm suggest that we should live with minimum rather than maximum impact on other species and on the Earth in general. Thus we see another aspect of our guiding principle: "simple in means, rich in ends." Further practical implications of these norms are discussed at length in chapters seven and eight.

A fuller discussion of the biocentric norm as it unfolds itself in practice begins with the realization that we, as individual humans, and as communities of humans, have vital needs which go beyond such basics as food, water, and shelter to include love, play, creative expression, intimate relationships with a particular landscape (or Nature taken in its entirety) as well as intimate relationships with other humans, and the vital need for spiritual growth, for becoming a mature human being.

Our vital material needs are probably more simple than many realize. In technocratic-industrial societies there is overwhelming propaganda and advertising which encourages false needs and destructive desires designed to foster increased production and consumption of goods. Most of this actually diverts us from facing reality in an objective way and from beginning the "real work" of spiritual growth and maturity.

Many people who do not see themselves as supporters of deep ecology nevertheless recognize an overriding vital human need for a healthy and high-quality natural environment for humans, if not for all life, with minimum intrusion of toxic waste, nuclear radiation from human enterprises, minimum acid rain and smog, and enough free flowing wilderness so humans can get in touch with their sources, the natural rhythms and the flow of time and place.

Drawing from the minority tradition and from the wisdom of many who have offered the insight of interconnectedness, we recognize that deep ecologists can offer suggestions for gaining maturity and encouraging the processes of harmony with Nature, but that there is no grand solution which is guaranteed to save us from ourselves.

The ultimate norms of deep ecology suggest a view of the nature of reality and our place as an individual (many in the one) in the larger scheme of things. They cannot be fully grasped intellectually but are ultimately experiential. We encourage readers to consider our further discussion of the psychological, social and ecological implications of these norms in later chapters.

As a brief summary of our position thus far, figure 5-1 summarizes the contrast between the dominant worldview and deep ecology.

Figure 5-1

Dominant Worldview	*Deep Ecology*
Dominance over Nature	Harmony with Nature
Natural environment as resource for humans	All nature has intrinsic worth/biospecies equality
Material/economic growth for growing human population	Elegantly simple material needs (material goals serving the larger goal of self-realization)
Belief in ample resource reserves	Earth "supplies" limited
High technological progress and solutions	Appropriate technology; nondominating science
Consumerism	Doing with enough/recycling
National/centralized community	Minority tradition/bioregion

III. BASIC PRINCIPLES OF DEEP ECOLOGY

In April 1984, during the advent of spring and John Muir's birthday, George Sessions and Arne Naess summarized fifteen years of thinking on the principles of deep ecology while camping in Death Valley, California. In this great and special place, they articulated these

69

principles in a literal, somewhat neutral way, hoping that they would be understood and accepted by persons coming from different philosophical and religious positions.

Readers are encouraged to elaborate their own versions of deep ecology, clarify key concepts and think through the consequences of acting from these principles.

Basic Principles

1. The well-being and flourishing of human and nonhuman Life on Earth have value in themselves (synonyms: intrinsic value, inherent value). These values are independent of the usefulness of the nonhuman world for human purposes.

2. Richness and diversity of life forms contribute to the realization of these values and are also values in themselves.

3. Humans have no right to reduce this richness and diversity except to satisfy *vital* needs.

4. The flourishing of human life and cultures is compatible with a substantial decrease of the human population. The flourishing of nonhuman life requires such a decrease.

5. Present human interference with the nonhuman world is excessive, and the situation is rapidly worsening.

6. Policies must therefore be changed. These policies affect basic economic, technological, and ideological structures. The resulting state of affairs will be deeply different from the present.

7. The ideological change is mainly that of appreciating *life quality* (dwelling in situations of inherent value) rather than adhering to an increasingly higher standard of living. There will be a profound awareness of the difference between big and great.

8. Those who subscribe to the foregoing points have an obligation directly or indirectly to try to implement the necessary changes.

Naess and Sessions Provide Comments on the Basic Principles:

RE (1). This formulation refers to the biosphere, or more accurately, to the ecosphere as a whole. This includes individuals, species, populations, habitat, as well as human and nonhuman cultures. From our current knowledge of all-pervasive intimate relationships, this implies

70

a fundamental deep concern and respect. Ecological processes of the planet should, on the whole, remain intact. "The world environment should remain 'natural'" (Gary Snyder).

The term "life" is used here in a more comprehensive nontechnical way to refer also to what biologists classify as "nonliving"; rivers (watersheds), landscapes, ecosystems. For supporters of deep ecology, slogans such as "Let the river live" illustrate this broader usage so common in most cultures.

Inherent value as used in (1) is common in deep ecology literature ("The presence of inherent value in a natural object is independent of any awareness, interest, or appreciation of it by a conscious being.")[5]

RE (2). More technically, this is a formulation concerning diversity and complexity. From an ecological standpoint, complexity and symbiosis are conditions for maximizing diversity. So-called simple, lower, or primitive species of plants and animals contribute essentially to the richness and diversity of life. They have value in themselves and are not merely steps toward the so-called higher or rational life forms. The second principle presupposes that life itself, as a process over evolutionary time, implies an increase of diversity and richness. The refusal to acknowledge that some life forms have greater or lesser intrinsic value than others (see points 1 and 2) runs counter to the formulations of some ecological philosophers and New Age writers.

Complexity, as referred to here, is different from complication. Urban life may be more complicated than life in a natural setting without being more complex in the sense of multifaceted quality.

RE (3). The term "vital need" is left deliberately vague to allow for considerable latitude in judgment. Differences in climate and related factors, together with differences in the structures of societies as they now exist, need to be considered (for some Eskimos, snowmobiles are necessary today to satisfy vital needs).

People in the materially richest countries cannot be expected to reduce their excessive interference with the nonhuman world to a moderate level overnight. The stabilization and reduction of the human population will take time. Interim strategies need to be developed. But this in no way excuses the present complacency—the extreme seriousness of our current situation must first be realized.

71

But the longer we wait the more drastic will be the measures needed. Until deep changes are made, substantial decreases in richness and diversity are liable to occur: the rate of extinction of species will be ten to one hundred times greater than any other period of earth history.

RE (4). The United Nations Fund for Population Activities in their State of World Population Report (1984) said that high human population growth rates (over 2.0 percent annum) in many developing countries "were diminishing the quality of life for many millions of people." During the decade 1974-1984, the world population grew by nearly 800 million—more than the size of India. "And we will be adding about one Bangladesh (population 93 million) per annum between now and the year 2000."

The report noted that "The growth rate of the human population has declined for the first time in human history. But at the same time, the number of people being added to the human population is bigger than at any time in history because the population base is larger."

Most of the nations in the developing world (including India and China) have as their official government policy the goal of reducing the rate of human population increase, but there are debates over the types of measures to take (contraception, abortion, etc.) consistent with human rights and feasibility.

The report concludes that if all governments set specific population targets as public policy to help alleviate poverty and advance the quality of life, the current situation could be improved.

As many ecologists have pointed out, it is also absolutely crucial to curb population growth in the so-called developed (i.e., overdeveloped) industrial societies. Given the tremendous rate of consumption and waste production of individuals in these societies, they represent a much greater threat and impact on the biosphere per capita than individuals in Second and Third World countries.

RE (5). This formulation is mild. For a realistic assessment of the situation, see the unabbreviated version of the I.U.C.N.'s *World Conservation Strategy.* There are other works to be highly recommended, such as Gerald Barney's *Global 2000 Report to the President of the United States.*

The slogan of "noninterference" does not imply that humans should not modify some ecosystems as do other species. Humans have modified the earth and will probably continue to do so. At issue is the nature and extent of such interference.

The fight to preserve and extend areas of wilderness or near-wilderness should continue and should focus on the general ecological functions of these areas (one such function: large wilderness areas are required in the biosphere to allow for continued evolutionary speciation of animals and plants). Most present designated wilderness areas and game preserves are not large enough to allow for such speciation.

RE (6). Economic growth as conceived and implemented today by the industrial states is incompatible with (1)-(5). There is only a faint resemblance between ideal sustainable forms of economic growth and present policies of the industrial societies. And "sustainable" still means "sustainable in relation to humans."

Present ideology tends to value things because they are scarce and because they have a commodity value. There is prestige in vast consumption and waste (to mention only several relevant factors).

Whereas "self-determination," "local community," and "think globally, act locally," will remain key terms in the ecology of human societies, nevertheless the implementation of deep changes requires increasingly global action—action across borders.

Governments in Third World countries (with the exception of Costa Rica and a few others) are uninterested in deep ecological issues. When the governments of industrial societies try to promote ecological measures through Third World governments, practically nothing is accomplished (e.g., with problems of desertification). Given this situation, support for global action through nongovernmental international organizations becomes increasingly important. Many of these organizations are able to act globally "from grassroots to grassroots," thus avoiding negative governmental interference.

Cultural diversity today requires advanced technology, that is, techniques that advance the basic goals of each culture. So-called soft, intermediate, and alternative technologies are steps in this direction.

RE (7). Some economists criticize the term "quality of life" because it is supposed to be vague. But on closer inspection, what they consider to be vague is actually the nonquantitative nature of the term. One cannot quantify adequately what is important for the quality of life as discussed here, and there is no need to do so.

RE (8). There is ample room for different opinions about priorities: what should be done first, what next? What is most urgent? What is clearly necessary as opposed to what is highly desirable but not absolutely pressing?

Interview With Arne Naess

The following excerpts are from an interview with Arne Naess conducted at the Zen Center of Los Angeles in April 1982. It was originally published as an interview in *Ten Directions*. [6] In the interview, Naess further discusses the major perspective of deep ecology. We include it at the conclusion of this chapter so that the reader can gain further information in preparation for reading the remaining chapters.

"The essence of deep ecology is to ask deeper questions. The adjective 'deep' stresses that we ask why and how, where others do not. For instance, ecology as a science does not ask what kind of a society would be the best for maintaining a particular ecosystem — that is considered a question for value theory, for politics, for ethics. As long as ecologists keep narrowly to their science, they do not ask such questions. What we need today is a tremendous expansion of ecological thinking in what I call ecosophy. *Sophy* comes from the Greek term *sophia,* 'wisdom,' which relates to ethics, norms, rules, and practice. Ecosophy, or deep ecology, then, involves a shift from science to wisdom.

"For example, we need to ask questions like, Why do we think that economic growth and high levels of consumption are so important? The conventional answer would be to point to the economic consequences of not having economic growth. But in deep ecology, we ask whether the present society fulfills basic human needs like love and security and access to nature, and, in so doing, we question our society's underlying assumptions. We ask which society, which education, which form of religion, is beneficial for all life on the planet as a whole, and then we ask further what we need to do in order to make the necessary changes. We are not limited to a scientific approach; we have an obligation to verbalize a total view.

"Of course, total views may differ. Buddhism, for example, provides a fitting background or context for deep ecology, certain Christian groups have formed platforms of action in favor of deep ecology, and I myself have worked out my own philosophy, which I call ecosophy. In general, however, people do not question deeply enough to explicate or make clear a total view. If they did, most would agree with saving the planet from the destruction that's in progress. A total view, such as deep ecology, can provide a single motivating force for all the activities and movements aimed at saving the planet from human exploitation and domination.

74

". . . It's easier for deep ecologists than for others because we have certain fundamental values, a fundamental view of what's meaningful in life, what's worth maintaining, which makes it completely clear that we're opposed to further development for the sake of increased domination and an increased standard of living. The material standard of living should be drastically reduced and the quality of life, in the sense of basic satisfaction in the depths of one's heart or soul, should be maintained or increased. This view is intuitive, as are all important views, in the sense that it can't be proven. As Aristotle said, it shows a lack of education to try to prove everything, because you have to have a starting point. You can't prove the methodology of science, you can't prove logic, because logic presupposes fundamental premises.

"All the sciences are fragmentary and incomplete in relation to basic rules and norms, so it's very shallow to think that science can solve our problems. Without basic norms, there is no science.

". . . People can then oppose nuclear power without having to read thick books and without knowing the myriad facts that are used in newspapers and periodicals. And they must also find others who feel the same and form circles of friends who give one another confidence and support in living in a way that the majority find ridiculous, naive, stupid and simplistic. But in order to do that, one must already have enough self-confidence to follow one's intuition—a quality very much lacking in broad sections of the populace. Most people follow the trends and advertisements and become philosophical and ethical cripples.

"There is a basic intuition in deep ecology that we have no right to destroy other living beings without sufficient reason. Another norm is that, with maturity, human beings will experience joy when other life forms experience joy and sorrow when other life forms experience sorrow. Not only will we feel sad when our brother or a dog or a cat feels sad, but we will grieve when living beings, including landscapes, are destroyed. In our civilization, we have vast means of destruction at our disposal but extremely little maturity in our feelings. Only a very narrow range of feelings have interested most human beings until now.

"For deep ecology, there is a core democracy in the biosphere. . . . In deep ecology, we have the goal not only of stabilizing human population but also of reducing it to a sustainable minimum without revolution or dictatorship. I should think we must have no more than 100 million people if we are to have the variety of cultures we had one hundred years ago. Because we need the conservation of human cultures, just as we need the conservation of animal species.

". . . Self-realization is the realization of the potentialities of life. Organisms that differ from each other in three ways give us less diversity than organisms that differ from each other in one hundred ways. Therefore, the self-realization we experience when we identify with the universe is heightened by an increase in the number of ways in which individuals, societies, and even species and life forms realize themselves. The greater the diversity, then, the greater the self-realization. This seeming duality between individuals and the totality is encompassed by what I call the Self and the Chinese call the Tao. Most people in deep ecology have had the feeling—usually, but not always, in nature—that they are connected with something greater than their ego, greater than their name, their family, their special attributes as an individual—a feeling that is often called oceanic because many have it on the ocean. Without that identification, one is not easily drawn to become involved in deep ecology. . . .

". . . Insofar as these deep feelings are religious, deep ecology has a religious component, and those people who have done the most to make societies aware of the destructive way in which we live in relation to natural settings have had such religious feelings. Rachel Carson, for example, says that we *cannot* do what we do, we have no religious or ethical justification for behaving as we do toward nature. . . . She is saying that we are simply not permitted to behave in that way. Some will say that nature is not man's property, it's the property of God; others will say it in other ways. The main point is that deep ecology has a religious component, fundamental intuitions that everyone must cultivate if he or she is to have a life based on values and not function like a computer.

". . . To maximize self-realization—and I don't mean self as ego but self in a broader sense—we need maximum diversity and maximum symbiosis. . . . Diversity, then, is a fundamental norm and a common delight. As deep ecologists, we take a natural delight in diversity, as long as it does not include crude, intrusive forms, like Nazi culture, that are destructive to others."

76

Now I see the secret of the making of the best persons.
It is to grow in the open air, and to eat and sleep
with the earth.
        —*Walt Whitman,* Leaves of Grass

CHAPTER 6

•

SOME SOURCES OF
THE DEEP ECOLOGY
PERSPECTIVE

Although ecology may be treated as a science, its greater and overriding wisdom is universal. That wisdom can be approached mathematically, chemically, or it can be danced or told as a myth. . . . It is manifest, for example, among pre-Classical Greeks, in Navajo religion and social orientation, in romantic poetry of the eighteenth and nineteenth centuries, in Chinese landscape painting of the eleventh century, in current Whiteheadian philosophy, in Zen Buddhism, in the worldview of the cult of the Cretan Great Mother, in the ceremonials of Bushman hunters, and in the medieval Christian metaphysics of light. What is common among all of them is a deep sense of engagement with the landscape, with profound connections to surroundings and to natural processes central to all life.

—*Paul Shepard,* The Subversive Science *(1969)*

Deep ecology is radically conservative in that it articulates a long-established minority stream of religion and philosophy in Western Europe, North America, and the Orient. It also has strong parallels and shared insights with many religious and philosophical positions of primal peoples (including Native Americans). In a certain sense it can be interpreted as remembering wisdom which men once knew.

In this chapter some of the sources of deep ecology are briefly described. This chapter is intended to help the reader place what seem like diverse and disparate writings into an ecological context.

Deep ecology derives its essence from the following traditions and philosophies which are mentioned in this chapter: the perennial philosophy, the pastoral/naturalist literary tradition, the science of ecology, the "new physics," some Christian sources, feminism, the philosophies of primal (or native) peoples, and some Eastern spiritual traditions. The writings of Martin Heidegger, Gary Snyder, Robinson Jeffers, John Muir, and David Brower have also contributed greatly to the deep ecology perspective. The reader is encouraged to explore further the sources of deep ecology in the essay on Baruch Spinoza and Western process metaphysics in appendix D.

I. THE PERENNIAL PHILOSOPHY

In *The Perennial Philosophy* (1945), Aldous Huxley surveyed many of the religions and philosophies of the world looking for common themes. He found that they characteristically began with a metaphysical account of the world or reality which placed humans in the wider scheme of things. Human psychology was then understood in terms of adjusting to this larger reality. Finally, a system of ethics or a way of life was the end result of the perennial philosophy approach. Spiritual growth and human maturity developed from the "enlightenment" of realizing that our narrow isolated socialized self is an illusion — that in reality, we are intimately connected with all the natural processes around us. Many people are familiar with these ideas from the Eastern traditions, but fail to realize that the perennial philosophy tradition also existed in the West for millennia. Good examples from Western philosophy include the systems of Pythagoras and Plato (see especially his "allegory of the cave" in the *Republic*) and the more Nature-oriented system of Spinoza. Philosopher Jacob Needleman discusses the Gnostic and other Western religious perennial philosophy traditions in *Lost Christianity* (1980) and *The Heart of Philosophy*

(1981), as does Roszak in *Where the Wasteland Ends* (1972), and *The Unfinished Animal* (1977).

The perennial philosophy tradition has direct relevance for us today for several reasons. Modern Western academic philosophy in the twentieth century has become very wedded to mechanistic science as its touchstone for reality and knowledge, along with a narrow preoccupation with the analysis of language, and has all but lost sight of the wisdom tradition in philosophy. Specialists in philosophy now, for example, do ethical theory entirely divorced from its metaphysical underpinnings or an awareness of the deep assumptions they are making. Philosophical specialists also ignore the history of philosophy and the cultural contexts in which the theories and ideas have arisen. All of this in its way tends to reinforce anthropocentrism and the existing technocratic-industrial society. Such specialists are of little help in developing the deep ecology worldview now needed.

Similarly, much of modern psychology has lost touch with the wisdom traditions and presents us with oversimplified and distorted socially oriented models of healthy mature human beings. Much of the interest in Eastern philosophy and psychology and techniques for spiritual development is an attempt to correct the impoverishment of Western philosophy and psychology.[1] The revival of the perennial philosophy tradition again unites metaphysics, psychology, theory of knowledge, ethics, and social and political theory to help provide us with a coherent and integrated view of the world and the meaning of human life.

Aldous Huxley points out that, "In all the historic formulations of the perennial philosophy it is axiomatic that the end of human life . . . is the direct and intuitive awareness of God; that action is the means to that end." Many Westerners see contemplation or meditation as mostly inactive sitting or an inward withdrawal from the world and its problems. But there is a very active strain to contemplative living which results from greater self-knowledge and integration of the person. Those who perform actions without a genuine awareness of their vital needs and real motives may actually be quite passive individuals. In Spinoza's version of perennial philosophy, the whole key to human maturity and freedom is an understanding of the world and ourselves which allows us to move from passive unreflective conditioned behavior to an active relationship with the world around us.

An appropriate metaphysics for the emerging ecological perennial philosophy would provide a structural account of the basic unity and interrelatedness of the universe, while at the same time accounting for the importance and uniqueness of individual beings. Similarly, this metaphysics of interrelatedness helps us realize that the natural world and other species are inextricably a part of us, and us of them (a mutual reciprocity). The truly active person will take direct action to help preserve the natural world, for in a profound mature sense, one sees that such preservation is in one's self/Self interest.

Western civilization as a whole now finds itself between dreams . . . [much as during the Renaissance when] Western man found himself between two dreams: behind him the dream of a Christianized world, before him the dream of the conquest of nature. The crisis of ecology, the threat of atomic war, and the disruption of the patterns of human life by advanced technology . . . [have resulted in the fact that] the lullaby of scientific progress, the dream of manipulating nature to suit our egoistic purposes, is ended.
—Jacob Needleman, *A Sense of the Cosmos* (1975)

II. THE LITERARY TRADITION OF NATURALISM AND PASTORALISM IN AMERICA

While a great deal of modern literature has the anthropocentric focus of humans coping with urban lifestyles and their inherent problems, there is also a rich pastoral and naturalist literary tradition in Europe and America that provides a source for deep ecological consciousness. The European Romantic movement, beginning with Jean-Jacques Rousseau's challenge to an overly civilized and refined Europe, and continuing with Goethe and the Romantic poets (Blake, Wordsworth, Coleridge, Shelley, etc.) can be viewed as a counterforce to the narrow scientism and industrialism of the modern world. This movement continued in America with Walt Whitman, the Transcendentalist Emerson, and Thoreau and Muir.

Literary critic Leo Marx (*The Machine in the Garden*, 1964) referred to this tradition during the excitement of Earth Day, when he criticized the scientific establishment for being so conservative and for not properly evaluating the severity of the environmental crisis. [2] Marx found the ecological perspective expressed in much of the American pastoral writing including Cooper, Emerson, Thoreau, Melville, Whitman, Twain and others. He claimed that the awareness of ecological interpenetration in these writers, together with a "sense of place," often produced "a kind of visionary experience, couched in a language of such intense, extreme, even mystical feeling that it is difficult for many readers (though not, significantly, for adherents of the [1960s] youth culture) to take it seriously."

In many ways, Melville's *Moby Dick* can be seen as the classic allegory of the West's (and particularly America's) self-destructive attempt to conquer Nature. Ahab as the captain of industry becomes increasingly insane in his efforts to outsmart and destroy Nature in the form of Moby Dick, the great white whale. But the hunter becomes the hunted and the whale destroys its tormentor.

This literary tradition, which also includes Mary Austin, D. H. Lawrence, Aldous Huxley, Robinson Jeffers, William Faulkner, Joseph Wood Krutch, Henry Beston, Anne Dillard, Wallace Stegner, Sigurd Olsen, Frank Waters, Wendell Berry, Edward Abbey, Barry Lopez, Gary Snyder, and others, has called to us to reject the technocratic-industrial worldview and reestablish our roots in Mother Gaia.[3]

While some of the Romantic and Transcendentalist writers were overly subjective and sentimental about the goodness of Nature and primal peoples (the "myth of the Noble Savage"), writers beginning with John Muir and Robinson Jeffers and continuing with Gary Snyder have developed a more objective view of humans and Nature. For example, D. H. Lawrence in his outstanding essay "Pan in America" (1924) surveys the overly sentimental pantheism of the European Romantics and then provides wonderful insight into the more realistic mystical sense of interrelatedness of the Native Americans of New Mexico.[4]

Among contemporary writers, no one has done more than Gary Snyder to shape the sensibilities of the deep ecology movement. In both his poetry and essays, Snyder has been laying the foundations for the "real work" of reinhabiting this continent. Fellow poet William Everson claimed in *Archetype West* (1976) that "Snyder has for two dozen years been hewing out the guidelines along which the greening of America must proceed, and his work has not been in vain."

In 1975, Snyder was awarded the Pulitzer Prize in Poetry for his book, *Turtle Island,* which contains some of his finest poems and most important essays and statements linking Zen Buddhism, the American Indian tradition, and deep ecology.

In his insightful essay, "Gary Snyder's Descent to Turtle Island," Edwin Folsom points out that as the Western frontier was closed, some poets began looking for a new direction for Americans. It became apparent that the religious/economic vision of urban-industrialism had destroyed the ecology and wildlife of this continent while also diminishing our lives. Snyder followed the lead of poets William Carlos Williams and Hart Crane, who suggested that we get in touch with the land itself and with the vision and traditions of early American primal peoples who lived in harmony with the land. Snyder has provided a well-rounded vision for a new tribe of "White Indians" to reinhabit the land based upon the "old ways." Folsom claims that:

Snyder's major accomplishment, then, is a rediscovery and reaffirmation of wilderness, a clear rejection of Turner's (and America's) closure of the frontier. Snyder announces the opening of the frontier again and attempts to push it eastward, to reverse America's historical process, to urge the wilderness to grow back into civilization, to release the stored energy from layers below us. [5]

Through the ancient enchanting use of the poetic voice, Snyder becomes the spokesman for Mother Gaia and all of her living creatures, calling upon us to return to sanity and "right livelihood" by readopting the old ways. This is the path of freedom for humans and the planet. In Snyder's words:

"Old" means true, right, normal: in the flow of the universe. Old also because it is the basic way to live—Taoism, Hinduism, Buddhism, are the younger brothers, slightly confused because passing through the temporary turbulence called civilization . . . People and places that will not be managed—they are called "wild" . . . "Self-thus," Chinese word for nature—not programmed—generating its own rules from within."

Readers are encouraged to further explore Snyder's ideas in his books listed in the bibliography.

———

Bob Steuding, in *Gary Snyder* (1976), makes a distinction between Romantic and ecological perspectives:

The theories of the contemporary poets, such as Snyder, seem distinctly non-Romantic in essence. These poets have an entirely different perception of Nature than that of the Romantics . . . the Romantics asked many valid questions, but they were unable to decode the answers they received because of clinging Judeo-Christian bias, a humanistic view of the universe; and, most importantly, lack of scientific knowledge. . . . The Transcendentalists read the Orientals, and agreed, as does Snyder, that all was interrelated. Yet they stood aside, viewing what they called "Nature" as something other than themselves. . . . In contrast to the perception of the world projected in Snyder's later work, the Romantics never *saw* nature. They were looking at their own minds.

―――――――――

III. THE SCIENCE OF ECOLOGY

The major contribution of the science of ecology to deep ecology has been the rediscovery within the modern scientific context that everything is connected to everything else. Thus, as a science, ecology provided a view of Nature that was lacking in the discrete, reductionist approach to Nature of the other sciences.

Furthermore, in the work of some ecologists and natural historians including Rachel Carson, F. Fraser Darling, Charles Elton, Aldo Leopold, Paul Sears, William Vogt, Eugene Odum, Frank Egler and others, deep ecological consciousness has existed side by side with the more narrow definition of ecology as the "study of natural interrelationships." Many of these ecologists were to develop in their own philosophies some version of a biocentric perspective on the equality of all nonhumans and humans.

Another contribution of the science of ecology was to encourage students to go into the field and really *see* interrelationships rather than just study them in textbooks or laboratories. Thus the scientist had to become a vital participant in the process. From the work of English pastor Gilbert White, through Thoreau, Muir, Charles Darwin, and others in the nineteenth century, to the more "radical" ecologists — Marston Bates, Frank Egler, Paul Ehrlich and others — ecologists have understood the need to go beyond the narrow definition of scientific data and look to their own consciousness to develop their own sense of place. [6]

In the 1920s and '30s, Aldo Leopold underwent a dramatic conversion from the "stewardship" resources management mentality to what he called an *ecological conscience*. His influential statement of ecological consciousness and the land ethic occurs in the now classic *Sand County Almanac* (1949). Leopold's biocentric equality is expressed in the claim that "we are only fellow-voyagers with other creatures in the odyssey of evolution." An adoption of the ecological conscience, he says, "changes the role of Homo sapiens from conqueror of the land-community to plain member and citizen of it. It implies respect for his fellow-members, and also respect for the community as such."

Leopold claimed that "the biotic mechanism is so complex that its working may never be fully understood," thus undercutting the possibility of its total successful domination and control by humans, and thereby also stressing the essential mysteriousness of the biotic process. Leopold also pointed to the contrasts between "man the conqueror *versus* man the biotic citizen; science the sharpener of his sword *versus* science the searchlight on his universe; land the slave and servant *versus* land the collective organism." He asserted:

. . . that man is, in fact, only a member of the biotic team is shown by an ecological interpretation of history . . . the combined evidence of history and ecology seems to support one general deduction: the less violent the man-made changes, the greater the probability of successful readjustment of the (ecological) pyramid.

Leopold was one of the first to formulate an egalitarian ecosystem ethic: "A thing is right when it tends to preserve the integrity, stability, and beauty of the biotic community. It is wrong when it tends otherwise."

Leopold's ideas are truly subversive and constitute a landmark in the development of the biocentric position. Conservationists have paid lip service to Leopold's outlook, but until recently, only a few other ecologists seem to have grasped the full impact of the radical nature of Leopold's ecological conscience. [7]

In the early 1960s, Paul Sears called ecology a "subversive subject" while other radical ecologists such as Frank Egler began looking to Eastern religions for an appropriate metaphysics of interrelatedness for ecology and the West. [8] Many radical ecologists who perceived this deep ecological insight began engaging in educational programs and public policy debates to protect ecological diversity for its own sake and for the connection humans have with the ongoing process. In particular, Marston Bates, John Livingston, David Ehrenfeld and Paul Ehrlich were active in exposing some of the basic assumptions of the dominant worldview and calling for political action to protect wilderness and other species.

John Livingston tried to come to grips with the tremendous failure to protect wildlife through public policy during this century. The arguments used in public debate, he saw, were all "rational," meaning based upon narrowly conceived human interests. Plants and animals were treated, in theory and practice, as only actual or potential resources to be consumed in various ways. In *The Fallacy of Wildlife Conservation* (1981) and his earlier *One Cosmic Instant* (1973), Livingston argued that without a major change in consciousness, a profound and inti-

86

mate sense of interrelatedness with the nonhuman world, there is no hope for turning the situation around and protecting wildlife from human destruction.

David Ehrenfeld made a major contribution in his criticism of the dominant worldview approach to management of wildlife and its technological solutions. In *The Arrogance of Humanism* (1978) he shows that the danger to civilization is the human-caused destruction of the natural world which he explains as being a logical outcome of acting under the dominant worldview assumptions. He proceeds to critically evaluate the practicality of these assumptions. Ehrenfeld was one of the first major ecologists to systematically look at the worldview from a perspective that is close to deep ecology in that he calls for a biocentric equality position.

Paul Ehrlich showed the way to political activism in the 1960s and '70s, bringing other professional biologists and ecologists into the political arena, working for the protection of natural diversity and postulating both the human values which are served by maintaining biological diversity and the inherent value of forest and ocean ecosystems.

Biologist Barry Commoner went even further than other ecologists in his social activism by becoming a candidate for president of the United States in 1980, running on a platform of changing the whole direction of environmental policies in the federal government, although he never explicitly stated the deep ecology perspective.

One of Commoner's major contributions was to summarize for an audience of laypeople the major "laws" of ecology which inform deep ecology perspectives. In *The Closing Circle* (1971) he listed these laws:

1. Everything is connected to everything else.
2. Everything must go somewhere.
3. Nature knows best.
4. There is no such thing as a free lunch, or everything has to go somewhere.

———

Barry Commoner comments on the Third Law of Ecology, "Nature Knows Best":

In my experience this principle is likely to encounter considerable resistance, for it appears to contradict a deeply held idea about the unique competence of human beings. One of the most pervasive features of modern technology is the notion that it is intended to "improve on nature"—to provide food, clothing, shelter, and means of communication and expression which are superior to those available to man in nature.

Stated boldly, the third law of ecology holds that any major man-made change in a natural system is likely to be *detrimental* to that system. This is a rather extreme claim; nevertheless I believe it has a good deal of merit if understood in a properly defined context.

I have found it useful to explain this principle by an analogy . . . in biological systems. It is possible to induce a certain range of random, inherited changes in a living thing by treating it with an agent, such as X-irradiation, that increases the frequency of mutations. Generally, exposure to X-rays increases the frequency of all mutations which have been observed, albeit very infrequently, in nature and can therefore be regarded as *possible* changes. What is significant, for our purposes, is the universal observation that when mutation frequency is enhanced by X-rays or other means, nearly all the mutations are harmful to the organisms and the great majority so damaging as to kill the organism before it is fully formed.

IV. THE "NEW PHYSICS" AND DEEP ECOLOGY

The guiding model for what a science should be from the seventeenth century onward has been physics. As architects of the Scientific Revolution, René Descartes and Isaac Newton envisioned the universe to be a gigantic machine explainable in simple linear cause-and-effect terms. According to Pierre LaPlace and others, it was just a matter of time before everything in the universe could be totally explained in these terms. The biological world could be explained by the principles of physics. The social sciences, including psychology and sociology, believed that in order to be respectable sciences, they too would have to model themselves after physics. The dominant Western metaphysics, from Democritus and Aristotle to the present, has viewed the world as a collection of discrete entities or substances. Modern physics was erected on this metaphysical view of reality as tiny bits of isolated matter—atoms. In addition, the objectivity of scientific knowledge was to be maintained by keeping the scientist distanced from what he was observing so that his emotions and subjective bias would not influence his findings.

With the "new physics" this whole picture of reality has been shattered, although the message has been slow to work its way out to the social (human) sciences. [9] The idea of discrete material, subatomic particles, is being abandoned for the view of Nature as a constant flux or flow of energy transformations. In a similar vein, the idea that the scientist can totally separate himself from the experiment or observation being conducted is also being abandoned as an illusion. It is important that Thoreau and Muir consciously rejected mechanistic scientific method in the nineteenth century and conducted participatory scientific studies. Michael Cohen in his outstanding book, *The Pathless Way*, explains how Muir arrived at his glacial theory of the formation of the Sierra Nevada by lying down on the glacial polished granite in order to "think like a glacier." The approaches of Thoreau, D. H. Lawrence, and Gary Snyder are also very sensuous, as well as participative. [10]

Theoretical physicist Fritjof Capra in *The Tao of Physics* (1975) has done an outstanding job of explaining the revolution of the new physics and how this has resulted in a metaphysical view of reality similar to those of Eastern religions and ecological interrelatedness. In *The Turning Point* (1982), Capra carries this new view of metaphysical interrelatedness on to an examination of the changes which need to be made in our social structures. He suggests that deep ecology would be the appropriate framework for future human societies.

If the new worldview and metaphysics of interrelatedness resulting from a deeper understanding of ecology is valid, then we should expect to see this same view of reality emerging in other fields. Medicine is an example where the "discrete problem" approach to illness is giving way to more holistic conceptions of health. We are now aware that physical health cannot be separated from mental health, and the health of the individual cannot be separated from the health of the environment. [11]

Morris Berman, author of *The Reenchantment of the World* (1981), sees some serious pitfalls to certain versions of the interconnected view of reality, especially as interpreted by New Age thinkers and proponents of the new physics, such as David Bohm. Berman claims that the process metaphysics which they expound, based on cybernetics systems theory, threatens to be disembodied. The sensuousness of the natural world is left out of their purely formal, computerized or mathematical abstractions. Much of scientific ecological theory is based on cybernetics systems theory—a continuation of the Cartesian seventeenth-century view of the universe as a machine—and should be held suspect for that reason. Similarly, attempts to model ecosystems by the use of computers inevitably distort the living reality. As the saying goes, "The map is not the territory." We believe the Earth is a living organism and should be treated and understood accordingly. There are no technological shortcuts to direct organic experiencing.

89

But most dangerous of all, in Berman's estimation, is that the New Age consciousness threatens to be "computer consciousness," just another abstract machine view of reality. [12]

━━━━━━━━━━━

Both the mystical traditions and the "new physics" serve to generate what we now call "ecological awareness," that is, awareness of the fundamental interrelatedness of all things — or, more accurately, all events.
—Warwick Fox, "The Intuition of Deep Ecology" in *The Ecologist* (1984)

I think what physics can do is help generate ecological awareness. You see, in my view now the Western version of mystical awareness, our version of Buddhism or Taoism, will be ecological awareness.
—Fritjof Capra, quoted in Warwick Fox, "The Intuition of Deep Ecology"

Our culture is starting, without much questioning or critical evaluation, to acquire a kind of "computer consciousness" . . . both video games and home computers create a similar view of the world for millions of people . . . both convey the notion that reality is a function of programming, and children as well as adults pick up a certain type of vocabulary from their use. The general result, I suspect, is a vast subculture that lives entirely in its head, that sees reality as essentially neutral, value-free, and especially disembodied, a form of pure mental process.
—Morris Berman, "The Cybernetic Dream of the 21st Century" (unpublished, 1984)

━━━━━━━━━━━

V. CHRISTIANITY AND DEEP ECOLOGY

Several thinkers in the Christian tradition are a source for the deep ecology perspective of organic wholeness and biocentric equality. In particular, St. Francis of Assisi (1181-1226) and Giordano Bruno (1548-1600) advocated this perspective.

Lynn White, Jr., in his article "The Historical Roots of our Ecologic Crisis," calls St. Francis the greatest spiritual revolutionary since Christ and suggests that he become the patron saint of ecology. White concludes:

The greatest spiritual revolutionary in Western history, Saint Francis, proposed what he thought was an alternative Christian view of nature and man's relationship to it; he tried to substitute the idea of the equal-

ity of all creatures, including man, for the idea of man's limitless rule of creation. . . .

The key to an understanding of Francis is his belief in the virtue of humility—not merely for the individual but for man as a species. Francis tried to depose man from his monarchy over creation and set up a democracy of all God's creatures. [13]

Francis's famous Canticle, "Brother Sun, Sister Moon," has a celebratory quality, acknowledging the equality of all God's creation.

Giordano Bruno's philosophy was based on a view of an infinite universe of vast interrelationships throughout time and space, including all phenomena, material and spiritual. Each part of the infinitely numerous worlds Bruno conceived to be moving on its own course, impelled by its own two-fold nature as part of the whole as an individual in relation to other worlds.

Before he was burned at the stake by the Inquisition for his heresy in expressing this kind of biocentric equality in the Square of the Flowers in Rome in 1600, Bruno had written in his major work, "So that the hindrance to natural knowledge and the main foundation of ignorance is the failure to perceive in things the harmony between substances, motions and qualities. . . . It is these things, many of which when seen from afar may be deemed absurd and odious, but if observed more nearly they will be found beautiful and true, and when known very closely they will be wholly approved, most lovely and certain withal. . . ."

A definitive statement of deep ecology from a Christian perspective has yet to be written, but the place to begin is in Scripture and tradition. A celebratory deep ecology, drawing from Scripture, might begin with a passage such as this:

> *But ask now the beasts,*
> *and they shall teach thee;*
> *and the fowls of the air,*
> *and they shall teach thee;*
> *Or speak to the earth,*
> *and it shall teach thee;*
> *And the fishes of the sea*
> *shall declare unto thee.*
> *(Job 12:7-8)*

91

CANTICLE OF BROTHER SUN, SISTER MOON

Most high, omnipotent,
good Lord,
Thine are all praise, glory, honor and
all benedictions.
To Thee alone, Most High, do they belong
And no man is worthy to name Thee.

Praise be to Thee, My Lord, with all
Thy creatures,
Especially Brother Sun,
Who is our day and lightens us
therewith.
Beautiful is he and radiant with great
splendor;
Of Thee, Most High, he bears expression.

Praise be to Thee, my Lord, for Sister
Moon, and for the stars
In the heavens which Thou has formed
bright, precious and fair.

Praise be to Thee, my Lord, for
Brother Wind,
And for the air and the cloud of fair
and all weather
Through which Thou givest
sustenance to Thy creatures.

Praise be, my Lord, for Sister Water.
Who is most useful, humble, precious
and chaste.

Praise be, my Lord, for Brother Fire,
By whom Thou lightest up the night:
He is beautiful, merry, robust and strong.

Praise be, my Lord, for our sister,
Mother Earth,
Who sustains and governs us
And brings forth diverse fruits with
many-hued flowers and grass.
   —St. Francis

VI. FEMINISM AND DEEP ECOLOGY

There are important parallels between the themes of some feminist writers and social activists and the ultimate norms and principles of deep ecology. Indeed, some feminists claim that deep ecology is an intellectual articulation of insights that many females have known for centuries.

Some feminist writers have provided intensive, critical examinations of major assumptions of the dominant worldview. In particular, persons such as Elizabeth Dodson Gray in *Green Paradise Lost* criticize the view of reality as "masculine" and the myth that Nature and human society are hierarchical. [14]

By calling us to mend our personal relationships, to examine more deeply how dominant modes of thinking in our culture condition us to egoism, competition, abstraction, and domination, and by bringing forth a "voice for nature" for itself rather than just for its utility to humans, feminists deepen our sense of wonder in our lives and our commitment to creative, nonviolent, empowering social activism.

Three women from different generations especially exemplify the cultivation of ecological consciousness through sophisticated articulation of their ecological insights, and in social activism, practicing from deep principles: Mary Austin, Rachel Carson, and Dolores LaChapelle.

Mary Austin (1868-1934), author of *Land of Little Rain* (1902), *The Basket Woman* (1904), and many other books set in the California desert country, has what her biographer called a "startling relevance for the late twentieth century." [15] Austin was a writer, naturalist and feminist who interpreted our abiding responsibility to and relationship with the Earth in eloquent prose and with deep understanding.

If one is inclined to wonder at first how so many dwellers came to be in the loneliest land that ever came out of God's hands, what they do there and why stay, one does not wonder so much after having lived there. None other than this long brown land lays such a hold on the affections. The rainbow hills, the tender bluish mists, the luminous radiance of the spring, have the lotus charm. They trick the sense of

time, so that once inhabiting there you always mean to go away without quite realizing that you have not done it.
    —Mary Austin, *Land of Little Rain*

    ▬▬▬▬▬▬▬▬▬

    Rachel Carson (1907-1964) combined contemporary scientific training in biology and ecology with a deeper ecological sensibility and sensitivity. In her books, *The Sea Around Us* (1950) and *Under the Sea Wind* (1941), she extolled the intrinsic value of oceans. She was alarmed at the use of science to further exploit the seas as natural resources. Ecology, for her, was the recognition of the organic, interconnected and interactive meaning of living within Nature. She provided classic tales of humility and attentive listening to rhythms larger than our own. [16]

    Finally, Carson engaged in debate over public policies concerning Resource Conservation and Development with her book on the ecological consequences of widespread use of pesticides, *Silent Spring* (1962). This book can probably date the beginnings of the "Age of Ecology." Her willingness to engage in public debate inspired a generation of social activists to ask important questions concerning the then taken-for-granted assumptions of the use of pesticides and herbicides. Carson's writings also directly affected many European ecoactivists, including Arne Naess.

    ▬▬▬▬▬▬▬▬▬

    The "control of nature" is a phrase conceived in arrogance, born of the Neanderthal age of biology and philosophy, when it was supposed that nature exists for the convenience of man. The concepts and practices of applied entomology for the most part date from that Stone Age of science. It is our alarming misfortune that so primitive a science has armed itself with the most modern and terrible weapons, and that in turning them against the insects it has also turned them against the earth.
    —Rachel Carson, *Silent Spring*

    ▬▬▬▬▬▬▬▬▬

    The ecofeminist connection to deep ecology is well exemplified by Dolores LaChapelle, who teaches and writes on deep ecology from the Way of the Mountain Center in Silverton, Colorado. Mountaineer, skier, ritualist, and author, LaChapelle has devoted her life to reestablishing the old ways of communicating with Nature. In the preface to *Earth Wisdom,* she writes that "communication, at its best, is called love; when it breaks down completely, we call it war. And it is a sort of war that is going on now between human beings and the earth. It's not that nature refuses to communicate with us, but that we no longer have a way to communicate with it. For millennia, primitives communicated with the earth and all its beings by means of rituals and festivals where all levels of the human were open to all levels of Nature."

Through her experiential education of walking and climbing in the mountains, teaching Tai Chi and drumming, and through her intellectual insights in various publications, LaChapelle is taking the beginning steps of restoring this lost communication into contemporary, damaged societies.

She leads rituals in Earth bonding and has written on the meaning of ritual in contemporary, Earth-alienated cultures. She provides the intellectual justification for doing what the Sierra Club and other reform environmental groups have been most reluctant to admit, that all the "information" on acid rain and deforestation will not provide the experiential linkage necessary for damaged people to reconnect with the land. Her essay "Ritual Is Essential" is reprinted in appendix F. [17]

In sum, the emergence of feminist-ecoactivist connections, through conferences, coalitions with reform environmental groups and antinuclear groups, in the writings of women such as LaChapelle, Carson, and Austin, as well as Carolyn Merchant, Anne Dillard, Susan Griffin and Elizabeth Gray, indicates that the process of exploring these connections to deep ecology is a very potent force for the future. Carolyn Merchant has researched the history of science (*The Death of Nature,* 1980) and the contribution of women to the environmental/ecology movement. In her essay, "Feminism and Ecology" (see appendix B), she uses Commoner's laws of ecology and makes explicit linkages between them and feminist concerns.

VII. PRIMAL PEOPLES AND DEEP ECOLOGY

The great sea
Has sent me adrift
It moves me
As the weed in a great river
Earth and the great weather
Move me
Have carried me away
And move my inward parts with joy.

When an Eskimo woman shaman, Uvavnuk, sings this song, the intuition of deep ecology, of connectedness, moves through it.

As deep ecologists reevaluate primal peoples, including the diverse nations and tribes of Native Americans, they seek not a revival of the Romantic version of primal peoples as "noble savages," but a basis for philosophy, religion, cosmology, and conservation practices that can be applied to our own society.

Indians have spoken of the *great spirit* and have given moving evocations to the land, to a sense of place. Chief Seattle, for example, in his famous surrender speech of 1851, said "One thing we know for sure. The earth was not made for man, man was made for the earth." But Europeans, and Western intellectuals, have not listened very carefully.

Supporters of deep ecology find much to inspire them in Native American thought and perception. As historian J. Donald Hughes concludes in his chapter on "Indian Wisdom for Today": "One of the inescapable facts which emerges when we contrast the Indian past with the present is that the American Indians' cultural patterns, based on careful hunting and agriculture carried on according to spiritual perceptions of nature, actually preserved the earth and life on the earth."[18]

Natural changes, cycles, rhythms, earthquakes, floods, mini ice ages all influenced the place in which Native Americans lived, but the people persisted in their spiritual ecology. Richard Nelson, in *Make Prayers to the Raven,* a study of the native natural history of the Koyukon of Alaska, says that the spiritual awareness of native peoples draws us into myth time. The Koyukon live in a world that watches. "The surroundings are aware, sensate, personified. They feel. They can be offended. And they must, at every moment, be treated with respect." The central assumption of the Koyukon worldview is that the natural

96

and supernatural worlds are inseparable; each is intrinsically a part of the other. Humans and natural entities are in constant spiritual interchange and reciprocity. [19]

Native Americans and other primal peoples can teach us reverence for the land, the *place* of being. Nature was used — beaver, bison, etc. — for sustenance, but richness of ends was achieved with material technology that was elegant, sophisticated, appropriate, and controlled within the context of a traditional society.

Native Americans also teach us the viability of communal societies based on mutual aid between people and bonding with nonhuman Nature. The modern, Western version of isolated individuals forever competitive, aggressive, and untrusting of other people is not the best of "human nature."

The Hopis prophesied in the 1600s that the whites would come and destroy the land and themselves, according to anthropologist Stan Steiner. The Indians would try to tell the whites how to live in peace and harmony with the land, but the whites would not, or could not, hear. Steiner explains the basic Indian philosophy of the sacred Circle of Life: "In the Circle of Life every being is no more, or less, than any other. We are all Sisters and Brothers. Life is shared with the bird, bear, insects, plants, mountains, clouds, stars, sun. To be in harmony with the natural world, one must live within the cycles of life." Steiner sensitively discusses the movement on the part of many American Indians to return to the old ways of life and to defend their land against ever-increasing industrial destruction. [20]

Evidence indicates that the primal mind holds the totality of human-centered artifacts, such as language, social organization, norms, shared meanings, and magic, within the first world of Nature. For the primal mind there is no sharp break between humans and the rest of Nature. Many deep ecologists feel sympathetic to the rhythm and ways of being experienced by primal peoples. Supporters of deep ecology do not advocate "going back to the stone age," but seek inspiration from primal traditions.

━━━━━━━━━━━

. . . the American Indians' cultural patterns, based on careful hunting and agriculture carried on according to spiritual perceptions of nature, actually preserved the earth and life on earth. . . . Indian conceptions of the universe and nature must be examined seriously, as valid ways of relating to the world, and not as superstitious, primitive, or unevolved. . . . Perhaps the most important insight which can be gained

from the Indian heritage is reverence for the earth and life. . . . It is important for us to learn from nature as the early Indians did, to keep an ear to the earth, and regain our perspective by frequent experiences with the non-artificial world, with animals and wild land. . . . The traditional Indian view valued people, the interrelated social group living in harmony with nature. . . .
—J. Donald Hughes, *American Indian Ecology* (1983)

VIII. MARTIN HEIDEGGER

When the early morning light quietly grows above the mountains . . .

The world's darkening never reaches to the light of Being.

We are too late for the gods and too early for Being. Being's poem, just begun, is man.
— Martin Heidegger

Martin Heidegger made three contributions to the deep, long-range ecology literature. First, he provided a major critique and indictment of the development of Western philosophy since Plato. He concluded that this anthropocentric development paved the way for the technocratic mentality which espouses domination over Nature. *Being,* a key ontological concept for Heidegger, was constrained into narrow Christian paths or into secular, humanistic, technological philosophy in the West.

Second, Heidegger called his readers to the "dangerous field of thinking." Thinking, for Heidegger, was closer to the Taoist process of contemplation than to Western analytical thinking.

Third, Heidegger called us to dwell authentically on this Earth, parallel to our call to dwell in our bioregion and to dwell with alertness to the natural processes.

Vincent Vycinas concisely translated Heidegger's meaning of dwelling:

Dwelling is not primarily inhabiting but taking care of and creating that space within which something comes into its own and flourishes.

98

Dwelling is primarily saving, in the older sense of setting something free to become itself, what it essentially is. . . . Dwelling is that which cares for things so that they essentially presence and come into their own. . . .

Heidegger called his readers to step back to a "reversal" of our usual analytical thinking and to use our intuitive power. By stepping back we may open the way for releasement of Being.

Heidegger drew intellectual inspiration from the pre-Socratic philosophers whom he saw as closer to the primal mind, and from Nature, from his own relationship with the fields and forests near his home. He seems to have had great difficulty in explaining to rationalist philosophers and Christian theologians his approach to thinking. Contemporary ecophilosophers face this same problem when constrained to use only the concepts and language of the rationalist Western philosophical tradition. Near the end of his life, Heidegger realized that the poetic voice was a clearer expression of intuition than formal philosophy. He arrived at a biocentric position in which humans would "let beings be."

Heidegger wrote:

Mortals dwell in that they receive the sky as sky. They leave to the sun and the moon their journey, to the stars their courses, to the seasons their blessing and their inclemency; they do not turn night into day nor day into a harassed unrest.

———————

When through a rent in the rain-clouded
sky a ray of the sun suddenly glides
over the gloom of the meadows . . .

We never come to thoughts. They come
to us.
That is the proper hour of discourse.
   —Martin Heidegger

———————

ON MARTIN HEIDEGGER'S
DEEP ECOLOGICAL PHILOSOPHY
Michael Zimmerman

Heidegger claims that the "essence" of technology is not technological devices, but the disclosure to man of all beings whatsoever as objective, calculable, quantifiable, disposable raw material which is of value only insofar as it contributes to the enhancement of human power. Heidegger says that the revelation of all beings as raw material for man is the culmination of the history of Western civilization and philosophy and at the same time it is the triumph of nihilism. It is this complex interrelationship of philosophy, technology, and nihilism that we must explore. . . .

This [new way of thinking about beings] would allow man to dwell within the world *not* as its master . . . being able to let the beings of the world display themselves in all their glory. . . . Heidegger agreed with many of the aims of the new [ecological] conscience, including its desire to halt the senseless pillaging of nature for profit. But he was more radical than most ecological thinkers, who continue to look upon man as "husbander" of nature, in the sense of having the "right" to manipulate nature as long as he does not cause too much damage in the process. For this still fails to see that the most important threat of the technological view is not a physical one, but a spiritual one. [21]

IX. EASTERN SPIRITUAL PROCESS TRADITIONS

Eastern sources include both Taoist and Buddhist writings. In particular, contemporary deep ecologists have found inspiration in the Taoist classic, the *Tao Te Ching,* and the writings of the thirteenth-century Japanese Buddhist teacher, Dōgen.

Eastern traditions express organic unity, address what we have called the minority tradition, and express acceptance of biocentric equality in some traditions. Furthermore, these sources relate to the process of becoming more mature, of awakening from illusion and delusion.

These traditions have also had a traceable influence in American intellectual development. Emerson and Thoreau were touched by the Eastern traditions and through them these traditions were transferred to Muir. The Eastern influence has been perpetuated in twentieth-century America in the works of F. C. S. Northrup, D. T. Suzuki, Alan Watts, Allen Ginsberg, Paul Goodman, Gary Snyder, and many others.

In the 1950s, the so-called Beat poets such as Ginsberg and Snyder began translating Japanese and Chinese poetry based on their own developing ecological consciousness. The poems and prose of Dōgen, Chuang-Tzu, Hua-yen and other Indian, Chinese and Japanese classic writers were taken down from the dusty shelves of libraries and out from the isolated classes on Eastern Philosophy or Chinese Writing and brought to groups of people engaged in the "real work" of cultivating their own ecological consciousness.

Writing on "Sattva: Enlightenment for Plants and Trees in Buddhism" in *CoEvolution,* William R. LaFleur concluded: "The point here, of course, is not to portray a sharp dichotomy between East and West. Neither the human mind nor historical accuracy can tolerate that. But there are materials and insights . . . which may be of use in coping with a set of crises given us and our world by men both in the East and the West of today."[22]

Zen master Robert Aitken Roshi has written an essay, "Gandhi, Dōgen and Deep Ecology," which clearly shows the connection between Gandhi's mature social activism, the meditations of Dōgen and the insights and ultimate norms of deep ecology. (See appendix C.)

X. ROBINSON JEFFERS

Robinson Jeffers dwelled on the California coastline near Big Sur for most of his long and productive life. He gave voice to the rivers, mountains and hawks of that coastline and placed twentieth-century human "achievements" in the cosmic context. Humans with their intellectual systems, nuclear bombs, and grand designs had become "a little too abstract, a little too wise. It is time for us to kiss the earth again." He clearly rejected anthropocentric subjectivism, or what he called *human solipsism,* and strove instead for objective truth.

Jeffers's deep ecology perspective is found in a statement of religious-scientific pantheism written in 1934:

I believe that the universe is one being, all its parts are different expressions of the same energy, and they are all in communication with each other, therefore parts of one organic whole. (This is physics, I believe, as well as religion.) The parts change and pass, or die, people and races and rocks and stars; none of them seems to me important in itself, but only the whole. This whole is in all its parts so beautiful, and is felt by me to be so intensely in earnest, that I am compelled to love it, and to think of it as divine. It seems to me that this whole alone is worthy of the deeper sort of love; and that there is peace, freedom, I might say a kind of salvation, in turning one's affections outward toward this one God, rather than inwards on one's self, or on humanity, or on human imaginations and abstractions—the world of spirits.

I think that it is our privilege and felicity to love God for his beauty, without claiming or expecting love from him. We are not important to him, but he to us.

I think that one may contribute (ever so slightly) to the beauty of things by making one's own life and environment beautiful, so far as one's power reaches.

Jeffers has been called by one critic "Spinoza's twentieth-century evangelist." His poetry is actually an expression of the psychology of the emotions. It alternates between joyous works describing the active emotion of increasing one's self-realization as part of the greater Self-realization by an identification with the totality of God/Nature, and dark tragedies of incest, murder and other calamities which beset those who are driven to their fiery destruction by overwhelming passions.

Jeffers involves humans in the spiritual quest for freedom in the whole of Nature/God, from galaxies to subatomic particles, but especially in the organic world of his immediate existence. This is clear in Jeffers's explanation of one of his most famous poems, "The Tower Beyond Tragedy": [23]

Orestes, in the poem, identifies himself with the whole divine nature of things: earth, man, and stars, the mountain forest and the running streams; they are all one existence, one organism. He perceives this, and that himself is included in it, identical with it. This perception is his tower beyond the reach of tragedy; because, whatever may happen, the great organism will remain forever immortal and immortally beautiful. Orestes has "fallen in love outward" not with a human creature, not with a limited cause, but with the universal God. That is the meaning of my poem.

Ecological consciousness seems most vibrant in the poetic mode. The poetic voices of Jeffers and Snyder, so rare in modern poetry but frequently found in primal people's oral tradition, are a virtual cascade of celebration of Nature/God and being.

Jeffers's poem, "Oh, Lovely Rock" from *Selected Poetry* (1938), illustrates that looking and seeing deeply are quite different. We can begin seeing ordinary things in their extraordinary perspective.

OH, LOVELY ROCK

We stayed the night in the pathless gorge of Ventana
 Creek, up the east fork.
The rock walls and the mountain ridges hung forest
 on forest above our heads, maple and redwood,
Laurel, oak, madrone, up to the high and slender
 Santa Lucian firs that stare up the cataracts
Of slide-rock to the star-color precipices.
We lay on gravel and kept a little campfire for warmth.
Past midnight only two or three coals glowed red in
 the cooling darkness; I laid a clutch of dead bay leaves
On the ember ends and felted dry sticks across them
 and lay down again. The revived flame
Lighted my sleeping son's face and his companion's, and the vertical
 face of the great gorge-wall
Across the stream. Light leaves overhead danced in the fire's breath,
 tree-trunks were seen; it was the rock wall
That fascinated my eyes and mind. Nothing strange: light gray
 diorite with two or three slanting seams in it,
Smooth-polished by the endless attrition of slides and
 floods; no fern nor lichen, pure naked rock . . . as
 if I were
Seeing rock for the first time. As if I were seeing
 through the flame-lit surface into the real and bodily
And living rock. Nothing strange . . . I cannot
Tell you how strange: the silent passion, the deep
 nobility and childlike loveliness: this fate going on
Outside our fates. It is here in the mountain like a
 grave smiling child. I shall die and my boys
Will live and die, our world will go on through its
 rapid agonies of change and discovery, this age will die,
And wolves have howled in the snow around a new
 Bethlehem: this rock will be here, grave, earnest,
 not passive: the energies
That are its atoms will still be bearing the whole
 mountain above: and I, many packed centuries ago
Felt its intense reality with love and wonder, this
 lonely rock.

XI. JOHN MUIR

John Muir's legacy to the deep, long-range ecology movement is his vision of the essential oneness of the Earth, his sense of participatory science, his expression of biocentric equality and his active leadership in issues of public policy affecting wild places. [24]

Again and again the reform and deep ecology movements have returned to the insights expressed by John Muir in these quotes: [25]

Let the Christian hunter go to the Lord's woods and kill his well-kept beasts, or wild Indians, and it is well; but let an enterprising specimen of these proper, predestined victims go to houses and fields and kill the most worthless person of the vertical godlike killers—oh! that is horribly unorthodox, and on the part of the Indians atrocious murder! Well, I have precious little sympathy for the selfish propriety of civilized man, and if a war of races should occur between the wild beasts and Lord Man, I would be tempted to sympathize with the bears. . . .

The world we are told was made for man. A presumption that is totally unsupported by facts. There is a very numerous class of men who are cast into painful fits of astonishment whenever they find anything, living or dead, in all God's universe, which they cannot eat or render in some way what they call useful to themselves. . . . Not content with taking all of earth, they also claim the celestial country as if the only ones who possess the kind of souls for which that imponderable empire was planned. . . .

Nature's object in making animals and plants might possibly be first of all the happiness of each one of them, not the creation of all for the happiness of one. Why ought man to value himself as more than an infinitely small composing unit of the one great unit of creation? . . . The universe would be incomplete without man; but it would also be incomplete without the smallest transmicroscopic creature that dwells beyond our conceitful eyes and knowledge.

In the conflict over building a dam inside the boundary of Yosemite National Park, at a place called Hetch Hetchy, Muir and his allies saw the broader implications of this dam while proponents of the dam saw only the narrower context of providing water to the expanding urban center of San Francisco.

In fighting for the protection of Yosemite Park, Muir was led into what he called the "political quag" and was later to write in his journal, "This playing at politics saps at the very foundation of righteousness." But he took direct action because he saw such action was necessary. In the 1980s the further damming and diversion of water from the Tuolumne River below Hetch Hetchy remains a controversial issue.

Muir's writings express his deep ecology principles, but he had difficulty writing for a general audience about his direct experiences in the Sierra. His reception by critics demonstrates a continuing dilemma for deep ecologists. The difficulty, as we see it, is the difference in perspective between the narrow definition of rational in the modern Western worldview and the deeper objectivism of Muir, Jeffers and the Eastern traditions discussed earlier in this chapter.

Michael Cohen in *The Pathless Way* discusses Muir's "stormy sermons" and his difficulties with the compromising political process of liberal-democratic societies where "interest group politics" means "power politics" (the mobilization of money and constituencies to influence legislators through numbers, not principles). [26]

Finally, Muir inspired the deep ecology movement by asking significant questions of his own life and of the human species. Can humans limit themselves and reverse the path of destruction done in the name of progress, exploitive economic development, and warfare on Nature itself? The word *ecocide* had not been coined during Muir's lifetime, but he certainly understood the concept and its implications.

In 1875, after spending several years roaming in the Sierra, exploring the glaciers and mountains and studying the increasing human impact of grazing domestic sheep on mountain meadows, Muir wrote in his journal:

I often wonder what men will do with the mountains. That is, with their utilizable, destructable garments. Will he cut down all, and make ships and houses with the trees? If so, what will be the final and far upshot? Will human destruction, like those of Nature—fire, flood, and avalanche—work out a higher good, a finer beauty? Will a better civilization come, in accord with obvious nature, and all this wild beauty be set to human poetry? Another outpouring of lava or the coming of the glacial period could scarce wipe out the flowers and flowering shrubs more effectively than do the sheep. And what then is coming— what is the human part of the mountain's destiny"? [27]

XII. DAVID BROWER

David Brower has been at the cutting edge of reform environmental politics for over thirty years. First as executive director of the Sierra

Club (1952-1969), then as founder and president of Friends of the Earth (1969-79), Brower has played an active role in some of the major public policy decisions concerning natural resources in the United States, including the controversy over Echo Park Dam in the early 1950s, the battles over dams on the Colorado River in the Grand Canyon in the 1960s, the legislation to create a National Wilderness Preservation System, the reform of the U.S. Forest Service, the creation of the Environmental Protection Agency and the many events, conferences and activities which internationalized the environmental movement during the 1970s.

In his public career and in his private intellectual/emotional growth, Brower showed the sometimes difficult interplay between reformist political action and the deeper ecological context. He grounded his philosophy in Jeffers's deep ecological insight that humans are only a small part of the biosphere, not lord and master of all. And he spoke frequently of the "rights of future generations" of humans and other beings to a "healthy environment."

———

In the foreword to *This Is The American Earth* (1961), David Brower wrote:

Although Thomas Jefferson argued that no one generation has a right to encroach upon another generation's freedom, the future's right to know the freedom of wilderness is going fast. And it need not go at all. A tragic loss could be prevented if only there could be broader understanding of this: that the resources of the earth do not exist just to be spent for the comfort, pleasure, or convenience of the generation or two who first learn how to spend them; that some of the resources exist for saving, and what diminishes them diminishes all mankind; that one of these is wilderness, wherein the flow of life, in its myriad forms, has gone on since the beginning of life, essentially uninterrupted by man and his technology; that this wilderness is worth saving for what it can mean to itself as part of the conservation ethic; that the saving is imperative to civilization and all mankind, whether or not all men yet know it.

———

Brower contributed especially to the deep ecology movement in two ways. First, he showed that environmental/ecology issues transcend political parties, transcend the expert opinion of Resource Conservation ideology and transcend nationalism. Second, through his publishing efforts he brought deeper ecological messages to two generations of readers.

Brower suggested in the 1950s that a broad coalition of environmental groups be formed. In the 1980s he took up the task of uniting the peace movement and the environmental movement. He created several Fate of the Earth conferences and sought "to evoke ecological conscience in all sectors of society, a few at a time." When asked if he thought John Muir would approve of this direction for the environmental movement, Brower responded with a quote from Muir: "When we try to pick out anything by itself, we find it hitched to everything else in the universe."

Through the Sierra Club and Friends of the Earth, Brower helped popularize deep ecology ideas by publishing beautiful exhibit format books on Thoreau, Muir, and Jeffers. He encouraged Paul Ehrlich to write *The Population Bomb*. The anthologies which Brower collected from the proceedings of the Sierra Club wilderness conferences of the 1960s often provided major statements of biocentric equality and the meaning of the wilderness experience as a vital human need. [28]

Finally, Brower contributed by questioning some of the assumptions of the dominant, modern worldview, especially the faith in unlimited technology. His own "conversion," as he called it, to the role of skeptic of unlimited technology he traced to the issue of siting a nuclear reactor at Diablo Canyon on the California coastline. Listening to scientists and technologists at several conferences, he realized that they did not have objective, neutral answers to technical problems and that they did not discuss ethical issues. In the issue of the Diablo Canyon reactor, Brower saw, over a twenty-year period, continuing deceit, fraud and manipulation of data by scientists to serve the corporate interests of a giant utility company. He further saw, in the political processes, a continuing pattern of compromise and supposed tradeoffs to "make a deal" which later had to be rectified as the failures of the decision-making process became more and more obvious. This has resulted in the continuing "radicalization" of Brower—"America's foremost conservationist." [29]

In sum, there are many diverse sources of the deep ecology perspective. The group of ideas which make up deep ecology are still being nourished by further understanding of the wisdom of the traditions discussed in this chapter. Historians, philosophers, and social scientists can contribute to the articulation of the deep ecology aspects of these traditions and suggest ways of cultivating ecological consciousness and ways to act from deep ecological principles in our own culture.

The mountains, the teacher says, are walking. . . . They are constantly at rest and constantly walking. We must devote ourselves to a detailed study of this virtue of walking. . . . He who doubts that mountains walk does not yet understand his own walking.
  —*Dōgen*, "The Mountains and Rivers Sutra"

CHAPTER 7
•
WHY WILDERNESS
IN THE NUCLEAR AGE?

What I have been preparing to say is this, in wildness is the preservation of the world. . . . Life consists of wildness. The most alive is the wildest. Not yet subdued to man, its presence refreshes him. . . . When I would re-create myself, I seek the darkest wood, the thickest and most interminable and to the citizen, most dismal, swamp. I enter as a sacred place, a Sanctum sanctorum. *There is the strength, the marrow, of Nature. In short, all good things are wild and free.*

—*Henry David Thoreau (1851)*[1]

For an advocate of deep ecology, wilderness is a landscape or ecosystem that has been minimally disrupted by the intervention of humans, especially the destructive technology of modern societies. The legal definition of section numbers and parcels is less relevant than the wild quality of the landscape. [2]

In this chapter we discuss the contact which humans can experience in undeveloped spaces, the intuitions of organic wholeness which many experience in such places, and the "rational" arguments which take place within the dominant worldview and which are presented in public policy debates over allocation of public lands to "wilderness" or "nonwilderness" designations in the law.

I. EXPERIENCING THE WILDERNESS

Experiencing the wilderness or the wildness of a place, from a deep ecology perspective, is a process of 1) developing a sense of place, 2) redefining the heroic person from conquerer of the land to the person fully experiencing the natural place, 3) cultivating the virtues of modesty and humility and 4) realizing how the mountains and rivers, fish and bears are continuing their own actualizing processes. The prototypical outcome of the active engagement between the mind and wilderness is seen in John Muir's encounter with the Sierra.

In the early 1870s, after spending several seasons in the high country, Muir was more fully realizing the supreme lesson that Nature is one living, pulsing organism. Theoretically he had believed in this unity before. Now he was experiencing it. He wrote at this time, "The whole wilderness is unity and interrelation, is alive and familiar . . . the very stones are talkative, sympathetic, brotherly. . . . No particle is ever wasted or worn out by externally flowing from use to use." [3]

Muir's intuition of unity influenced his study of Nature. For Muir, as for the process philosophers and contemporary ecologists, the purpose of science is not just to classify and manipulate bits and pieces of the planet, but to explain while fully experiencing. As a deeper ecologist, informed by his quest for ecosophy or ecowisdom, Muir was looking into the landscape, not just at it. He began to understand grasshoppers; pine trees and rocks were not to be understood just as separate entities but interwoven.

In his studies in the Sierra, Muir struggled to express his intuition in the form acceptable to his materialist-reductionist contemporaries. First he used the metaphor of an *open book* but found that too static and fixed in the past. Then he attempted to view Nature as a path or several paths but he came to realize that true wilderness is pathless. He had been following, he realized, the pathless way.[4]

On his extensive questing in the Sierra, Muir sometimes took only bread, tea and an overcoat to keep him warm during storms. He loved storms of all sorts and was especially alert to their possibilities. He went to free-flowing Nature, to wild mountain landscapes, rivers and valleys, ". . . not as a mere sport or plaything excursion, but to find the law that governs the relations subsisting between humans and Nature."[5]

This type of approach to wild places is in sharp contrast with much contemporary recreation — especially what is called "outdoor recreation," with its emphasis on easy access to some lake or river, comfort and convenience for the traveler, and extensive focus on recreational equipment such as all-terrain vehicles or snowmobiles.

We suggest that humans have a vital need for wilderness, wild places, to help us become more mature; but beyond our psychological needs, wilderness is the habitat of other beings which have a right to live and blossom for themselves (inherent value). Thus on both the grounds of self-realization and biocentric equality, the wilderness issue as public policy decision and as re-creative experience assumes great importance from a deep ecology perspective.

There is a great deal of talk these days about saving the environment. We must, for the environment sustains our bodies. But as humans we also require support for our spirits, and this is what certain kinds of places provide. The catalyst that converts any physical location — any environment if you will — into a place, is the process of experiencing deeply. A place is a piece of the whole environment that has been claimed by feelings. Viewed simply as a life-support system, the earth is an environment. Viewed as a resource that sustains our humanity, the earth is a collection of places. We never speak, for example, of an environment we have known; it is always places we have known — and recall. We are homesick for places, we are reminded of places, it is the sounds and smells and sights of places which haunts us and against which we often measure our present.

—Alan Gussow, "A Sense of Place" (1971)[6]

The question concerning wilderness is part of the larger question, "How shall we live and what shall we live for?"

111

Presented with the question from the resource economist, "Why not plastic trees?" the deep ecologist responds, "That's absurd," or he tries to show the benefits in dollar terms of setting aside some parcel of land as "designated wilderness." But he intuits that there is greater meaning and importance to the quality of wildness than can be described by the calculations of resource economists.

In our technocratic-industrial society there are many who share these deep intuitions and the experience of the ritual journey into wilderness as *sacred space*. And this journey has been shared by many people in diverse cultures and times. People in primal cultures, dwelling in ecosystems, bonded to place, having communion with wild animals and realizing that spirit and matter are not inherently separated, have experienced this deeper sense of place.

━━━━━━━

Paul Shepard in his essay on sense of place describes the ritualistic journeying of the Australian:

In going on the pilgrimage called walkabout, the Aborigine travels to a succession of named places, each familiar from childhood and each the place of some episode in the story of creation. The sacred qualities of each are heightened by symbolic art forms and religious relics. The journey is into the interior in every sense, as myth is the dramatic externalization of the events of an inner history. To the archive where the individual moves simultaneously through his personal and tribal past, renewing contact with crucial points, a journey into time and space refreshing the meaning of his own being. [7]

━━━━━━━

This questing includes appreciation of nonhuman self, and for some, experiential understanding that mountains and rivers are actualizing. Mountains actualizing may be a most difficult concept, at least for modern persons. Yet Leopold's evocative phrase "thinking like a mountain" calls up this consciousness. To paraphrase Leopold, we might say, "I dreamed I was thinking like a mountain but when I awoke I did not know if I was a man thinking like a mountain or a mountain thinking like a man."

In his famous essay, "Mountains and Rivers Sutra," Dōgen says:

As for mountains, there are mountains hidden in jewels; there are mountains hidden in marshes, mountains hidden in the sky; there are mountains hidden in mountains. There is a study of mountains hidden in hiddenness. An ancient Buddha said, "Mountains are mountains and

112

rivers are rivers." The meaning of these words is not that mountains are mountains, but that mountains are mountains. Therefore, we should thoroughly study these mountains. When we thoroughly study the mountains, this is mountain training. Such mountains and rivers themselves spontaneously become wise men and sages. [8]

Without such depths of consciousness as Dōgen expresses, perhaps, but with elan for the physical excitement, open vistas and flow of intuition, the contemporary wilderness traveler has some sense of following the simple way to richer ends.

Statements by two persons who have experienced wilderness and who have worked to defend wilderness areas in the arena of public policy are worth quoting. The first is Dolores LaChapelle's description of powder skiing, the second is David Brower's recounting of his trips in the Sierra during the 1920s: [9]

Long before I had heard of Martin Heidegger . . . I was experiencing what he calls the "round dance of appropriation," the interrelationship of the fourfold: earth, sky, gods, and mortals in *my* world of powder snow skiing — one of the few sub-cultures in modern industrial society still open to the fourfold. . . .

In an authentic "world," the mortals are in togetherness not only with the others of the fourfold — the earth, the sky, and the gods; but mortals are together with one another. The freedom, grace, and joy of this togetherness in the powder "world" occurs in response to the gift of the sky: unbroken snow. This is most easily skied in direct response to the earth's gravity — down the fall line — but the dips and contours of the earth automatically lay out the "way" to follow; and for the skillful skiers, there is only one best "way" for each, so all can ski together at top speed and still flow with one another and with the earth. . . . Just as in a flight of birds turning through the air, no *one* is the leader and none are the followers, yet all are together; so also the powder snow skiers are all together effortlessly, because they are appropriating, responsively conforming themselves to the earth and sky in their "world," thus there are no collisions. Each human *being* is free to follow his own path.

— Dolores LaChapelle, *Earth Wisdom* (1978)

I am partial . . . to the moving trip that can give the visitor the feel of a big, continuous wilderness — one in which you can cross pass after pass and know that on the other side you don't drop into civilization, but stay in wilderness instead. In big wilderness you learn how important size itself is to the viability of the wilderness. It needs enough buffer to keep its heartland essentially free from the pervasive influences of technology. Such big wilderness is scarce, and is vanishing at the rate of

about a million acres a year, chiefly to the chainsaw. People who know it can save it. No one else.
—David Brower, in his tribute to John Muir, in *Gentle Wilderness* (1968)[10]

━━━━━━━━━

But we live, as Thoreau said, a "sort of border life" between the first world of Nature and the second world of technocratic-industrial society. And, Thoreau continued, "you never gain something but that you lose something." As some humans greatly increase their analytical power and their power to dominate landscapes with vast construction projects, missile systems, etc., they seem to lose some of their power of understanding, of thoughtfulness and meditative dancing in the wonder of the cosmos. Even to mention this joyful wonderment and sense of place within the narrowly defined constraints and constructs of the resource economist and materialist is seen by some people as heresy, or overly sentimental.[11]

So arguments for and against wilderness preservation are usually presented within the confines of the dominant worldview. In the following section of this chapter we look at some of the major wilderness-related arguments within the dominant worldview and criticize them from a deep ecology perspective.

━━━━━━━━━

Only by going alone in silence, without baggage, can one truly get into the heart of the wilderness. All other travel is mere dust and hotels and baggage and chatter.
—John Muir

━━━━━━━━━

II. WILDERNESS ARGUMENTS WITHIN THE DOMINANT SOCIAL WORLDVIEW

The most frequently used legal definition of wilderness is contained in the Wilderness Act of 1964:

A wilderness, in contrast with those areas where man and his works dominate the landscape, is hereby recognized as an area where the earth and its community of life are untrammeled by man, where man himself is a visitor who does not remain. An area of wilderness is further

114

*defined to mean in the Act an area of undeveloped Federal land retain-
ing its primeval character and influence, without permanent improvement of human habitation, which is protected and managed so as to
preserve its natural conditions and which (1) generally appears to have
been affected primarily by the forces of nature, with the imprint of
man's work substantially unnoticeable; (2) has outstanding opportunities for solitude or a primitive and unconfined type of recreation;
(3) has at least five thousand acres of land or is of sufficient size as
to make practicable its preservation and use in an unimpaired condition; and (4) may also contain ecological, geological or other features
of scientific, educational, scenic or historical value.*

It is within the framework of this legal definition, or some adaptation of it, that arguments are formed in the political arena of the United
States.

1. Resource Economists Look at Wilderness
(But Are Not Seeing It)

The Resource Conservation and Development ideology has been
defined as that ideology which sees Nature as material for human use,
consumption and development. Nature is primarily a storehouse of
natural resources for humans. The intrinsic value of Nature, or the
spirit of a place, has no sanction in this ideology.

Designating certain areas or parcels of land, rivers, islands or oceans
as "official wilderness" is a bone that sticks in the throat of those
natural resource economists who favor rapid economic development
based on narrowly perceived human needs and wants. When wilderness is included in the calculations of these resource economists, some
incommensurables enter into the equation. Preservation of any area
as wilderness is based on a convoluted economic argument. Different
goals may not be qualitatively comparable. When the economist tries
to put value on some area by adding the dollar values of use by snow-
mobilers, backpackers, Native American shamans using the area to
"make medicine," and the market value of timber, then those commodities with high market value win. As John Rodman concludes,
"When recreation, scenic beauty, wilderness and wildlife habitat protection were incorporated by the Conservationist as resource uses, the
result was not only subtly to degrade wilderness to the status of something useful but also to introduce something alien, ultimately indigest-
ible into the body of Resource Conservation."[12]

Even welfare economists who have attempted to use the tools of
economic rationality to defend a wilderness, such as the free-flowing

Snake River in Hell's Canyon, Idaho, eventually are unable to defend anything but a degraded concept of wilderness. John Krutilla, for example, argues that present value should be determined by future benefits. He begins with the assumption that Nature is irreproducible as compared to the commodities which can be obtained from Nature (timber and water, for example). Materials can be substituted for each other, but the supply of natural environments which can be designated wilderness will remain constant or decrease if existing wild areas are converted into intensely managed "tree farms," or dams are built on the few still free-flowing rivers in North America or vast ecosystems are massively altered by humans during a short time frame. In more economically developed nations, at least, the demand for wilderness-dependent recreation will increase in the future, assuming larger populations of humans want a wilderness experience. Because it is possible to find substitutes for materials derived from wilderness areas but difficult to create a wilderness, the reproducibility cost is much higher than the benefits of logging a wilderness old-growth forest. Because it is assumed people will pay to have a wilderness experience in the future, preservation for the future keeps the options open of using that wilderness area for recreation or for extracting resources with more advanced and less environmentally impacting technology in the future. [13]

But this argument in favor of wilderness for small areas (less than ten percent of the Federal lands in the lower forty-eight states in the United States is even considered for wilderness designation) is discounted by other economists who argue that the amenity values are not as valuable as commodities. Refraining from current use, they argue, is costly, and Nature is reproducible. Some argue that natural "appearances" can be restored "so that nobody will even know the difference."

Another critic of the welfare economist's arguments in favor of wilderness argues that there is no intrinsic value in "rare" landscapes and that "the supply" of natural environments is affected by technology in that with technology humans can manipulate both biological processes and information and significance. [14]

Roderick Nash, author of *Wilderness and the American Mind,* has developed a theory of "exporting wilderness," in which more affluent persons in economically developed nations could contribute money through some appropriate organization (such as World Wildlife Fund) or through buying touristic experiences in Third World nations. If tourists spend money to see wildlife in its habitat then the reserves

116

would be converted to a higher economic value rather than using them for grazing of domestic livestock, which might yield a lower "rate of return" on investment. [15]

The difficulty with this argument is that it still is based on a definition of preservation within a short-term, narrowly conceived human economy. If some mineral were discovered in a Nature reserve in Brazil, for example, which was used by tourists from the United States (spending their money to see wildlife in habitat) but the mineral would yield X times more money on the world market if extracted than tourism does, then the economically rational action would be to extract the mineral even if it disrupted the habitat of wildlife and drastically reduced the income derived from tourists.

In sum, there is no consideration of intrinsic worth for wild Nature in the calculus of Resource Conservation and Development. And there is no permanent assurance of protection for wilderness and wildlife since it all depends on the fluctuations of the world economy and transient subjective tastes. At best, some of the worst abuses of the market could be mitigated by exposing low cost/benefit ratios of development. But the assumptions of this ideology rest on the assertion of human chauvinism. Even extended utilitarian arguments that try to place a dollar value on the clean air and water derived from wilderness for the benefit of humans assume that Earth exists primarily for human use.

The deep ecology perspective on natural resource economics is quite different for it involves questions of inherent value and right livelihood. A system of economics consistent with deep ecology principles needs to be developed but is beyond the scope of the introduction to deep ecology in this book.

However, E. F. Schumacher provides an example of what we mean when he contrasts the conventional economist with what he calls the *Buddhist economist*. [16] The Buddhist economist sees "the essence of civilization not in the multiplication of wants but in the purification of human character." And, Schumacher continues, "While the materialist is mainly interested in goods, the Buddhist is mainly interested in liberation. . . . The study of Buddhist economics could be recommended even to those who believe that economic growth is more important than any spiritual or religious values. It is not a question of choosing between 'modern growth' and 'traditional stagnation.' It is a question of finding the right path of development, the Middle Way between materialist heedlessness and traditional immobility, in short, of finding 'Right Livelihood.'"

The only acceptable strategy of economic development is *ecodevelopment,* a strategy that flows with the natural processes of a specific bioregion and leaves vast areas free as untrammeled wild places. [17]

2. Wilderness as National Heritage

In technocratic-industrial societies, only a few places have secular, symbolic value and are in some cases "saved" from massive resource extraction projects. In the United States such places include the Grand Canyon of the Colorado River, Yosemite Valley, Death Valley, and the Florida Everglades. But all these places have been and are being severely impacted by land use patterns outside the artificial boundaries of the national parks — strip mining, diversion of rivers, oil and gas extraction, housing developments, industrial tourism, and so on.

The cultural embodiment or national heritage argument is deeper than the economist's argument that land is "created" by people who seek personal profit and have no goals besides maximizing profit. People who identify with a place, with Yosemite Valley or some very small local valley or mountain, could speak of "our river" or "our mountains" and could oppose damming the river or strip mining the mountain. [18]

We seek a renewed stirring of love for the earth
We plead that what we are capable of doing is
not always what we ought to do.
We urge that all people now determine
that a wide untrammeled freedom shall remain
to testify that this generation has love for the next.
If we want to succeed in that, we might show, meanwhile,
a little more love for this one, and for each other.
— Nancy Newhall, *This Is The American Earth* (1961)

Some leaders of environmental organizations have encouraged reservation of special places which are part of the world cultural heritage. UNESCO and the International Union for the Conservation of Nature through their world biosphere program have institutionalized this concept by listing "significant" areas or places, including Redwood National Park in northern California. National governments are called upon to protect these places for future generations of world citizens. Such places are established by "popular demand." If enough people lobby the Congress of the U.S. to "set aside" a place as a park, through the political process, then it can be saved from logging or massive mining projects or other development.

Critics of this argument assert that national and international symbols are arbitrary and easily changed. Resource economist Martin Krieger in his article, "What's Wrong with Plastic Trees?" presents almost a manual for the destruction of a sense of place. "It is possible," he asserts, "that by manipulating memory through the rewriting of history, environments will come to have new meaning. Finally, we may want to create proxy environments by means of substitution and simulation. In order to create substitutes, we must endow new objects with significance by means of advertising and social practice." Krieger's vision is one of dystopia. "Artificial prairies and wildernesses have been created, and there is no reason to believe that these artificial environments need be unsatisfactory for those who experience them. . . . We will have to realize that the way in which we experience nature is conditioned by our society—which more and more is seen to be receptive to responsible interventions."[19]

Something like this is occurring during the years of the Reagan administration in the United States, as national leaders call upon symbolic fears and values such as national energy self-sufficiency and national security and economic growth to manipulate citizens to fear the "locking up" of resources in designated wilderness areas.

The propaganda of the modern worldview for human domination of vast ecosystems and for scientific management indicates the power of those who influence the mass media and teaching institutions in modern nations. Some corporations and New Age thinkers look to the Disney Enterprises' "prototype community of tomorrow" carved out of the swamps of central Florida as the visionary goal of a corporate state where wild Nature is reduced to simulated experiences and plastic alligators.[20]

Krieger is certainly correct in pointing out that the dominant institutions of modern societies, including churches, corporations with their ability to condition the public with constantly repeated advertisements, leaders of government, and most teachers in public schools and colleges, are propagandizing for more and more humanization of the planet. When children enthusiastically troop off to computer camps during the summer rather than take backpacking trips in the mountains or practice river running in kayaks, then indeed there is

119

little possibility they will engage in the process of bonding during their formative years. Rather, we should be encouraging those recreational activities which will help the child and adult be in balance with the Earth. Krieger's arguments against the wilderness as cultural embodiment actually tend to highlight the intense alienation of many urbanites from a sense of place, and the pathological elements of personal development in technocratic-industrial societies (discussed further in chapter ten).

3. Obligations to Future Generations (of All Creatures, Rocks and Trees)

In a previous section we discussed the economist's view that preservation of wilderness presents "opportunity costs" for a present generation and that wilderness may not even be desired by near or far-future generations. Indeed, if future generations have no wilderness then they will never experience the loss of wilderness that is so intensely traumatic to many persons in the present generation. For example, the destruction of wildness in East Africa could be seen as of little importance to future generations. [21]

But for the deep ecologist, preservation of the flow of wildness demonstrates hope and faith that humans have a future and that humans can show some restraint on the will to power, to dominate and destroy. It would seem that deep ecologists are more hopeful concerning the future than many leaders of modern nations. Keep the wildness wild, a reserve of species diversity and genetic heritage for future generations of humans who will have the opportunity to experience unspoiled Nature. This view is expressed by David Brower in his introduction to *Galápagos: The Flow of Wildness.* Brower's concern is that civilization is a thin veneer over man's biological heritage. He chose the Galápagos Islands in the South Pacific, made famous by Charles Darwin's visit in 1835 where Darwin found inspiration for his ecological theory of evolution, for recognition as an Earth International Park. [22]

4. Wise Stewardship

The wise steward argument has several variations which can be classified under four headings: Narrow Christian Version, Revised Christian Version, Secular Version Based on the Gaia Hypothesis, and the New Age/Aquarian Conspiracy Version. A response from a deep ecological viewpoint is then offered.

A. Narrow Christian Version

In the narrow Christian version, there is little place for wilderness. Furthermore, humans are considered superior to other species, and separate from the rest of Nature. The domination of Nature is tempered only by the responsibility of the herdsman. The herdsman protects "his sheep," his domesticated livestock, from wolves or coyotes.

The steward is not just interested in maximizing short-term profit from "his land." He is interested in sustainability of the resource base. He, of course, may take a *noblesse oblige* approach as suggested by biologist René Dubos and "enhance" the productivity of the land for human purposes or even plant "genetically superior" trees and breed "genetically superior" animals. There are anthropocentric reasons for preserving some margins or "ecological islands of species diversity" for those plants and animals which contribute to the health of a bioregion upon which the farmer depends. Furthermore, wilderness is looked upon as a reminder of the natural world "out of which humans emerged."

Thus the first world of Nature, in the wise steward argument, is only a backdrop for humans, whereas in the second world of high technology, humans have the aristocrat's responsibility as "managers of Nature."

In the introduction to *Galápagos: The Flow of Wilderness* (1968), David Brower wrote:

Man is prolific enough to explore across the land, but he can only do so at the expense of the organic diversity essential to the only world that he can live upon. . . . Man needs an Earth International Park, to protect on this planet what he has not destroyed and what need not be destroyed. In this action, all nations could unite against the one real enemy—Rampant Technology. Here might be rescued, for the improved men we should hope will be born in centuries and millennia to come, the natural places where answers can always be sought to questions man may one day be wise enough to ask.

During the flurry of environmental concern of the 1970s, David Brower worried that not enough attention was being paid to wilderness protection. Attention was narrowly focused on pollution and urban problems. But the failure to recognize the importance of wilderness protection has also come from those advocating rural reform.

Wendell Berry is an eloquent spokesman against the evils of modern industrial society and for a return to an agrarian America based on the organic ecological farm. In his *The Unsettling of America* (1977),

121

Berry was one of the first to point to the ecological crisis as primarily a crisis of character and culture. But in his focus on the Jeffersonian agrarian model, he fails to see the ecological necessity for large wilderness areas. [23]

Berry presents an excellent critique of reform environmental organizations such as the Sierra Club for its elitism in wanting to preserve wilderness as "scenery" and as places to take vacations and escape the city. These anthropocentric reasons merely perpetuate the industrial way of life and the lack of rootedness and a sense of place in modern America. But Berry misses the deeper ecological reasons for wilderness preservation held by John Muir and modern ecologists such as Paul Ehrlich.

Berry is very much in the Christian stewardship tradition when he argues that the land must be "used" by humans. While he argues that we should consider "the good of the whole of Creation, the world and *all* its creatures together" (emphasis added), he also holds that we can't preserve "more than a small portion of the land in wilderness." But wilderness or near-wilderness is required as habitat for *all* of the Earth's wild creatures. Berry apparently fails to see the contradiction and falls short of deep ecological awareness.

Saint Benedict is frequently cited as the patron saint of narrow Christian stewardship. René Dubos, in *A God Within* (1972), describes Benedictine stewardship:

Benedict of Nursia . . . can be regarded as the patron saint of those who believe that true conservation means not only protecting nature against human misbehavior but also developing human activities which favor a creative, harmonious relationship between man and nature. . . . The first chapter of Genesis speaks of man's dominion over nature. The Benedictine rule in contrast seems inspired rather from the second chapter, in which the Good Lord placed man in the Garden of Eden not as a master but rather in the spirit of stewardship. Throughout the history of the Benedictine order, its monks have actively intervened in nature—as farmers, builders, and scholars. . . . Saint Bernard believed that it was the duty of the monks to work as partners of God in improving his creation or at least in giving it a more human expression. Implicit in his writings is the thought that labor is like a prayer which helps in recreating paradise out of chaotic wilderness.

B. Revised Christian Stewardship

A revised Christian version of stewardship suggests that the rights of all God's creation be respected.

For example, Jeremy Rifkin has called for a "second Christian Reformation," a radical reevaluation of the stewardship doctrine based on ecological principles of diversity, interdependence, and decentralization:

Maintenance replaces the notion of progress, stewardship replaces ownership, and nurturing replaces engineering. Biological limits to both production and consumption are acknowledged. . . . If the Christian community fails to embrace the concept of a New Covenant vision of stewardship, it is possible that the emerging religious fervor could be taken over and ruthlessly exploited by right-wing and corporate interests. [24]

This version of stewardship comes close to a deep ecology perspective, provided that the necessity for vast unmanaged wilderness areas is recognized.

C. Gaia Hypothesis

The third stewardship version is presented by James Lovelock, based on his Gaia hypothesis (the Earth as living organism) which ". . . postulates that the physical and chemical condition of the surface of the Earth, of the atmosphere and of the oceans has been and is actively made fit and comfortable by the presence of life itself. This is in contrast to the conventional wisdom which held that life adapted to the planetary conditions as it and they evolved their separate ways." [25]

During the last three hundred years, the human species and its domesticated livestock have grown substantially as a proportion of the total biomass. Human-induced pollution and interventions into bioregions (such as massive clearing of tropical rain forests) disrupt the delicate homeostasis of the Earth. Lovelock suggests that some parts of the Earth organism are "vital organs" which, if disrupted, would cause the whole Earth (Gaia) to malfunction. Humans, says Lovelock, should live in Gaia as wise stewards by restraining human activities that impair her functioning. He concludes:

It seems therefore that the principal dangers to our planet arising from man's activities may not be the special and singular evils of his urbanized industrial existence. When urban industrial man does something ecologically bad he notices it and tends to put things right again. The really critical areas which need careful watching are more likely to be the tropics and the seas close to the continental shores. It is in these regions, where few do watch, that harmful practices may be pur-

123

sued to the point of no-return before their dangers are recognized; and so it is from these regions that unpleasant surprises are most likely to emerge. Here man may sap the vitality of Gaia by reducing and by deleting key species in her life-support system; and he may then exacerbate the situation by releasing into the air or the sea abnormal quantities of compounds which are potentially dangerous on a global scale.[26]

Lovelock seems overly optimistic about the ability of industrial man to solve his problems. The "wise husbandry" or wise management of the Earth therefore requires large regions to be left as margins. Zoned or designated as "Earth international conservation areas" or "Nature preserves," these areas would be off limits to urban industrial development.

Philosopher/ecologist John Phillips gives a succinct statement of this approach:

The biosphere as a whole should be zoned, in order to protect it from the human impact. We must strictly confine the Urban-Industrial Zone, and the Production Zone (agriculture, grazing, fishing), enlarge the Compromise Zone, and drastically expand the Protection Zone, i.e., wilderness, wild rivers. Great expanses of seacoast and estuaries must be included in the Protection Zone, along with forests, prairies, and various habitat types. We must learn that the multiple-use Compromise Zone is no substitute, with its mining, lumbering, grazing, and recreation in the national forests, for the scientific, aesthetic, and genetic pool values of the Protection Zone. Such zoning, if carried out in time, may be the only way to limit the destructive impact of our technocratic-industrial-agri-business complex on earth.

D. New Age/Aquarian Conspiracy Version of Stewardship

The fourth version of stewardship is that of the New Age/Aquarian Conspiracy, which carries the stewardship argument to its logical extreme. This New Age ideology is more thoroughly discussed in the next chapter. Briefly, however, for the proponents of this position, there are virtually no ethical restraints on human manipulation of the biosphere. The Earth is not God's and humans are not trustees of the Kingdom, keeping their own demands small in terms of the larger Creation. The only restraints are technical, political and economic (lack of capital for development of projects).

Some areas of the Earth, perhaps Antarctica or the Amazon Basin, could temporarily be placed off limits to massive human interventions (clear cutting the forests of the Amazon, for example) until the managers develop ways to "manage" the area productively for human economy and develop the technology for extraction. For example, some industry spokespeople, testifying on development of mineral resources on the continental shelf of the United States, said that they wanted the territory to explore for minerals, but would not have the technology to "develop the resources" until at least the year 2000. The implication was that the resources would be developed when there was a demand in the market for them, when capital was available for drilling and when the technology came "on line."

The major metaphor of New Age is that the Earth is a spaceship and technologically advanced humans have a destiny to become "copilots" of the spaceship. Teilhard de Chardin claimed that the destiny of humans in this generation would be to "seize the tiller of creation."

E. Deep Ecological Response to Stewardship

The deep ecologist response to the revised Christian version of stewardship and to Lovelock's version is to agree in some respects on practical grounds but not on philosophical grounds.

In Lovelock's proposal, vast areas of the Earth might be zoned off limits for further human intervention on a massive scale. The polar regions, the Amazon Basin, vast portions of the ocean estuaries, shallow water areas of the continental shelf, and possibly the great mountain systems of the Earth could be designated wilderness. No massive weather modification experiments, dumping of nuclear wastes, further deforestation of tropical rain forests, massive dam construction in the Amazon Basin or huge and disruptive mineral development projects would be allowed. The krill and marine environment around the Antarctic continent could be zoned wilderness to protect the chain of life which ecologists have identified as dependent on that marine area.

If margins are defined very widely, then riparian, or streamside habitat, and large portions of all variety of ecosystems from mountains to deserts would have strict legal protection from logging, farming, or energy development projects. Much of the American southwest, now regarded as roadless, might be designated as official wilderness.

One major philosophical disagreement with the wise steward position is that it still incorporates the premise of instrumental rationality—the narrowly utilitarian view—of natural resources primarily for human use, and fails to distinguish vital human needs from mere desires, egotistical arrogance and adventurism in technology ("if we have the technology, let's use it").

Zoning in the interim could be supported while recognizing that, over the long run, zoning by national and international agencies is not consistent with the minority tradition whereby local communities (bioregional in nature), which appreciate and respect the vital needs of nonhumans, reach decisions by consensus.

For the supporter of deep ecology, however, the most damaging aspect of the wise steward argument is the continued radical separation of person from wilderness (wild Nature, the flow of wilderness). It is in all versions anthropocentric and dualistic. "We have emerged from the first world of Nature," the wise steward seems to say, "and can never return to our place crackling with spirit." There is no norm of biocentric equality. The major implication for wilderness is to leave smaller and smaller areas wild as public policy while we have more and more technocratic-industrial "solutions" to the contradictions and convolutions of the economy.

5. The Ecologist's Imperative of Protecting Habitats of Nonhuman Beings

As we have indicated in previous chapters, ecologists are warning us of the unprecedented rate of species extinction due to massive human interventions in their habitats. [27] The concern with endangered species is now widely understood. Several types of programs have been proposed to protect genetic diversity and to propagate specific species. But habitat preservation, or wilderness preservation, is the only possible way to protect the flow of wildness, species diversity, genetic diversity, and ongoing intermingling of species-in-habitat. Species diversity and the processes of evolution *cannot* be maintained by keeping plants and animals in zoos and laboratories. Old-growth forests are necessary for the survival of many species and to maintain genetic diversity.

The biocentric intuition that species have a right to exist and follow their own evolutionary destinies was established in the United States in the Endangered Species Act of 1973. This Act has been severely attacked by those who defend the belief that the Earth exists for human use. But the Endangered Species Act still has major limitations. The Act includes complex procedures for designating a species endangered, although it rejects the economist's narrow approach of a cost/benefit analysis on each species. Nevertheless, it includes the concept of balance between human needs and species habitat preservation. Ecologists who seek to defend the California condor or the snail darter are asked to justify habitat preservation based on the prin-

126

ciple of equity for some landowner of the habitat and balance between economic growth and preservation of a "useless" species. Economizing ecology within the dominant worldview only leads to either a technocratic solution (such as artificial breeding programs for condors) or to benign neglect (allowing certain species of flora or fauna to go into extinction). In the balance, humans are valued more highly individually and collectively (a corporation owning lands which are California condor habitat, for example) than is the endangered species.

Excessive human intervention in natural processes has led other species to near-extinction. For deep ecologists the balance has long since been tipped in favor of humans. Now we must shift the balance back to protect the habitat of other species.

Protection of wilderness and near-wilderness is imperative. While primal peoples lived in sustainable communities for tens of thousands of years without impairing the viability of ecosystems, modern technocratic-industrial society threatens every ecosystem on Earth and may even be threatening to drastically change the pattern of weather in the biosphere as a whole.

Technocratic-industrial society is moving into areas of the planet never inhabited by humans before, including the oceans and the Antarctic continent. Tropical rain forests in Asia, Africa, South and Central America, Oceania and Australia are under attack by an unprecedented array of technology and plans for exploitation and development. [28] Tropical rain forests contain the greatest biological diversity of any type of ecosystem on Earth. *The Eleventh Annual Environmental Report to the President* (1980) concluded:

A most serious threat to the biosphere is the rapid disappearance of tropical forests. In many tropical forests, the soils, terrain, temperature, patterns of rainfall, and distribution of nutrients are in precarious balance. When these forests are disturbed by extensive cutting, neither trees nor productive grasses will grow again. Even where conditions are more favorable to regrowth, extensive clearance destroys the ecological diversity of tropical forests. These forests are habitat for the richest variety of plant and animal species on earth. [29]

Wilderness preservation is necessary to preserve the process of species formation, the flow of wildness and the natural evolutionary process itself. There is no substitute for wilderness preservation. Zoos, botanical gardens, artificial insemination and breeding programs for endangered species, small enclaves of parks in the midst of large-scale mining or other industrialized processes, gene banks where genes of endangered species are frozen for later possible use, and captive

127

breeding programs are all completely unsatisfactory to meet the challenge of protecting biological diversity.

In the United States various wilderness acts setting aside some public lands as designated wilderness have been enacted by Congress during the 1970s and 80s. All of these are weak compromises. Boundaries of designated wilderness areas are more the product of political dealing than for the protection of the integrity of old-growth forests, deserts, and other types of ecosystems. The more extensive wilderness proposals for North America made by the environmental group Earth First! provide a realistic base to begin the real process of protecting wilderness on this continent. Reform environmental groups must recognize that the "problem of wilderness" is not solved by the passage of compromised, weak and inadequate wilderness legislation by the U.S. Congress.

Until the dominant, modern worldview changes in the direction of deep ecology, perhaps the most important priority for reform environmentalist efforts is the protection of wilderness. Biologists, anthropologists, soil scientists and others are beginning to realize that they must lobby in the political arena for protection of habitat. In many cases the population of animals or plants, natural processes, and even the preliterate or primal human populations they were studying have been destroyed by technocratic-industrial society before they have completed their study. Dian Fossey, author of *Gorillas in the Mist* (1983), for example, recorded the complete destruction of one of her study groups in Africa, apparently as the result of a collection effort. Anne Ehrlich comments on this collection effort of gorillas: "Since it is estimated that only a fraction of the infants captured in this way survive to reach their destination zoo, each successfully collected specimen may have cost the lives of ten to twenty gorillas and the destruction of several family groups."[30]

While Africa has been spotlighted in many news stories, the threat to marine environments is less noticed. The fate of the great whales aroused public opinion worldwide, but international organizations, such as the International Whaling Commission, continue to offer only weak alternatives to a total ban on commercial whaling.[31]

All of the oceans of the world face enormous problems with pollution, harvesting of fish and mineral exploration and development. The establishment by the Reagan administration of a 200 mile "Exclusive Economic Zone" around all United States territory without adequate consideration for marine environment preservation is viewed with alarm by many environmentalists.[32] In Australia, deep ecologists continue to focus on protecting remnant rain forests in New South Wales and Queensland and protection of the Great Barrier Reef.[33]

Scientists working in Antarctica conclude that it is a fragile ecosystem subject to disruption by humans who build airports, scientific study stations and other structures. Many of the scientists who have conducted studies of Antarctica as well as ecoactivists working through ecological groups such as Greenpeace (formed in the 1960s) are actively lobbying the signatory nations of the Antarctic Treaty to establish designated wilderness on that continent and its marine waters.[34]

The full powers of national law, international treaties and United Nations efforts should be directed to the protection of world wilderness areas. In principle, no further massive developments should be allowed at all. Bioregional development serving the demonstrated vital needs of local residents which will not impair biological diversity and natural processes is the only type of development that is consistent with preservation of the flow of wilderness.

No testing of nuclear weapons or disposal of nuclear reactor wastes should be permitted in wilderness areas, on land or water. Effective efforts to drastically reduce acid rain generated from sources in technocratic-industrial societies should be undertaken immediately.

On balance, biocentric principles should be followed in deciding issues of public policy affecting biological diversity, wilderness preservation and economic development.

> *I swear I see what is better than to tell the best.*
> *It is always to leave the best untold.*
> —*Walt Whitman,* A Song of the Rolling Earth

CHAPTER 8
·
NATURAL RESOURCE CONSERVATION OR PROTECTION OF THE INTEGRITY OF NATURE: CONTRASTING VIEWS OF MANAGEMENT

There are only people and natural resources.
—Gifford Pinchot (1947)

The times are changing. Today it's a matter of dollars and cents. That makes it tough on uses (of the national forests) that don't produce much income, such as recreation.
—U.S. Regional Forester Craig Rupp (1983)

Old-growth forests remind me of an old folks home, just waiting to die.
—Official of the Reagan administration (1984)

In the previous chapter we discussed wilderness protection as a public policy issue and as an issue of cultivating ecological consciousness. In this chapter we discuss the broader notion of human uses of Nature or natural resources.

We begin with a historical sketch of the Resource Conservation and Development ideology as expressed in the United States and then discuss the New Age/Aquarian Conspiracy as a radical extension of this ideology.

We then make some comments on the assumptions of these dominant positions from a deep ecology perspective and offer some tentative suggestions for deep ecological management.

I. STEWARDSHIP IN PRACTICE

1. A Brief History of Resource Conservation and Development (RCD)

After spending three nights with President Theodore Roosevelt under the oaks and pine trees of Yosemite National Park in 1903, John Muir proclaimed in his journal, "Now Ho! for righteous management." Muir was hopeful at the beginning of the twentieth century that under the leadership of wise managers, the national parks and forests would be left essentially wild, preserved as watershed and wildlife habitat. The national parks would remain largely wilderness. Utilitarian uses of the national forests would respect the ongoing, healthy functioning of ecosystems. But his hopes for the wise management of the nation's forests and wild lands were soon to be destroyed.

The story of professionalized, scientific management of natural resources and public land by new experts working within the framework of centralized corporations and national legislation in the United States begins with Gifford Pinchot. Pinchot was trained in Germany in forest management and fought under the label of the "conservation movement" to change the then-prevalent attitude, especially in the western United States, that all land was open for taking minerals, grazing on open range, cutting timber, plowing fields, and appropriating water without planning for the future or considering what the economists were to call "externalities"—air and water pollution, for example. [1]

While Muir was striving to protect large areas of land from the machines of technocratic-industrial society, first through the institution of national forests and then through the institution of national parks, Pinchot was striving to develop a professional cadre of managers to develop resources and encourage legislation which would institutionalize scientific management of renewable resources.

Pinchot's ideology was adopted in law and through the actions of public agencies and private organizations. Conservation became a way of allocating natural resources more efficiently through scientific management and manipulation of natural systems on an ever-larger scale. The "wise use" and multiple use of natural resources meant management for development and economic growth.

As Pinchot said:

The first great fact about conservation is that it stands for development. There has been a fundamental misconception that conservation means nothing but the husbanding of resources for future generations. There could be no more serious mistake. . . . The first principle of conservation is the use of the natural resources now existing on this continent for the benefit of the people who live here now. [2]

It now seems obvious that we are in the midst of an environmental and spiritual crisis more severe than the one that sent Muir to his grave defending wild Nature in Yosemite. For now the whole planet is threatened by the possible holocaust of nuclear war and by the continued "peaceful" development of natural resources in the tropical rain forests and in the oceans. "Balanced use of resources," "wise use," "scientific management," and "genetic improvement" of forests are all central concepts of the management ideology based upon the assumption that humans are the central figures and actors in history, together with the idea that the whole of Nature is to be understood as resources for humans and thus is open for unlimited human manipulation.

In the United States these assumptions were enacted in land use laws passed by most county governments and federal agencies such as the U.S. Forest Service and Bureau of Reclamation as well as the Tennessee Valley Authority, and form the dominant ideology taught in professional schools of forestry, wildlife management, water resources management, range management and agriculture.

Various types of natural resources were given to special recreation managers, soil scientists, foresters, range managers, environmental engineers, and energy managers, for example. Some reform environmental groups developed their own professionals specializing in these fields. Historian Stephen Fox in his history of the conservation movement argues that radical amateurs arose time and again to revitalize reform groups such as the Audubon Society and Sierra Club, but the experts continue to dominate the normal decision-making processes.[3]

The experts found a congenial home in colleges and universities, which were interested in keeping student enrollment up by training hordes of these experts. In some ways the modern university is like a sponge, sopping up new professions. The university has been called the citadel of expertise. It is not surprising that some of the leading theorists of reform environmentalism have been university professors who wish to appear progressive and professional.

"Expert Testimony" became something of a growth industry. Frequently, in congressional committee hearings or in administrative hearings, or in court cases concerning some natural resource issue, expert was pitted against expert. Theodore Roszak calls this strategy one of "countervailing expertise" and contends that it is a shallow practice because:

. . . while undeniably well-intentioned and capable of stopgap success on specific political issues, it leaves wholly untouched the great cultural question of our times. It does not challenge the universally presumed rightness of the urban-industrial order of life. Therefore it cannot address itself to the possibility that high industrial society, due to its scale, pace, and complexity, is inherently technocratic, and so inherently undemocratic. At most, it leaves us with the hope that the bastardized technocracies of our day might be converted into ideal technocracies.[4]

2. Resource Conservation and Development Ideology

Among resource managers there seems to be some awareness of the philosophical assumptions underlying the anthropocentric resource ideology. But generally the problems that arise in this kind of management are perceived to be technical, economic, or political issues. Many people trained in this ideology see themselves as being "value-free" and beyond politics in their decisions. In keeping with this ideology, when environmentalists try to discuss forestry management with public agencies such as the Forest Service, their positions and arguments are viewed from the subjective standpoint of a "special interest" group. The generally nonreflective position of RCD managers makes it almost impossible to discuss issues on a deeper philosophical level. The anthropocentric versus biocentric worldviews of land use managers and environmentalists generally mean that they share little common ground and, as a result, they talk past each other. The basic philosophical differences tend to be obscured or deflected into discussions of technical issues. For example, those who oppose aerial spraying of herbicides on forests are trapped into arguing over the research data of very technical studies of dispersion rates, the effects on pregnant women, and so on. But the chains of interrelationships in an ecosystem are so complex that the results of such studies are usually tentative and inconclusive. And if the burden of proof is on those opposed to the spraying to demonstrate its harmful effects, then the spraying will continue. Those with a philosophically biocentric perspective that respects all of Nature and its processes would most likely arrive at a contrary conclusion.

The usual rhetoric of "conservation," "stewardship," and "wise use" in the contemporary version of RCD now means in practice the development of resources as quickly as is technically possible with the available capital to serve human "needs." The whole of Nature and nonhuman species are not seen as having value in themselves and the right to follow out their own evolutionary destinies. In the ideology of RCD, humans are not understood or experienced to be an integral part of natural processes, but rather as rightfully dominating and controlling the rest of Nature based on principles of scientific management. This means altering Nature to produce more or "better" commodities for human consumption and directing Nature to do the bidding of humans on the utilitarian principle of the "greatest good for the greatest number" of humans.[5]

The ultimate foundations of RCD scientific management of Nature appear to be a profound faith, almost a religion of management. A commissioner of the Bureau of Reclamation, in a speech defending the Reagan administration's management policies, said:

Research, engineering, and resource management all have a role in solving our water resource problems. We need better water resource technology, especially for ground water resources. Although the Bureau of Reclamation is recognized internationally for its engineering excellence, we're constantly working to improve our engineering. And the quest for better management is practically a religion in America. *(Emphasis added.)*[6]

The value-free managers, the experts and technocrats, even if they do not espouse some extreme version of Christian stewardship and domination, do profess a secular religion of faith and hope— a faith in never-ending technological progress and a hope that what they do will work. Even technological failure on an alarmingly regular basis, as in the case of nuclear power, only seems to generate more faith, more hope, and a stronger belief that we need more and more

135

managers and technical experts to solve the problems. Case after case of technological fixes that produce even greater environmental backlash seem not to daunt them in the least.[7]

The metaphor of the Earth as just natural resources to be exploited and consumed by humans remains the dominant image embedded in the psyches of modern RCD managers. As sociologist William Burch wrote, "Though the conversion of all the world into a commodity is periodically challenged and even modified, it remains the basic metaphor in high energy societies both communist and capitalist."[8]

Modern managers can rationalize that they are only serving the needs of the people because of their commitment to unlimited growth and ever-expanding markets. As Karl Polanyi points out, the modern consumer society in which everything is marketable and is assigned an economic value is a completely new social form of society that involves "no less a transformation than that of the natural and human substance of society into commodities. Yet labor, land, and money are *not* commodities. Labor is simply another name for human activity. But on the basis of the fiction that labor, land and money are commodities, markets are organized."[9] The trinity of beliefs underlying the ethics of RCD is the metaphor of the market, the Earth as a collection of human resources or commodities, and the Earth as a machine or spaceship. The dominant quest for better management in modern industrial societies, however, is *not* righteous management as envisioned by John Muir.

The RCD position easily translates into the economizing of forests, rivers and anything defined within the specific human economy as a natural resource. When this degeneration of the RCD position is coupled with the anthropocentric assumptions which are its underpinning, and when it is believed to be natural and desirable for human populations to increase indefinitely together with the assumption that it is desirable for humans to continue expanding their demands and wants, then there is very little room to consider any rights of dolphins, spotted owls, or California condors to their own habitats. Indeed, the logical outcome is to consider other species as just genetic resources whose DNA can be frozen and stored in gene banks for manipulation by scientist-technologists at the command of corporations or government agencies.

Within the assumptions of the dominant worldview, the basic challenge of the forester, water resource manager, range manager, fisheries manager, etc., is to produce more and more commodities in shorter and shorter periods of time.

Nature and its processes are too slow and inefficient in terms of the economizing model. Indeed, "efficiency of production," virtually without regard for the larger ecological context, is the major slogan of managers who take a homocentric rather than biocentric position.

For example, the rotation cycle, the number of years between cutting a stand of timber and its recutting after regrowth, has been progressively reduced from perhaps 120 years to eighty, sixty, or forty. One official of a major corporation in the western United States asked his scientific managers and technologists to develop and plant "genetically enhanced" trees which could be "harvested" in twenty years. "Trees are just a crop, like corn," say many commercial foresters.

Relatively small natural areas and stretches of free-flowing rivers are allowed to exist in the context of RCD, but only if they do not intrude upon basic resource production. As one forest products industry official said, "Maybe 100 acres of old-growth redwood would be enough for our grandchildren to see." "Nonproductive" land may be left as wilderness, but the borders get smaller and smaller and environmentalists find themselves arguing with forestry officials over fifty-foot buffer strips along streams where logging will not be allowed. At best, under RCD, the "environmental effects" of proposed development projects will be studied and *some* effort will be made to "mitigate" the known negative environmental impacts.

Recent Forest Service efforts to develop a "decision procedure" for differing recreational uses on forest lands have fared little better than economic analyses of forest values, and continue to highlight the failure of land use managers to recognize more objective ecological criteria. For example, in a recent study of "scenic preferences" as baseline data for decisions concerning "scenic management," a sample of persons was shown photos of various kinds of scenes ranging from clear-cut forests to super freeways. They were asked to rate their preferences on a subjective scale and then the averages were tabulated. The average preference ratings were then considered to be public opinion concerning the types of landscape to be valued for recreational purposes. [10]

The older imagery of RCD sees humans as happy gardeners and stewards weeding the Earth of "undesirable pests" and predators. Biologist René Dubos has presented this image in his book, *The Wooing of the Earth,* along with the claim that humans are simply "bringing out the potential" of the planet. But even Dubos admits that "The belief that we can manage the Earth and improve on Nature is probably the ultimate expression of human conceit, but it has deep roots in the past and is almost universal."[11]

―――――

W. D. Hagenstein, an official of the Industrial Forestry Association, in a speech entitled "The Old Forest Maketh Way for the New," gives a succinct statement of the Resource Conservation and Development ideology:

I know firsthand what happens to an old-growth forest left entirely to the whims of nature. What all this background is leading to is my philosophy of the use of old-growth timber. First, do not waste the asset. Second, if the timber is needed to satisfy social needs like housing and other construction, use it. . . .

Professional foresters are trained to accept the philosophy that the conversion of old-growth unmanaged forest . . . to a managed forest, with its favorable distribution of age classes, is desirable from a social, economic, and forestry point of view. The annual allowable harvests determined by the Forest Service are simply a scheme to regulate the harvest of the old growth. By the time the last of it has been harvested, there is sufficient young timber of merchantable size, brought about by reforestation and protection, to prevent any hiatus in the timber supply to meet Americans' needs for both products and jobs. . . .

Just as the medical profession is bound to protect public health in general, the forestry profession is likewise duty-bound to protect public health by preventing the waste of trees. . . . Therefore, any artificial restriction on the protection or salvage of damaged old-growth forests poses the ethical question of whether the forestry profession is performing in its highest tradition and in accordance with its full responsibilities to society. . . . When there are homeless people in the world, there is no more a right to waste wood than there is a right to waste food when there are hungry people. Whether people like it or not, the old forest must make way for the new. [12]

―――――

3. New Age/Aquarian Conspiracy

The New Age/Aquarian Conspiracy version of scientific management is the most systematic, technocratic and domineering version of Resource Conservation and Development ideology. It is the logical extension of the dominant worldview of the Earth as a collection of natural resources to be used primarily for humans. Proponents of this view frequently speak of the elimination, by planned human intervention, of most of the natural evolutionary process. The only "ulti-

138

mate resource" is humans who, with their brains and technocratic abilities, will develop grander and grander schemes for "humanizing" the Earth. [13]

In *An Operating Manual for Spaceship Earth* (1971), Buckminster Fuller likens the Earth to a machine, asserts that there is no world population problem, and says that the world's problems can be solved by computers. Engineering, coupled with cybernetics systems and information theory, can provide a purely technological solution to the world's ills.

On the issue of genetic engineering and the rapid development of this industry, Jeremy Rifkin in *Algeny* (1983) points out that the Darwinian view of natural evolutionary processes is now being replaced by genetic manipulation and development of species to conform to limited human purposes and desires. The computer/information revolution is a mere prelude to the genetic transformation of all life on Earth. [14]

New Age/Aquarian Conspiracy futurists are planning for newly contrived biological organisms to provide the energy base for the expanding industrial society as the fossil fuel era phases out. By redesigning life on Earth, this conveniently eliminates the natural evolutionary process, for it is too slow and inefficient. Similarly, natural ecosystems are not geared to the modern pace of industrial production and efficiency, although some representative samples can be preserved in museum-like settings as a luxury item to satisfy the aesthetic and recreational tastes of certain elite minorities.

████████

Dick Russell has explored the new corporations which see the potential to make a profit from the biotechnological revolution. "The tree of knowledge," he says, "grows on Wall Street": [15]

A revolution of unprecedented scope and incalculable social effects is taking place around the globe in corporate board rooms and allied scientific laboratories. Its practitioners bear company names right out of yesterday's science fiction: Cetus, Biogen, Genetech, Agrigenetics. Its financial backers are giant multinational corporations like Environmenton, DuPont, Dow Chemical and Eli Lilly. And its sources of wisdom are university researchers from Harvard, MIT, Stanford and elsewhere, many of whom are becoming overnight millionaires by affiliating with the new "growth industry of the '80s." The industry is biotechnology, or genetic engineering. . . . The potential of this ability to alter the basis of nature is staggering, and beginning to manifest itself in nearly every arena of life. Besides offering an eventual cure for

1,000 genetically-related diseases and possibly cancer, the bioengineers talk of new types of crops designed to take nitrogen from the air, farm animals that will grow faster, and manufactured life forms to carry out industrial processes.

————

Domestic animals and humans are now being bred through artificial insemination while "cloned" animals and plants are also being widely developed. Even some zoos have developed an endangered species program which includes freezing sperm and eggs and matching animals through computerized systems.

The New Age/Aquarian Conspiracy ideas for scientific management are presented against the backdrop of the possibility of all-out nuclear warfare, which would be the most devastating human-caused event in the history of the world. But the possible destruction of up to twenty-five percent of all species on Earth due to "business-as-usual" economic growth and development during the next forty to sixty years is seen by some as "reparable" by the advances in genetic engineering.

At the same time, multinational corporations and government resource agencies are building, or have on the drawing boards, projects to "tame" the Amazon Basin by clear-cutting the old-growth tropical rain forests and through "vegetative conversion" to monocultures. Almost all old-growth rain forests from Sri Lanka to Australia and South America are threatened by multinational corporations bent on extracting resources.

Centralized government agencies are drawing plans for even vaster projects using larger construction equipment. Massive pipelines are planned to run from Siberia to western Europe. Soviet planners envision damming and diverting the major river systems of western Siberia from running north to the Arctic to running south to the Caspian Sea. There are plans to further divert northern California waters to southern California through massive canals, and even plans to ship water from the Great Lakes to Texas. Oil, gas, and mineral development on one billion acres off California is presented as a "new frontier" for economic development. "Harvesting" krill and other resources on the Antarctic marine shelf and possible mineral developments on that continent have been discussed for years by the scientists working for those nations having a claim to the continent. The list of projects for major technological modification of the Earth goes on and on.

But New Age/Aquarian Conspiracy proponents see this future as bright with human promise. In his book *Doomsday Has Been Cancelled,* J. Peter Vayk says:

Once we come to understand the heat balancing mechanisms more thoroughly, we can begin to supplement existing regulatory interactions with consciously implemented mechanisms. Should we find it desirable, we will be able to turn the Sahara Desert into farms and forests, or remake the landscape of New England, while we create the kind of future we dream.... We are the legitimate children of Gaia; we need not be ashamed that we are altering the landscapes and ecosystems of Earth. But we do owe our mother careful attention to our handiwork and to our treatment of Gaia's other species of life. [16]

In this vision, humans are the center of the historical process, with the duty, as René Dubos says, to "humanize the earth." He asserts that, "Earth has potentialities that remain unexpressed until properly manipulated by human labor and imagination." [17]

The logical next move for New Age/Aquarian Conspiracy advocates is the "leap into space." "Spaceship Earth" became a popular image in the 1960s, the decade of the first space flights. And space has been called the "high frontier," in which modern technological man can do productive work, mine minerals on the moon and other planets and plant human civilization on previously "undomesticated" planets. James M. Beggs, administrator of the National Aeronautics and Space Administration in 1984, outlined this kind of scenario: U.S. space stations could "open space to a limitless range of opportunities" and lead to a moon colony by the year 2010 and a manned base on Mars by 2060.

■

After building a permanently manned space station we must learn how to tug it out, or move it in other ways to geosynchronous orbit, 22,300 miles up where the station rotates at the same rate as Earth and thus remains stationary over one area.

As we enter the twenty-first century, or shortly thereafter, we will have established a manned space station in lunar orbit, which will allow us to exploit the moon's resources. At about the year 2010, we could establish a colony on the moon, beginning with a small research station. By 2020 or 2030 we might have an operating productive activity on the moon.

In about the year 2040 the colony on the moon would be flourishing. Twenty short years after that the colony on Mars would be healthy and growing. And with the technology being developed today, we could be mining large amounts of material, expanding our economic activities in space and bringing the benefits back to Earth.

The technology to carry out the scenario is in our hands today. We need the will, imagination and vision to use it to reach our goals.

—James Beggs, National Aeronautics and Space Administrator (1984)

Some proponents of the New Age/Aquarian Conspiracy look to Teilhard de Chardin as their godfather. Teilhard's spiritual evolutionary Christianity is expressed in *The Phenomenon of Man* (1959) and other writings. Teilhard has appeared as an avant-garde theologian to many because he has combined Christian spirituality with evolutionary ideas. But as Christian scholar Frederick Elder (*Crisis In Eden,* 1970) pointed out in his survey of Christianity and the environment, Teilhard is "fiercely anthropocentric." Teilhard envisioned "man's evolutionary movement toward a point of complete humanization" of the planet—what Teilhard called the *Omega point.* Teilhard was writing largely before the human overpopulation crisis had been brought to public consciousness by ecologists and others. Similarly, Teilhard was also writing in a preecological era. His faith in human ingenuity through technology seemed to be almost unbounded.

Teilhard was himself a paleontologist and student of biological evolution. But in his case, his awareness of species extinction over the ages may have led to a profound distrust, alienation, and fear that the natural evolutionary processes would eventually result in the extinction of humans. This fear of Nature seemed to pervade his theology and cannot be overestimated in assessing the theme of domination and control over Nature expressed in much New Age writing. Teilhard also harkened back to the story of the Fall in Genesis. On this view, Nature as well as man fell from divine grace and so "both needed to be redeemed." There is spiritual transformation for humans, but there is also "creative transformation" of the nonhuman world. What this means is that the planet must be humanized and converted over to human purposes. This is an old theme in Western thought and was used as a justification by English philosopher Francis Bacon, who was largely instrumental in developing the modern worldview. Unfortunately, the large-scale human transformation of the nonhuman world is profoundly dangerous and unecological, as professional ecologists ceaselessly point out.

142

Teilhardian scholar Thomas Berry is aware of the antiecological anthropocentrism of Teilhard's thought and has struggled to revise it in biocentric ways. But he realizes how difficult it is for humans to go beyond anthropocentric thinking in all its forms: [18]

Probably the adjustment of thinkers from a pre-evolutionary context to an evolutionary context of interpretation is the best parallel, in the order of magnitude of its adjustment, to the adjustment from an anthropocentric to a biocentric orientation of consciousness. This latter is the adjustment we are suggesting for the vision of Teilhard. . . .

[For Teilhard] the sense of progress was irresistible, the feeling that the great mission of the human was to exploit natural resources, to build civilization, to release mankind from the age-old tyrannies of the natural world. The ancient mystique of communion with the natural world was seen simply as ignorance and superstition. . . . A world under rational control was the ideal to work toward. . . . While he rejected the mechanistic worldview in favor of a mystical worldview, he fully accepted the industrial and technological exploitation of the planet as a desirable human activity. . . . Teilhard became the heir to the imperial tradition in human-earth relations, the tradition of human control over the natural world. The sublime mission of scientific research and of technological invention was to support this advance into the ultra-human. . . . Teilhard is the most faithful of all followers of Francis Bacon, in his assertion that human intelligence should subordinate the natural world to human heights. . . . The damage done to the natural world was incidental, a price to be paid, a normal expenditure of energy for every advance in the evolutionary order. Teilhard is deeply involved in the total religious and humanist traditions of the West out of which this exploitative attitude developed. . . . The opinion is correct that Teilhard does not in any direct manner support the ecological mode of consciousness. . . .

Teilhard establishes the human as his exclusive norm of values, a norm that requires the human to invade and to control rationally the spontaneities of nature. . . . [For Teilhard] there is no question of accepting the natural world in its own spontaneous modes of being and establishing as an ideal a basic intercommunication with the total earth community, a communion whereby the human would "live lightly" upon the earth. This would be a treachery to the demands of the evolutionary process. . . .

On his own principles of totality we might say that the evolutionary process finds its highest expression in the earth community seen in its comprehensive dimensions, not simply in a human community reigning in triumphal dominion over the other components of the earth community. The same evolutionary process has produced all the living and nonliving components of the planet.

—Thomas Berry, *Teilhard in the Ecological Age* (1982)

The New Age movement is a powerful and vocal force in today's world of futurologists and "think tanks." One reason it is so influential is that it is telling people what they are used to hearing: more and more massive technology and conquest of the planet and outer space. This is merely the most sophisticated and glamorous thrust of the Western tradition of anthropocentric domination and control. But Teilhardian scholars such as Berry are already defecting from the ranks. The New Age scientists, technologists, and businessmen will have to face the fact that their philosophical/religious base is now rapidly eroding. They will have to join the Age of Ecology sooner or later. One hopes for the sake of person/planet that it is sooner rather than later.

████████████

A NEW AGE ANTI-ECOLOGICAL VISION

In the life/death struggle between man and nature . . . the question has been . . . *who* would win: Man or Nature? Man has won—or is winning. . . . Man has loved his earth; it nourished him. But he has also hated it for its relentless attempt to annihilate him. . . . Man is on the threshold of setting controls over ever-larger forces of nature—climate and earthquakes, for instance. The control of life and evolution is near . . . man may eventually establish control on a cosmological scale. We might alter the orbit or the tilt of the earth. . . . Man is now in process of taking control of his own evolutionary destiny and, by default, the destiny of all other living creatures on his planet. . . . [This is] part of the grand transition man is now undergoing, the transition from being a *passively produced organism* to being the *active controller* of life and destiny. . . . Controls have now spread to almost every area of human experience. Lagging behind, of course, is control of man himself, but this appears to be the area wherein the next giant steps will be taken.

—James Christian, *Philosophy* (1981)[19]

(Viewed from the perennial philosophy wisdom tradition of Spinoza or Buddhism, the kind of power over Nature described here is not being *active,* as New Age thinkers believe, but rather as being *passive* to our fears and unhealthy desires.)

████████████

II. A DEEP ECOLOGY PERSPECTIVE

1. Some General Suggestions

An alternative approach to that suggested by resource economists and current versions of the Resource Conservation ideology is suggested in this section.

Our first principle is to encourage agencies, legislators, property owners and managers to consider flowing with rather than forcing natural processes. Second, in facing practical situations we favor working within the minority tradition, in the local community, especially the bioregion.

One of the criticisms of scientific management as now practiced is the attention to building "abstract models" which in our estimation have little relevance to site-specific situations. For example, the U.S. Forest Service has attempted to develop and implement decision-making by setting goals for each forest. The goals are "commodity outputs" per time frame (usually every ten years). A computer model (Forplan) takes data collected by sampling techniques, adds numerous questionable assumptions and yields output tables telling the managers how many board feet or cubic feet of trees can be cut to meet the goals. This abstracting of Nature is a dangerous and uncaring approach and lulls the manager into thinking he has the relevant variables under control. We need to take seriously the ecologists' principle that Nature is more complex than we now know and more complex than we possibly can know.

This is not to say we don't see some value to scientific data collection. But it should be specifically addressing a more local site, valley or bioregion. Many primal peoples were excellent observers of natural processes, knowing the weather, pattern of changes in the seasons, habits of wildlife and so forth. Science and technology can be an aid but they are no substitute for this kind of direct land wisdom.

This knowledge was used to serve vital needs for food collection, materials for building shelters, and so forth. Therefore, drawing upon the distinction in wildlife management between "hands-on" and "hands-off" techniques, Muir's righteous management (biocentric ecological management) would be essentially hands-off management. [20]

Righteous management would also be consistent with Taoist philosophy and ways of life wherein human activities fit in and flow with the larger cycles of Nature rather than attempt to modify Nature on a large scale to fit grandiose human projects and whims. There is some indication that this is what Muir had in mind for the national forests when they were established in the 1880s and 1890s, and his concluding essay, "The Bee Pastures of California," in *The Mountains of California,* presents a vision of righteous management which has been long overlooked by planners and reform environmentalists.

Muir saw the national forests as places where the flow of wild Nature would be protected against the ravages of expanding industrial civilization. When he saw Pinchot's plans being implemented for the exploitation of the national forests as commodities for economic growth and development, he turned to the concept of national parks as places where wilderness would predominate. It is perhaps ironic that now in the United States nearly every national park is also being threatened by encroaching industrial civilization. And as ecologists such as Paul Erlich call for vast unmanaged wilderness ecosystems as essential for human survival, the Forest Service has launched a publicity campaign through its pamphlets and other means to condition the public to accept "tree farms" in place of natural forests. "Is Nature Always Right?" one pamphlet asks. "Nature often works in slow, ponderous rhythms which are not always efficient" and "natural growth results in a crowded haphazard mix." The forester can give Nature a helping hand to provide forest products for growing human needs.

There seems to be a general principle involved here that, in terms of hands-on, manipulative management, increasingly intensive management produces a host of unintended consequences which are perceived by the managers and the general public, and especially by the environmental/ecology movement, as real and severe problems. The usual approach, however, is to seek ever more intensive management, which spawns even more problems. And each of these problems is seen as separate, with separate experts and interest groups speaking to each other across a chasm of different technical vocabularies, hidden agendas and very narrow ideas of their own self-interest.

An extreme example of this situation, well documented by historians, ecologists and government agencies, is the situation in California's Central Valley, where the intensively managed agri-industry, which claims as its goal, "feeding the hungry of the world," is now creating an unhealthy, almost unfit environment for many human inhabitants of the Valley. Massive construction projects designed to bring more water to more acres of land have caused desertification, air and water pollution, failure of the underground water system and destruction of fisheries and estuaries in the San Francisco Bay and Sacramento River delta. [21]

Alternatives can be derived from Aldo Leopold's land ethic, which he states as a general principle for maintaining the integrity of natural processes. The land — birds, plants, soil, etc. — is included in the community along with humans, and consideration of vital human needs is placed in the context of the needs of others for self-realization. Both individuals and collectives of organisms and ecosystems are considered when making decisions.

For example, when it is shown that a proposed project will threaten a rare or endangered species, much more careful consideration is given to the project. Mitigation by removing some individuals of the endangered species, such as California condors from their nests or eggs from their nests, breeding some of these in captivity or freezing their genes as genetic resources for future generations are *not* acceptable alternatives.

The killing of the remaining whales to "serve the food needs" or the "needs for jobs" of a few people for a few years in the whaling industry is not an acceptable alternative. Furthermore, ecologists and others interested in preserving wild species should not be required to solve all the problems of jobs, urbanization, and industries in order to advocate protection of other species. Environmentalists are never against jobs as some opponents charge, but are certainly proponents of jobs which are ecologically benign.

2. "Not Do"

Many of the specific goals of preservation of habitat of other species consistent with biocentric equality are summarized in the phrase "Let the river live," where the "river" includes a broader definition of living — not just human populations or even the trees along the river, but the ecosystem of flowing energy. Another perspective on management consistent with Naess's key slogan, "simple in means, rich in ends," is "not do."

It is well documented, for example, that huge areas of the American West have been overgrazed by domestic livestock during the last hundred years so that the carrying capacity, the ability of the range to support certain "head" of livestock over the long term, has diminished. But federal subsidies in the form of low grazing fees (in comparison to fees charged on private lands) and letting ranchers (because of their political pull) continue running livestock on overgrazed lands in herds which are too large for sustainability, increase the problem.

147

A simple "not do" solution is to end federal subsidies and restrict use of public lands for grazing to a level consistent with recovery of grasslands as estimated by professional ecologists.

A second simple "not do" example is the Great Barrier Islands legislation in the United States Congress. The numerous Barrier Islands along the Atlantic seaboard and the Gulf of Mexico are noted for their fragility and unique lifeforms but also the desirability by humans for second home developments and commercial industrial development. One way to protect the intrinsic values and human amenity values of some of these islands is to establish national parks or wildlife reserves at a cost of buying private lands.

However, the "not do" solution in this case was removal of all government financial subsidies for building on Barrier Islands—no funds for roads, schools, sewer systems, marina developments nor government subsidies or guarantees for storm damage insurance (a major issue since hurricanes frequently sweep through some of the islands). The government stated that it would not provide emergency relief funds to help people resettle if they lost their property in a storm.

Result: The rate of development of the Barrier Islands has decreased, habitat has been protected and some people are relieved that "big government" is not taking their property.

3. Living in Mixed Communities of Humans and Nonhumans

While the bioregional, minority tradition seems appropriate to us for cultivating ecological consciousness, allowing for biological diversity and simplicity of means, there are tough, practical decisions to make. We cite several examples.

Consistent with our ultimate norms, it seems that one principle is protection of endangered species of plants and animals as part of the general norm of unity in diversity.

Another norm is bioregional responsibility. The local community is the place for decisions. However, what happens when a local community's needs conflict with the norm of protecting species diversity?

Such a situation occurred on the north slope of Alaska where native Eskimos were hunting bowhead whales in the 1970s. The International Whaling Commission ruled that this was an endangered species of whale and considered a total ban on the killing of bowheads. However, the native Eskimos pleaded that it was part of their tradition to kill whales. Their myths and lifestyle were dependent on it. If they didn't kill whales they would be more dependent on canned meat from the "lower forty-eight" given them by welfare departments.

148

This somewhat split the environmentalists. Many groups supported a total ban on the killing of bowheads until ecologists determined that their population had "sufficiently increased," but Friends of the Earth took the position that Eskimos be allowed to take a regulated number of bowheads using their traditional methods (no advanced technology for killing them was allowed).

Arne Naess provides an example from the bioregion of northern Norway where farmers and herders, through expansion of farms and number of sheep, were rapidly encroaching on habitat of wolves and bears. Some suggested killing all bears since a few bears seemed to be eating some sheep. But others suggested identifying the problem more carefully. Was a specific bear becoming more and more interested in sheep? Could that bear be enticed to refrain from eating sheep? Could it be removed to another location? Could the farmers agree to keep their sheep out of areas where bears were known to have dens or graze? Only as a last resort would the community consider the option of killing that bear. [22]

This approach is in great contrast with that favored by some ranchers and farmers in the American West. When a "predator" is defined — such as wolves, coyotes, eagles, etc. — then systematic efforts are undertaken to eliminate it, including aerial hunting of wolves (in Alaska), spreading of poison "1080," shooting eagles with high-powered rifles and destroying habitat (denning areas, riparian habitat of rats, etc.).

4. Forms of Agriculture

Most agriculture as now practiced as agri-industry with massive use of herbicides, pesticides and other chemicals, major changes in the natural flow of energy through irrigation systems, monocultural systems of cropping and deletions of "border" regions such as riparian habitat, would be wrong insofar as this type of agriculture threatens the integrity and stability of wild ecosystems.

In practice, of course, given the realities of world population and the amount of human-induced changes in landscapes, some less-pure-than-desirable forms of agriculture are necessary, if we are trying to work within a deep ecology perspective.

Thus we are especially encouraged by some of the work on *permaculture* by Australians, including Bill Mollison. Working within a bioregion, sharing experiences and knowledge, experimenting with self-reliance and leaving areas of habitat for other species, they are working toward a sustainable and more locally based agriculture. [23]

149

The organic farming techniques publicized by many writers in the context of specific bioregions is another example worth exploring. For example, an interesting proposal for a return to primitive agriculture in one of the most industrialized nations of the world, Japan, is explained by its founder, Masanobu Fukuoka, in his book *The One-Straw Revolution*. [24] Fukuoka is particularly useful from a deep ecology perspective because he discusses the metaphysical and epistemological assumptions of agriculture in technocratic-industrial societies and presents some alternative proposals.

Much work remains to be done to expose the assumptions and the consequences of the dominant worldview on agriculture and grazing, perhaps along the lines of Denzel Ferguson's *Sacred Cows on the Public Lands* (1983). [25] Further specification of types, modes and assumptions of agriculture within deep ecology principles is needed.

The reason for all the confusion is that there are two paths of human knowledge — discriminating and non-discriminating. . . . I deny the empty image of nature as created by the human intellect, and clearly distinguish it from nature as experienced by the non-discriminating understanding. If we eradicate the false conception of nature, I believe the root of the world's disorder will disappear. . . . Nature as grasped by scientific knowledge is a nature which has been destroyed; it is a ghost possessing a skeleton, but no soul.
—Masanobu Fukuoka, *The One-Straw Revolution* (1978)

Wendel Berry, in *The Unsettling of America* (1977), makes the point that modern agriculture and land use in general is the result of our contemporary distortion of values:

The exploitive always involves the abuse or the perversion of nature and ultimately its destruction. Thus, we saw how far the exploitive revolution had penetrated the official character when our recent secretary of agriculture remarked that "Food is a weapon." This was given a fearful symmetry indeed when, in discussing the possible use of nuclear weapons, a secretary of defense spoke of "palatable" levels of devastation. Consider the associations that have since ancient times clustered around the idea of food — associations of mutual care, generosity, neighborliness, festivity, communal joy, religious ceremony — and you will see that these two secretaries represent a cultural catastrophe. The concerns of farming and those of war, once thought to be diametrically opposed,

150

have become identical. Here we have an example of men who have been made vicious, not presumably by nature or circumstances, but by their values.

Food is not a weapon. [26]

Berry demonstrates that older, more intuitive ways of interacting with the land are being swept away and labeled "superstitious" when in actuality they contain a great deal of ecological understanding. Modern technocratic societies have pinned their hopes for increased production and efficiency on technologies based on partial, and in many cases, inadequate theoretical scientific models. There is no reason to believe that scientific theories and models will ever capture the full intricacy of natural ecosystem functioning.

The adequacy of technology is only as good as the theoretical models upon which it is based. The idea of Gaia treated as a scientific theory rather than myth is an example of a theoretical model and its limitations. Myth is encompassing, intuitive, comforting, involving. The model is limited, cold, manipulative, distant from reality.

The science of ecology as defined narrowly in academia with its thermodynamic studies of energy flows modeled on our current understanding of the laws of physics, the economically modeled concepts of producers and consumers, and quantitative analyses of predator-prey relationships, is itself replete with theoretical concepts and models. The very concept of an ecosystem is based upon cybernetics systems theory which is an attempt to apply a machine model to natural organic processes.

The massive failure of modern technologies when applied more intensively to complex organic systems should lead to widespread healthy skepticism toward scientific modeling together with its associated technologies. It seems appropriate that ecologists and other scientists, and certainly the Resource Conservation and Development scientific managers of Nature, should take heed. But treated with due caution, modesty, a basically conservative attitude, and an awareness of its inherent limitations, ecological science can help us in our search for righteous management. But science and technology alone are a dangerous substitute for land wisdom. And so underlying the search is the constant process of asking deeper and more probing questions. [27]

At the level of politics, land use planning, and other decision-making, every proposal which involves an alteration of a natural ecosystem must be subjected to intensive questioning. What are the social and environmental impacts? Why this project? Will it disrupt the far-future generations of other species, in addition to humans?

Revisioning the quest of human living, we need to ask the fundamental question posed by twentieth-century anthropologist and naturalist Loren Eiseley: "How can we reenter the first world of Nature, from which we have alienated ourselves?" And we need to ask how we can rediscover the enchantment of Gaia, the sacredness of Gaia, and thus heal ourselves.

5. Recovery of Damaged Ecosystems

We have argued that Muir's righteous management is management based upon a worldview and a spiritual way of life similar to the outlook of Taoism, the American Indians, and other primal societies wherein the best management is, in principle, the least management. But we also realize that vast areas of the Earth have been seriously distressed and disrupted by careless and highly exploitive human activity. Strip mining and deforestation are only two obvious examples in the United States. Should these kinds of environmental degradation be left to heal naturally or should humans intervene to help the healing process?

Aldo Leopold defined land health in terms of the naturally evolving processes of an ecosystem in dynamic equilibrium. He used undamaged wilderness as a baseline from which to gauge the health of human-occupied ecosystems. It would seem to be compatible with deep ecology principles and righteous management that, in general, if humans have distressed an ecosystem, they have an obligation to help heal that system. The recovery of human-damaged ecosystems is not strictly a scientific matter, for reasons mentioned earlier, but would involve a combination of art, science, and most importantly, a sense of place. [28] That is, those humans involved in reinhabiting or restoring an ecosystem to health would need to be sensitive to the spiritual as well as the biological needs of that place.

Only in recent years have professional ecologists begun to consider, in a systematic way, the scientific, ethical, and practical issues involved in the recovery of damaged ecosystems. In the introduction to his book on the art of ecosystem healing, ecologist John Cairns poses some interesting questions:

How is recovery defined? What criteria are important in measuring recovery? Do societal perturbations (e.g., strip mining) have a different effect upon natural communities than natural perturbations (e.g., floods)? Should the term "restoration" include, for example, replace ment of stripmined forests with prairie grassland where the latter do not naturally occur (e.g., West Virginia)? How do perturbation-dependent communities differ from other communities relative to the recovery process? Are certain species likely to be primary colonizers of all disturbed systems? . . . Even the selection of an appropriate word to describe the overall process is difficult. One might use rejuvenate, restore, renew, regenerate, rebuild or reconstitute. All of these imply a return to the original (or a new) state of recreation or a youthful strength. Such terms are synonyms for "restoration" and may make it easier for readers of ecological literature to understand and identify the results expected from the recovery phase. [29]

Cairns attempts to answer critics who claim that restoration or rehabilitation has nothing to do with the concept of conservation:

If one views conservation as saving for future generations, reclamation may be as important as preservation. If complete recovery is indeed possible, a distant future generation may not be able to distinguish the reclaimed area from a preserved one. It is also worth noting that reclamation will be better understood and the degree of recovery more precisely determined if untouched reference areas are preserved to serve as models. [30]

Over the years, various environmentalists have proposed dismantling the Bureau of Reclamation. Cairns's use of the term *reclamation* might provide the basis for a new positive ecological function for the Bureau. Cairns's philosophical grounding in anthropocentric conservation might also be widened to include the rights of other species to their own habitats as further criteria in the restorative process. Those committed to deep ecology principles will look with interest on ecological models and prescriptions as provided by Cairns while also keeping in mind the deeper religious/philosophical understanding of person in Nature.

The following are two examples which are symbolic and provocative metaphors for those seeking to heal human-damaged ecosystems. The first example is the significant move in the direction of implementing deep ecology and land ethic principles that has been taken by the U.S. National Park Service in their recent efforts to rehabilitate portions of Redwood Creek in California's Redwood National Park. This small watershed has been studied as intensively as any in the state and could serve as an example of possible rehabilitation in other watersheds. However, the first chapter of *Watershed Rehabilitation in Redwood*

National Park and Other Pacific Coastal Areas provides restoration managers with a vexing dilemma:

Rehabilitation is the restoration to a former state or capacity. Implicit in the term is the assumption of a degraded condition. In wildlands, the greater the degradation, the greater the public visibility and, therefore, the greater the pressure for restoration or rehabilitation. Unfortunately, the greater the perceived "need" for rehabilitation, the lower the probability that rehabilitation efforts will be successful. Thus this dilemma: The greater the public outcry that "something be done," the smaller the opportunity to actually succeed. [31]

This dilemma may again point to the need for land use agencies to move away from policy decisions based on subjective criteria such as public opinion to more objective criteria based upon sound ecological principles.

When the patient is in a state of crisis, the healers need both skills and luck to stabilize the condition. This was the case with Redwood Creek. Until the 1880s, this watershed was inhabited by old-growth redwoods, black bear, Roosevelt elk, oak trees, egrets, river otter, Pacific salmon, and a small tribe (two to four hundred) of Chilula Indians. The Chilula led lives filled with rituals and with a sense of place. Their "churches" were rocks and waterfalls and small lakes where they prayed, held puberty rites, communed with the spirits, and sought to understand. They ate salmon from Redwood Creek and engaged in some prescribed burning, allowing grasses to continue to grow which they used in making baskets. [32] After 1880 the Indians were removed to the Hupa reservation and the lands of Redwood Creek passed to large timber corporations. As late as 1950, however, most of the old-growth redwood forests (which were considered the only commercially valuable wood in the forests) were still intact.

By 1978, only 9,500 acres of old-growth redwoods remained. Clearcuts on steep slopes were eroding. Exotic species of trees had been planted in some areas by the timber corporations. In the Act establishing Redwood National Park, Congress directed the Park Service to undertake ". . . the rehabilitation of areas within and upstream from the park contributing significant sedimentation because of past logging disturbances and road conditions. . . ." [33] The land managers agreed that, "Successful management of erosion is as much a philosophical and political problem as a technical one."

In the first three years of rehabilitation, sites were selected on the basis of the seriousness of the "wounds," estimates of the potential for increasing sediment to the drainage, and "complications" such as gullying from the failure of culverts on logging roads. Each site had a "prescription" written for it.

An example of a site-specific prescription is found in the recommendations for the Tall Trees Grove, an alluvial flat of old-growth redwoods containing some of the tallest trees on Earth. This grove is surrounded on three sides by Redwood Creek, which is still carrying heavy quantities of man-induced erosion material, and by clear-cuts on the uphill slopes. The report claimed that: "Most likely the Tall Trees Grove has a long history of flooding and sedimentation, as with other similar groves on alluvial flats, and it is necessary to see that this continues with minimum adverse change. This will be difficult, because the past half-century has been one of major changes on the watershed related to human use." A whole series of subtle conditions relating to rates of sedimentation, fine sediment versus coarse bedloads, rates of tree growth, and seedling survival was found to be necessary for maintaining these groves. The long, slow, inexorable processes of Nature could not be circumvented by technological ingenuity if these groves were to continue to prosper. It was concluded that, "Management of these groves with the objective of their preservation must allow for such events and their maintenance."

The ecological and rehabilitation studies which resulted in the prescriptions for maintaining the redwood groves, together with other practices such as allowing forest fires to burn in uninhabited areas, further underscores Commoner's law that "Nature knows best." It is encouraging to see the U.S. Park Service begin to incorporate ecological wisdom in their management plans and as an ideal by which to guide management and rehabilitation policy. [34]

The second example of the difficult job of rehabilitating a human-damaged area is the proposal to make the Los Angeles Basin again habitable by the California condor. The condor is an endangered species caught up in the machinations of an exploitive hands-on scientific management plan. Instead of attempting to protect the remaining birds and enlarge and restore their habitat, some biologists have weighed and measured and generally disturbed the condors while hopes for their survival hinge mainly on captive breeding in zoos. But captive wild animals have been removed from the natural evolutionary processes. As David Brower has pointed out, the condor is a condor only in *place*, in natural habitat, and this principle holds as well for other wild animals, as well as humans. The goal is to restore the Los Angeles Basin to condor habitat. The symbol of the condor and condor habitat for the Los Angeles Basin provides a provocative metaphor for this and future generations of humans as they begin the process of reinhabitation of these areas. [35]

The fate of the California condor is a symbolic issue for Brower and many other people. Brower asked a rhetorical question: "If we cannot save a receptive environment for the condor, symbol of the global threat to endangered species, what can we save? What condors need most right now is our sense of their place," he concluded. Brower suggested that a practical ecotopian vision would be to restore the Los Angeles Basin to condor habitat. He concluded his essay on "The Condor and a Sense of Place" with the following statement:

The Condor Question, we hope, will enhance the opportunity for the rest of us to keep intact the wildness and wild living things that remain in the sea, on the land, and in the air, to prevent a wake for them and their not-so-distant relatives, ourselves. We and they need our places, our islands of sanctuary.

Let it speed the California condor's recovery to measure the bird arbitrarily about like this: A condor is five percent feathers, flesh, blood, and bone. All the rest is *place*. Condors are soaring manifestations of the place that coded their genes. That place requires space to nest in, to teach fledglings, to roost in unmolested, to bathe and drink in, to find other condors in and not too many biologists, and to fly over wild and free. If it is to be worthy at all, our sense of ethics about other living things requires our being able to grant that their place transcends our urge to satisfy our curiosity, to probe, to draw blood, to insult, to incarcerate. We can respect the dignity of a creature that has done our species no wrong — except, perhaps, to prefer us at a distance.

We tend to view the kind of management designed to regulate and halt further environmental destruction by modern humans as *interim management*. And since the current urban-industrial onslaught must be slowed and stopped as quickly as possible, then surely the success of interim resistance measures will be equally important in its own way as are the creative steps taken toward deep ecology futures. We are arguing that interim management measures, while a necessary condition at present, are not sufficient to provide a long-range solution to our environmental plight. As Gary Snyder suggests, "We need to work on all levels simultaneously."

We recognize the absolutely crucial importance of maintaining the natural evolutionary/ecological processes on this planet and of resisting the dominance of the managed "artificial world." Another interim management strategy, justified in anthropocentric terms, is the "World Conservation Strategy" developed by the International Union for the Conservation of Nature and Natural Resources (IUCN) and backed by the United Nations Environmental Program. This worldwide plan has been worked out in considerable detail and might actually help provide a transition to deep ecology decentralized futures.[36]

In October 1982, the United Nations General Assembly adopted a World Charter for Nature (which had been prepared by the IUCN) which includes a more biocentric orientation. The General Assembly is convinced that:

... *Every form of life is unique, warranting respect regardless of its worth to man, and, to accord other organisms such recognition, man must be guided by a moral code of action.* ... *Nature shall be respected and its essential processes shall not be disrupted.* ... *Ecosystems and organisms* ... *which are utilized by man shall be managed to achieve and maintain optimum sustainable productivity, but not in such a way as to endanger the integrity of those other ecosystems or species with which they coexist.*

While the Charter for Nature is to be applauded, we have suggested the ambiguities in the concept of management, and various incompatibilities in achieving optimum productivity on the one hand while not disrupting ecological processes and the integrity of Nature on the other.

We are caught in a series of complex dilemmas. We have argued that contemporary RCD ideology is generally hands-on management, and that the overall manipulation of Nature is both ecologically disastrous and ethically unacceptable. It violates the integrity of Nature, and further, it is unethical, as Heidegger and others have argued, to pervert living beings by mechanizing and genetically altering them. Environmental disaster is the end result of the unrestrained freedom of societies to exploit Nature. We believe that genuine freedom for humans and nonhumans lies in deep ecology futures.

It is crucial that interim management plans do not include practices that are ecologically harmful or questionable, thus foreclosing the possibilities for deep ecology futures. Many forms of hands-on management — taking wild animals from their natural habitats to serve

157

as breeding stock in zoos, or being lulled into complacency by setting up genetic sperm banks of wild stock—may be examples of such practices.

6. Deep, Long-Range Goals and Interim Management

Some will no doubt say that deep ecology proposals for holistic management and reinhabitation are overly idealistic and impractical on a global scale. As a sociological fact, deep ecological consciousness and interest in bioregionalism are on the increase in many parts of the Earth.

However, there are public policy decisions which are being made by corporations and national governments which include the fate of vast areas of the planet where humans have never made significant impact before—the oceans, sky, antarctic and polar regions, Siberia, many mountain regions, and all remaining rain forest areas where bioregional peoples have lived for centuries but which are now being destroyed. [37]

In our estimation, at present we must use all political avenues open to us, including the mechanism of the United Nations, to protect vast expanses of ecologically viable habitat to insure species survival.

Furthermore, in order to insure the compatibility of interim measures with long-range ecology futures, restoration managers and interim managers need to cultivate a biocentric perspective. Some are just beginning to understand the relationship between cultivating one's own ecological consciousness and "managing." Any real understanding of the land means atuning oneself to the land, to a specific bioregion, and developing a sense of place. Otherwise, land management will continue to "manage" on the basis of subjective economic criteria to the detriment of the Earth and the future.

If enough citizens cultivate their own ecological consciousness and act through the political process to inform managers and government agencies of the principles of deep ecology, some significant changes in the direction of wise long-range management policies can be achieved.

Nothing is said in this book about the export of commodities—water, plants, timber, etc.—to cities, nor anything about managing cities, their size or design, nor the political power of cities to take natural resources from far away for their own uses. Nor do we discuss jobs, the structure of decision-making in natural resource extraction and the creation of jobs for ever-growing human populations. These are vital issues for individuals and for public policy and deserve careful, thoughtful consideration based on deep ecology norms and principles. We encourage readers to draw from their own experiences, whether living in large cities, suburbs or the countryside, to make more specific decisions based on their own knowledge, information, and intuitions within the deep ecology framework.

Forest workers and private landowners of small and large parcels of damaged forest lands, for example, can adopt a holistic forestry strategy based on maintaining biological diversity rather than making decisions based on short-term return on invested capital. [38]

As Gary Snyder concludes, "Like it or not we are *all* finally 'inhabitory' on this one small blue-green planet. . . . It's clearly time to put hegemonial controversies aside, to turn away from economics that demand constant exploitation of both people and resources, and to put Earth first!" [39]

This living flowing land
is all there is, forever

We are *it*
it sings through us —

We could live on this Earth
without clothes or tools!
    — Gary Snyder, from "By Frazier
    Creek Falls" in Turtle Island *(1974)*

CHAPTER 9

•

ECOTOPIA:
THE VISION DEFINED

It would be a grave injustice to dismiss utopian thought as mere fantasy, visionary and impractical; to consider it restricted to literary forms that bear its label is to underestimate its wide prevalence, at many levels and in all cultures. However expressed, it is essentially a critique of defects and limitations of society and an expression for something better.

—Paul Sears, "Utopia and the Living Landscape" (1965)

Developing ecotopian visions is part of our environmental education. In a society famous for dystopian visions, such as *Brave New World* and *1984*, ecotopian visions present affirmations of our bonds with Earth.

Creating ecotopian futures has practical value. It helps us articulate our goals and presents an ideal which may never be completely realized but which keeps us focused on the ideal. We can also compare our personal actions and collective public decisions on specific issues with this goal. We suggest that ecotopian visions give perspective on vain-glorious illusions of both revolutionary leaders and the propaganda of defenders of the status quo. Furthermore, ecotopian visions help us see the distance between what ought to be and what is now reality in our technocratic-industrial society.

In this chapter, we use ecotopia in the broad sense of all visions of a good society placed in the context of deep ecological norms and principles. We present the ecotopian visions of Loren Eiseley, Baker Brownell, Aldous Huxley, Gary Snyder and Paul Shepard. We should keep in mind that ecotopian visions are always tentative; the examples given in this chapter are first approximations and not complete statements. [1]

In addition to acting as a provocative catalyst for public debate, creating ecotopian visions is also useful for the development of ecological consciousness in people who struggle with these visions. This process enables one to sharpen both the image of the ecotopian future, and the rational skills needed in public debate to argue the points.

We feel this process is an essential part of environmental education for high school- and college-age students. This may help them see viable alternatives to the status quo which they can incorporate into their own lives. Even grammar school children can gain from this activity. With some ingenuity on the part of teachers, deep ecology principles can be introduced using the deep questioning process.

Inspiration for ecotopian visions can be drawn from the anthropological literature on hunter/gatherers, small-scale agricultural communities, and contemporary primal cultures. A direct transition from our own culture into an ecotopia is beyond the imagination of most people. And so deciding on what is the "best" of contemporary culture to include in the ecotopian vision is part of the educational process. This can help us understand the difference between vital and nonvital human needs and bring us to a greater realization of the implications of applying deep ecology norms.

162

When we look back through history we can recognize the practical significance in shaping the direction of society of Plato's *Republic,* Augustine's *City of God,* and the visions of Karl Marx. Our contemporary technocratic-industrial worldview and society owes much of its present form to the vision presented in Bacon's *New Atlantis,* to various Enlightenment utopian visions, and to science fiction from H. G. Wells to Isaac Asimov.

Some ecotopias are very broad in scope whereas others are more specifically bioregional. It would be valuable to develop more ecotopias which address the problems and issues of the differing unique bioregions. For example, Ernest Callenbach's novels, *Ecotopia* (1975) and *Ecotopia Emerging* (1981), provide specific visions for America's Pacific Northwest region. The city of Saint Francis (San Francisco) becomes an ecological model for future urban areas. Callenbach discusses appropriate technology, emphasizing local grassroots politics, consensus decision-making, and the importance of providing opportunities for women to be major political leaders. There are discussions of ecological education for children, and ecological rituals. The basic philosophy of the Ecotopians tends to be patterned after the American Indian.

QUESTIONS TO ASK
IN DEVELOPING ECOTOPIAN VISIONS

How can imperfect persons reach toward Self-realization in the broader sense discussed in this book?

How can humans begin the process of integrating body-mind-spirit?

What kinds of social structures are more conducive than others to both individual self-realization and the broader Self-realization?

What kinds of social structures are truly sustainable?

What kinds of technology are appropriate to deep ecology principles?

How do communities of people and individuals relate to this technology?

How can vital needs be defined?

How can vital needs be served fully with minimal impact on the requirements of vital needs of nonhumans?

What is the role of emotion in human life?

What kinds of cosmology, religion and education are most conducive to deep ecology principles?

I. LOREN EISELEY

In his essay "The Last Magician," which appeared in his collection of essays, *The Invisible Pyramid* (1970), Eiseley says that humanity now faces a magician who will shape its final form:

. . . a magician in the shape of his own collective brain, that unique and spreading force which in its manipulations will precipitate the last miracle, or, like the sorcerer's apprentice, wreak the last disaster. The possible nature of the last disaster the world of today has made all too evident: man has become a spreading blight which threatens to efface the green world that created him . . . the nature of the human predicament is: how nature is to be reentered; how man, the relatively unthinking and proud creator of the second world — the world of culture — may revivify and restore the first world which cherished and brought him into being. [2]

In the hunting/gathering cultures of the first world — the world of ecosystem people — man "projected a friendly image upon animals: animals talked among themselves and thought rationally like men; they had souls. . . . [Man was still] inside that world; he had not turned it into an instrument or a mere source of materials."

The second world — the world of culture — is a world of man's creation. It was made possible, in Eiseley's estimation, as a result of more advanced forms of symbolizing, of the linguistic phenomenon of displacement, of the invention of historical time. Man separated himself from the rest of Nature, became more urban and alienated from the "spirits in every tree or running brook. His animal confreres slunk like pariahs soulless from his presence. They no longer spoke." The Pan-power has been lost. Now the life of humanity is felt to be "unreal and sterile":

Perhaps a creature of so much ingenuity and deep memory is almost bound to grow alienated from his world, his fellows, and the objects around him. He suffers from a nostalgia for which there is no remedy upon earth except as is to be found in the enlightenment of the spirit — some ability to have a perceptive rather than an exploitive relationship with his fellow creatures. . . . Yet as the growing crust of his exploitive technology thickened, the more man thought that he could withdraw from or recast nature, that by drastic retreat he could dispel his deepening sickness.

If modern humans are to overcome this growing alienation and sickness, what will be required is:

. . . the act of a truly great magician, the man capable of transforming himself. For what, increasingly, is required of man is that he pursue the paradox of return . . . [but] man does not wish to retrace his steps down to the margins of the reeds and peer within, lest by some magic he be permanently recaptured. Instead, men prefer to hide in cities of their own devising.

Eiseley was writing at the juncture of two historic human events: the landing on the moon and the advent of space travel coupled with the explosive awareness of the global environmental crisis. Two competing images of the future seem to be vying for our attention — "the starship and the canoe." He gently warns us to set our priorities straight:

At the climactic moment of his journey into space [man] has met himself at the doorway of the stars. And the looming shadow before him has pointed backward into the entangled gloom of a forest from which it has been his purpose to escape. Man has crossed, in his history, two worlds. He must now enter another and forgotten one, but with the knowledge gained on the pathway to the moon. He must learn that, whatever his powers as a magician, he lies under the spell of a greater and a green enchantment which, try as he will, he can never avoid, however far he travels. The spell has been laid on him since the beginning of time — the spell of the natural world from which he sprang.

While Eiseley as an evolutionary voyager claims no aversion to space travel, he is nevertheless concerned with the motivations of some who advocate it most ardently. The great axial religions tried to "persuade man to transcend his own nature" but modern science has held out to humans "the prospect of limitless power over exterior nature. Its technicians sometimes seem, in fact, to have proffered us the power of the void as though flight were the most important value on earth." One space engineer of Eiseley's acquaintance claimed that "We have got to spend everything we have, if necessary, to get off this planet" because the Ice Age is returning. A space agency administrator claimed in print that "Should man fall back from his destiny . . . the confines of this planet will destroy him." Eiseley finds the expression of this kind of continuing psychic alienation from the planet shallow and dangerous:

It is not fair to say this planet will destroy us. Space flight is a brave venture, but upon the soaring rockets are projected all the fears and evasions of man. He has fled across two worlds, from the windy corridors of wild savannahs to the sunlit world of the mind, and still he flees. Earth will not destroy him. It is he who threatens to destroy the earth.

165

Eiseley concludes with a challenge and a utopian direction for the future survival of mankind:

Today man's mounting numbers and his technological power to pollute his environment reveal a single demanding necessity: the necessity for him consciously to reenter and preserve, for his own safety, the old first world from which he originally emerged. His second world, drawn from his own brain, has brought him far, but it cannot take him out of nature, nor can he live by escaping into his second world alone. He must incorporate from the wisdom of the axial thinkers an ethic not alone directed toward his fellows, but extended to the living world around him. He must make, by way of his cultural world, an actual conscious reentry into the sunflower forest he had thought merely to exploit or abandon. He must do this in order to survive. If he succeeds he will, perhaps, have created a third world which combines elements of the original two and which should bring closer the responsibilities and nobleness of character envisioned by the axial thinkers who may be acclaimed as the creators, if not of man, then of his soul.

II. BAKER BROWNELL

Baker Brownell, a social philosopher at Northwestern University during the 1930s and 40s, deserves credit for the first post-World War II ecotopian vision. Brownell proposed redirecting technocratic-industrial society away from its destructive path and toward simplified lifestyles in balance and rhythm with the natural world. Brownell realized that human existence is sustained by the larger natural world and the social order proposed in an ecotopian vision must be articulated with constant awareness of that fact. [3]

In Brownell's words, man's life:

. . . has been laid out through millions of years in association with living animals and plants and the vast music movement of the natural world . . . the beasts and the plants participate primevally in our communities. They enter our philosophies; mold our natures; help make us fully human. They are among our greatest teachers.

This sense of evolutionary continuity and ecological interrelatedness and reciprocity has implications for value determinations. In characterizing Brownell's position, Thomas Colwell, the educational philosopher, says:

By making value determination a function of an environmental field in which human interests are only one of a number of contending considerations, Brownell hopes to avoid the subjectivity inherent in social determinism. The process of deciding what is good for man would have to be framed in the context of what is good for components of the natural world other than man. [4]

From this ecological worldview and value orientation so reminiscent of Leopold's land ethic, Brownell sees that standards of human health and the meaningfulness of human existence must also be framed within the wider context of Nature:

We are continuous with Nature and the world. This sense of functional unity with the natural world is a basic condition, we may assume, of what is called a meaningful and stable life. . . . This functional . . . conception of life establishes normality on the broad basis of man's associations with his fellow plants and animals as well as with his own kind. . . .

Brownell is now faced with an epistemological problem and Colwell describes his dilemma:

But how is Nature to be known such that we may not only learn its own requirements for sustained existence, but that human values may be articulated within its purview? What method of knowing is appropriate to value judgment that is construed ecologically rather than socially? And how do we find in this method a place for human individuality and uniqueness? How, in short, is man's relationship to Nature to be understood if we are to derive a scheme of social practice from it?

He was forced to reject science as a way of knowing in the relevant sense, for science is statistical and generalized by its very nature and thus tends to "subsume the concrete under the relational." But for Brownell, the "concrete thing is the ultimate datum in existence." A method was needed that would retain the concrete reality of each individual thing even within the wider sphere of ecological interrelatedness, and Brownell found this method in direct mystical experience. This experience, for Brownell, is a kind of Gestalt in which individuality is retained even within the field of ecological relationships:

Mysticism enables man to comprehend the unity of direct experience which is denied to science, and in so doing he is in touch with the influence of environmental forces and relationships contextually rather than through the inadequate symbolic formulations of scientific method. In Brownell's mysticism, man is more fully aware of the sanctions and limits of the natural world because he is sensitive to their direct intervention in his daily life, and so is better able to overcome his anthropocentrism and shape his social life in accordance with ecological norms. . . . [In an ecologically healthy man/nature environment] sub-

167

jectivity is transformed and judgment begins to be conditioned by respect for the normativeness of ecosystemic relationships and sanctions. Thus, the ground of objectivity for Brownell's mysticism is in the world, in an environment ordered on the basis of ecologically sound principles.

From this ecological metaphysical/epistemological base, Brownell launches his attack on the urban/industrial worldview. The gargantuan size and complexity of modern industrial societies eliminates the possibility for direct concrete experience:

Industrial man, fragmented by the divisive specialization he is forced to engage in, vainly compensates for his lack of direct experience by vicarious cultivation of still other specializations, either as spectator, participant in extroverted pursuit of pleasure and material goods, or as lone practitioner of highly wrought technical and professional skills. For Brownell, our culture is a culture of escape and substitutive behavior. . . . Substitutive behavior forces us to separate emotion from direct action; and this separation, Brownell thought, is the essence of decadence.

Brownell was especially critical of urban life:

The greater aggressiveness and violence of city life stemmed from an excessive concentration of the specialized functions and organizations. But because the activities of corporate organizations increasingly reached out to include the remotest of rural areas, they too became affiliated with the extensive urban culture. All industrial life is lived in the urban context. . . . [Urban men] have learned to value false gods. They have been seduced by bright, divisive cultures, specialized perfections and privileges, glittering fragments, gadgets, ready-made arts, and importations bought promiscuously without relevance to the basic making-using rhythm that is central in any good life. They live on the loot of the world, on trinkets and odds and ends, the only value of which is often the thrill of acquisition.

Colwell sums up Brownell's critique of industrial society in his review of Brownell's writing:

In limiting concrete experience and reinforcing acquisitiveness, the goal of urban culture becomes the perpetual expansion of the scope of acquisitive experience. . . . An acquisitive culture is a man-centered culture. . . . It is morally narrow in its outlook and suicidal in its course; it fails to realize that the destiny of man, his well-being and happiness, must be framed in accordance with the welfare of the life of the whole of Nature and not just his own immediate desires.

168

To achieve a healthy, ecologically integrated human community, Brownell called for the decentralization of society: "The true human community is incompatible with corporate mass society." The reform of education, even in ecological ways, is by itself insufficient. Education as a social institution is part and parcel of the larger social context. As Colwell says:

The goal of the school is to promote the self-realization of each community member, and this leads to an appreciation of the broad world beyond the culture itself. Man is a part of Nature, his full humanity is realized when he has defined his own particularity in relation to Nature's totality. . . . The community is the supreme educational environment, and however much educators may try to institute instructional reform in the schools designed to enhance self-realization and overcome alienation, their efforts will fail as long as the community is organized on the principles of mass-society. Education must therefore become the agency of social reconstruction to make the small community the primary environment for educational activity. . . . In so heavily emphasizing the dependency of educational reform on social reconstruction, Brownell has made the possibility of educational reform hinge on what amounts to utopian social innovation. [5]

It is significant that Brownell had been a student of George Santayana. Upon his retirement in 1911, Santayana had made a scathing attack upon the anthropocentrism of the European philosophical/religious tradition. He had also rejected urban life and the direction of technocratic society for the virtues of rural life.

III. ALDOUS HUXLEY

Aldous Huxley came to an ecological perspective gradually during his long career, and as a result of his long association with D. H. Lawrence. Huxley's last novel, *Island* (1961), was an ecotopian vision. [6]

The novel is set on the island of Pala in southeast Asia, a Buddhist community which had isolated itself for 200 years from industrialization and colonization. A Scottish physician had introduced Western science to Pala in the nineteenth century, but the prevailing Buddhism set the contemplative direction of the community. The village was the mode of human community. Population had been stabilized, and technology was appropriate to meet basic needs—the island was self-sustaining. Much of the plot revolves around the attempt by Pala to resist commercialization from a neighboring community and to resist exploitation of its oil reserves by outside corporations.

169

Buddhism is the vehicle by which the youth are taught to have direct mystical experience and to experience their identity with the ecological whole. A great deal of the book is concerned with the nurturing and education of the young. Mountain climbing is one of the ways Huxley proposes to integrate the individual and overcome the mind-body split so endemic in Western civilized education:

Specialization . . . is necessary and inevitable. And if one educates the whole mind-body along with the symbol-using intellect, that kind of necessary specialization won't do much harm. But you people don't educate the mind-body. Your cure for too much scientific specialization is a few more courses in the humanities. . . . By themselves the humanities don't humanize. They're simply another form of specialization on the symbolic level. Reading Plato or listening to a lecture on T. S. Eliot doesn't educate the whole human being; like courses in physics or chemistry, it merely educates the symbol manipulator and leaves the rest of the living mind-body in its pristine state of ignorance and ineptitude.

Huxley further claimed that the primary scientific emphasis would be on the life sciences, not physics and chemistry. The islanders had "not the faintest desire to land on the backside of the moon. Only the modest ambition to live as fully human beings in harmony with the rest of life on this island at this latitude on this planet." Young children began their science training with the study of ecology. When asked whether this was too complicated for children, Huxley replied:

That's precisely the reason why we begin with it. Never give children a chance of imagining that anything exists in isolation. Make it plain from the very first that all living is relationship. Show them relationships in the woods, in the fields, in the ponds and streams, in the village and the country around it.

Children are taught ecological truths in animal fables. They are shown examples of erosion and ecological damage in places where "greedy, stupid people have tried to take without giving, to exploit without love or understanding." For Huxley, an understanding of ecology leads to an understanding of morality:

Confronted by [examples of ecological damage], it's easy for the child to see the need for conservation and then to go on from conservation to morality—easy for him to go on from the Golden Rule in relation to plants and animals and the earth that supports them to the Golden Rule in relation to human beings. . . . The morality to which a child goes on from the facts of ecology and the parables of erosion is a universal ethic. . . . Conservation morality gives nobody an excuse for feeling superior, or claiming special privileges. "Do as you would be done by" applies to our dealings with all kinds of life in every part of the world. We shall be permitted to live on this planet only for as long as we treat all nature with compassion and intelligence. Elementary ecology leads straight to elementary Buddhism.

IV. GARY SNYDER

Gary Snyder has provided an admirably concise yet comprehensive ecotopian vision in "Four 'Changes'" (1969). Snyder's ecological perspective results from a combination of Zen Buddhism, Native American religion, the ways of life of the primal peoples on many continents, and the insights of the contemporary science of ecology.[7] This spiritual ecology is in evidence when he claims:

Man is but a part of the fabric of life—dependent on the whole fabric for his very existence. As the most highly developed tool-using animal, he must recognize that the unknown evolutionary destinies of other life forms are to be respected. . . . There are now too many human beings, and the problem is growing rapidly worse. . . . The goal would be half of the present world population, or less. . . . Let reverence for life and reverence for the feminine mean also reverence for other species, and future human lives, most of which are threatened. . . . I am a child of all life, and all living beings are my brothers and sisters.

And in anticipation of Schumacher in *Small Is Beautiful,* Snyder asserts:

Most of the production and consumption of modern societies is not necessary or conducive to spiritual and cultural growth, let alone survival . . . mankind has become a locust-like blight on the planet that will leave a bare cupboard for its own children— all the while in a kind of addict's dream of affluence, comfort, eternal progress—using the great achievements of science to produce software and swill. . . . Balance, harmony, humility, growth which is mutual growth with redwood and quail— to be a good member of the great community of living creatures. True affluence is not needing anything. . . . Economics must be seen as a small sub-branch of ecology.

Snyder's broad utopian visionary statement clearly sets him in direct opposition to the artificial environment vision contained in much New Age/Aquarian conspiracy literature. Snyder calls for an *unobtrusive technology* in a world environment which is left natural:

We have it within our powers not only to change our "selves" but to change our culture. If man is to remain on earth he must transform

171

the five-millennia long urbanizing civilization tradition into a new ecologically-sensitive harmony-oriented wild-minded scientific/spiritual culture . . . nothing short of total transformation will do much good. What we envision is a planet on which the human population lives harmoniously and dynamically by employing a sophisticated and unobtrusive technology in a world environment which is "left natural." . . . Master the archaic and the primitive as models of basic nature-related cultures—as well as the most imaginative extensions of science—and build a community where these two vectors cross.

V. PAUL SHEPARD

Perhaps the most challenging, uncompromising, and in some ways disturbing ecological utopian proposal has been advanced by Paul Shepard in *The Tender Carnivore and the Sacred Game* (1973).[8] Shepard develops his thought from a very sophisticated anthropological basis and does an admirable job of clearing away the myths and distortions which have been heaped upon hunting/gathering societies since the advent of agriculture. Shepard asks, "Can we face the possibility that hunters were more fully human than their descendants?" In his view, the ecological crisis has been ten thousand years in the making:

As agriculture replaced hunting and gathering it was accompanied by radical changes in the way men saw and responded to their natural surroundings. Although hundreds of local forms of farming developed . . . they all shared the aim of completely humanizing the earth's surface, replacing wild with domestic, and creating landscapes from habitat.[9]

Not only is farming itself an ecological disease, according to Shepard, but the traditional peasant has led "the dullest life man has ever lived." While the pioneer subsistence farm is in fairly close ecological harmony, farmers in a monocultural setting "require constant social supercharging to remain sane and human." Rural life is hopeless in modern industrial irrigation farming. Domestic plants and animals are biological disasters, he claims; they are "genetic goofies." Shepard agrees with Brownell that humans need wild animals in their natural habitat to model themselves after and become fully human; domesticated pets and farm animals provide pathetically inadequate substitutes. For Shepard, an ecologically sane future requires that almost all forms of farming together with genetically-altered plants and animals must go. Another requirement for the

172

future is the full recognition that humans are genetically hunters and gatherers:

Most people seem to agree that we cannot and do not want to go back to the past; but the reason given is often wrong: that time has moved on and what was can never be again. The truth is that we cannot go back to what we never left. Our home is the earth, our time the Pleistocene Ice Ages. The past is the formula for our being. Cynegetic man is us. [10]

Unlike some of the earlier utopian literature, Shepard squarely comes to grips with the recent anthropological/genetic literature on Homo sapiens. In any realistic utopian planning for the future, it is necessary for our physical and emotional health that we incorporate into our lives the central features of a hunting/gathering way of life (rituals, exercise, etc.). Secondly, modern ecological findings support the existence of huge expanses of unmanaged wilderness to ensure the integrity of ecosystems and wildlife habitat. Shepard also addresses this issue in his utopian proposal. As he points out:

It is impossible to overestimate the ecological crime of species extinction, which is the only irreparable environmental damage by man. Extinction is caused by alteration of the habitat. The measures necessary to avoid it are the same that preserve the biosphere as a whole. The prevention of extinction should be the criterion for a plan or policy of environmental activity of any kind. [11]

Shepard's proposal is somewhat desperate in that he plans for the world population to stabilize at about eight billion people by the year 2020. In order to meet the requirements for hunting/gathering existence, he argues that cities of the kind designed by Doxiadis or Paolo Soleri might be strung in narrow ribbons along the edges of the continents and islands while the center of the continents would be allowed to return to the wild.

If eight billion people . . . were to live in some 160,000 cities (of 50,000 inhabitants), and these cities were uniformly distributed over the earth's fifty million square miles of land, only some three hundred square miles of land would surround each city (allowing two square miles for each city itself). Cities would then be only about seventeen miles apart, and no true wilderness would be possible. If, instead of being dispersed in the interiors of continents, they were constructed in a broken line on the perimeters of the continents, the whole of the interior could be freed for ecological and evolutionary systems on a scale essential to their own requirements and to human cynegetic culture. [12]

173

What would provide the basic diet for humans living in these great ribbons of cities stretching endlessly around the continents with agriculture gone, only occasional gardens, and meat brought back from hunting/gathering forays into the wilderness? Surprisingly, Shepard's answer is a food technology based on microbial life:

Biochemistry and microbial biology make possible the recovery of a livable planet complementing ecology rather than opposing it . . . the transition to non-land-based subsistence might take half a century . . . but perhaps three-quarters of the earth could be freed from its present destructive use. [13]

Shepard's long, detailed discussions of the maturation and education of future cynegetic people are fascinating. For example:

I believe that every child under ten has three ecological needs: architecturally complex play space shared with companions; a cumulative and increasingly diverse experience of non-human forms, animate and inanimate, whose taxonomic names and generic relationships he must learn; and occasional and progressively more strenuous excursions into the wilderness where he may, in a limited way, confront the non-human. . . . The collection and study of plants and animals is more important than any other learning activity. . . . In the cynegetic society [the child] would be introduced gradually to the great wilderness, which . . . would occupy the centers of islands and continents, unmodified by human action. All travel in three-quarters of the earth's land surface would therefore be on foot. . . . Cynegetic man by definition is a hunter and a gatherer. From the age of thirteen the adolescent youth would move into a series of increasingly extended and arduous expeditions for which childhood and juvenile skills and his knowledge of natural history had prepared him. [14]

Shepard has some harsh words for mystical experience but, like most Western intellectuals, he is not aware of its use by Brownell, Zen Buddhism, and many other traditions including the primitive, in which individual concrete reality is stressed:

Primitive man is often said to feel an "identity with nature." This observation stems from an erroneous concept of continuity in nature in which distinctions and boundaries evaporate. Hunting/gathering men are not lost in a fuzzy emotional merger with their surroundings; they are sensitive to delicate nuances that separate and relate . . . mysticism is hardly a way of advancing to a mature life on this earth. [15]

VI. CRITIQUE OF ECOTOPIAN VISIONS

Much of the antimodernist movement in the West during the last 300 years has been a resistance to the urban-industrial in favor of the pastoral. Contemporary New Age thinking glorifies the urban-industrial high technology future at the expense of both the rural and the wilderness/ecological. Shepard appears to want to combine the New Age visions of Doxiadis and Soleri and biochemical food technology with the hunting/gathering wilderness/ecological vision and, in *some* ways, his solution echoes Thoreau, as described by Roderick Nash:

In providing a philosophical defense of the half-savage, Thoreau gave the American idealization of the pastoral a new foundation. Previously most Americans had revered the rural, agrarian condition as a release both from wilderness and from high civilization. They stood, so to speak, with both feet in the center of the spectrum of environments. Thoreau, on the other hand, arrived at the middle by straddling. He rejoiced in the extremes and, by keeping a foot in each, believed he could extract the best of both worlds. [16]

The virtues of "high civilization" have paled considerably since Thoreau's day. And the prospects of modern cynegetic man as also modern urban man filling those apartment-house cities encircling the continents of the world is unsettling, to say the least. As Shepard puts it:

Nature would be separated from the works but not the lives of men, for men would live in both worlds. The confusion that has plagued mankind for ten millennia between what is made by him and what is not made by him would be ended. [17]

This seems an unusually high price to pay for these kinds of advantages and we wonder if Thoreau, given this option in today's world, would have closed with the deal. Traditional hunters traveled in small bands, isolated from other humans and totally surrounded by and integrated with their natural environment. On special occasions they came together as a larger society or nation. Shepard thinks this kind of tribalization can occur within Soleri's cities and, "Properly designed, such an arrangement would seem less crowded than present city life. Architecture will take into account our mammalian and primate nature as well as our human values and customs." [18]

Whether cities like this could be so designed remains largely conjectural. We have suspicions that those who go on the hunting expeditions into the center of the wilderness, lasting for weeks, months, and perhaps years in some cases, might on occasion just decide not to return. Those cynegetic genes, having grown used to the true freedom of wilderness and solitude, a steady diet of wild game and plants, and encountering highly desirable living space, might come to look with acute displeasure on the microbial diet and the multitudes of people awaiting their return. The continents would gradually be repopulated with what ecologist Raymond Dasmann calls *ecosystem people* living a mixed hunting/gathering subsistence-agricultural appropriate technology way of life. Our sympathies would lie with them. The future primitive would not live in two worlds but would be integrated with the surroundings.

We find the visions of Gary Snyder and Raymond Dasmann more appealing and realistic in the long run than Shepard's. [19] Snyder has respect for a great deal of modern theoretical science and for small-scale appropriate technology and, like Shepard, he is fully aware of the hunting/gathering biological basis of Homo sapiens and of the ecological necessity for vast unmanaged natural areas. Snyder, however, has much less respect for cities but more tolerance for subsistence and small-scale organic farming. With Raymond Dasmann and Peter Berg, he has been exploring bioregional proposals for reinhabiting the land whereby ecosystem people ways of life can be reinstituted. Which vision is ultimately more practical? Shepard acquiesces in the prospect of an Earth inhabited by eight billion humans. With Snyder's vision, carrying capacity of continents and islands at ecosystem people levels would have to be determined and then all efforts would have to be made to reduce human population to those levels by humane means. Utopian proposals which are less specific and less global in scope may increase the likelihood that cultural as well as biological diversity will be preserved as each area works out its own unique version of reinhabitation.

The overall claim here has been that the explicit or implicit utopian visions of the technocratic social worldview—of humans dominating and managing Nature as a resource in the production of the "artificial environment" or as an expendable launching pad in the journey to outer space—are indefensible. Human attention must now rapidly shift to an ecological worldview and utopian vision to serve as a guide for individual and social values and action. Intellectual debate must focus on the refinement of these visions together with appropriate social strategies. Educational goals and strategies must follow suit.

One of the poems of the *Tao Te Ching* expresses one vision of ecotopia clearly:

Better to keep
Your country small
Your people few
Your devices simple—
And even those for
Infrequent use.

Let people measure life
By the meaning of death
And not go out of their way
To visit far off places.
With nowhere to travel

And little care for display
Great ships, fine carriages,
And shining weapons become
Mere relics of the past.

Let people recover
The simple life:
Reckoning by knotted cords,
Delighting in a basic meal,
Pleased with humble attire,
Happy in their homes,
Taking pleasure in their
Rustic ways.

So content are they
That nearby towns,
So close the sound
Of dogs and roosters
Forms one chorus,
Folks grown gray with age
May pass away never having
Strayed beyond the village.

—Translated by Tom Early

CHAPTER 10
•
CHARACTER
AND CULTURE

In prevalent individualistic and utilitarian political thinking in western modern industrial states, the terms "self-realization," "self-expression," "self-interest" are used (in ways that assume) the ultimate and extensive incompatibility of the interests of different individuals. In opposition to this trend there is another, which is based on the hypothesis (that) self-realization cannot develop far without sharing joys and sorrows with others, or more fundamentally, without the development of the narrow ego of the small child into the comprehensive structure of a Self that comprises all human beings. The ecological movement—as many earlier philosophical movements—takes a step further and asks for a development such that there is a deep identification of people with all life.
—Arne Naess (1977)

179

I n the previous chapter we suggested that one question to be discussed in stating an ecotopian vision is, how can imperfect persons reach toward self-realization within the larger ultimate norms of self-realization and biocentric equality?

We seek to encourage development of mature persons who understand the immutable connection between themselves and the land community or person/planet. We need a theory of acting which acknowledges the way culture impacts on or directs personal growth. And we need a theory of acting that recognizes the way the dominant worldview, as defined in this book, has conditioned our psyches and contributed to our predicament. Finally, we need some suggestions for acting in this culture which serve both the vital needs of persons and nonhumans.

The relation between psychological development and culture or religious tradition has been discussed by many great thinkers in different traditions. In the Christian tradition, the self-discipline and practice required for growth is discussed by, among others, Augustine, the great mystics St. John of the Cross and Meister Eckhart, Soren Kierkegaard, and the anonymous author of *The Cloud of Unknowing*. In philosophy, theories of psychological growth are articulated by Plato, Spinoza, Rousseau, and many others. Eastern traditions abound with theories and practices for psychological-spiritual growth.

During the twentieth century, major work on psycho-social development grounded in extensive empirical observations has been presented by Sigmund Freud, Carl Jung, Jean Piaget, Karen Horney, Erik Erikson, Erich Fromm and C. Wright Mills. Edith Cobb and Joseph Pearce have given special attention to children and their relation to nonhuman nature.[1] The ways in which our culture inhibits the development of psychological maturity in women is brought forth in the works of Dorothy Dinnerstein, Susan Griffin and Jesse Bernard.[2] This body of work is large and provides many valuable insights and theories which can contribute to our understanding of psycho-social development.

However, we contend that, generally speaking, these theories are either too internal, relying only on the narrow psycho-social theories of self, or too external, by conceding too much to cultural determinism. Furthermore, the external environment tends to be defined as the community of other persons, especially the immediate family or kin group and school. Even some of the most recent texts which incorporate what they call an "ecological" or "systems model" use as their main reference the "social system."

Nature, in the broad sense used in this book, or even nonhuman animals and natural settings, have been frequently absent from these theories altogether, although some recent work by psychologists and sociologists has begun to explore the importance of wilderness and other natural settings for personal growth.[3]

One other exception to the general rule of the exclusion of non-humans from the community is the recent surge of articles on "pet therapy," on relations between domestic animals as pets and "special populations of lonely children and retarded or older people." In keeping with the dominant modern worldview, this literature tends to be anthropocentric.

One theory which suggests how to achieve the balance between internal (psyche) and external nature is the provocative theory of Paul Shepard. Shepard gave special attention to relations between humans and wild animals in his book *Thinking Animals,* and returned to this theme in *Nature and Madness.*[4] His basic theory is that our culture, with its dynamics of education, dominant messages in the mass media and from the family, encourages persons to remain stuck in a period of early adolescence, psychologically, throughout their lives.

Before presenting Shepard's thesis in more detail, we will summarize some of the commentary by several perceptive critics on the way the educational system in our culture encourages this predicament. We then review Shepard's theory of cultural history in the West, and discuss the dilemma of persons raised and socialized in technocratic-industrial culture. In the concluding section we make a few suggestions, drawing particularly from the work of Dolores LaChapelle, which can encourage maturity based on deep ecological norms in our culture.

Our major theme is that direct action is necessary to develop human ecological consciousness and maturity in its fullest sense.

I. CRITICISMS OF THE EDUCATIONAL SYSTEM UNDER THE DOMINANT WORLDVIEW

Many educational critics have pointed to the consequences of educating children within the framework of the dominant worldview.

Contemporary educational overspecialization has led to a decline in the liberal arts requirements and programs in which Western humanistic values and ideals have traditionally resided. The rise in influence of social scientists in the educational establishment has helped enshrine the positivist fact/value distinction in educational decision-making processes. This has led to an educational value relativism and subjectivism in which one value is no better than any other—the pursuit of truth and wisdom is educationally of no more value than, for example, taking a real estate degree. Plato's analysis of the mob rule of the undisciplined, undiscriminating democratic masses has come to pass in the educational establishment. One of the most perceptive and influential novels of the 1970s, Robert Pirsig's *Zen and the Art of Motorcycle Maintenance,* was a search for *quality* in our lives in a society which was rapidly losing any sense of quality. Having succumbed to the value relativism and the business mentality of the "give-the-customers-whatever-they-want-so-long-as-it-makes-a-profit" of the society-at-large, the educational establishment is no longer in a position to make sound judgments concerning a quality education. As one critic points out, "Once considered an essential enterprise for the improvement of American society, higher education has become the handmaiden of successful career planning."[5]

The rise of academic and vocational overspecialization, together with the new "democratic" value relativism and the decline of the influence of the liberal arts, has thus played into the hands of certain governmental and corporate business interests. Liberal educational reformers, and even some radicals, are of the opinion that if we can disentangle government and corporate business influences from the schools, and if we can reestablish the pursuit of knowledge and liberal arts orientation at the center of the educational process once again, all will be well. While there is considerable merit to these proposals, this analysis only begins to scratch at the surface of our malaise. While the reestablishment of the centrality of the liberal arts may help overcome pervasive value relativism and reassert basic Western humanistic ideals, these same values are, in part, under attack from a different quarter. *That is, the humanistic anthropocentrism of the Western liberal arts orientation has been deeply implicated in the global environmental crisis.*

We cannot conclude that contemporary education is ignoring values. Education is surely teaching values both explicitly and implicitly; it is teaching the worldview and values of the scientific/technological society. It is teaching by precept and example that values (and maybe facts as well) are all subjective and relative, that it is "rational" to compromise on all issues, and that Nature exists as but a commodity to be enjoyed and consumed by humans. It teaches that there is a technological solu-

182

tion to all problems. Education is preparing young people for careers in the highly exploitive, ecologically disastrous technological society.

The educational establishment is itself now infected with the values and procedures of the technological worldview, from the training of administrators and the rise of huge bureaucracies to the attempt to teach using electronic gadgets and computers whenever possible. The rise of teacher labor unions has brought technocratic politics onto the campus; teachers are often seen as just another special interest group in their battles with that other special interest group, the management. Further, education is now seen as a "commodity" and the students as "consumers." Management techniques are used to "sell the product." The suggestion by liberal educational reformers to reinstitute the liberal arts core might help mitigate the worst of the vulgarization and commercialization of contemporary education. But this suggestion does not go to the roots of the anthropocentric technological social worldview itself.

Resource Conservation and Development is the official technological version of environmental education that has been taught in schools throughout most of the twentieth century. As a high school student during the 1950s in the rich agricultural San Joaquin Valley of California, one of the authors experienced "Conservation Week," sponsored by the school each year. His memories are of movies depicting scientific forestry management for "sustained yields," extolling the virtues of huge hydroelectric dams spewing water sky-high as the wild rivers were "harnessed" and put to work for a growing, productive California.

After his conversion from anthropocentric resource management to a biocentric perspective, Aldo Leopold pointed out in 1949:

Despite nearly a century of propaganda, conservation still proceeds at a snail's pace; progress still consists largely of letterhead pieties and convention oratory. . . . The usual answer to this dilemma is "more conservation education." No one will debate this, but is it certain that only the volume of education needs stepping up? Is something lacking in the content as well?[6]

Paul Shepard draws on the work of psychologists Erik Erikson, Erich Fromm and others. His theory is that there is a natural, psychogenetic development for humans. Some cultures foster this more than others. In particular, primal peoples, hunters/gatherers, encourage passage through this normal process which includes intimate relating to wild nature and wild animals.[7]

Our present urban-techno-industrial lifestyles tend to preclude such processes of intimate relationship with nonhuman Nature, restricting our experiences primarily to the fabricated environment, massive in scale and unprecedented in history. According to Shepard, this failure to properly relate to wild Nature and thus to develop into more fully mature humans may be one of the root causes of vandalism, destructive behavior and excessive intervention by humans into natural processes.

Shepard boldly presents a theory linking the history of Western culture and the psychosocial history of the individual in contemporary technocratic society. He asserts that the domination of Nature in Western cultures began with the waning of hunter/gatherer societies. He traces the beginnings of mental disorientation and emotional impoverishment to the development of agriculture and the "desert edge" conditions of the Middle East. Agriculture and the rise of Judeo-Christian monotheism broke the bonds of sacredness with the Earth. According to Shepard, the "desert fathers" who defined the major stream of Christian thought denied the cyclic pattern of events and insisted on linear time and the pursuit of abstract, self-confirming truth.

Contrasting polytheism and monotheism, Shepard concludes that "Monotheism socially becomes fascism, imperialism or capitalism; philosophically is unmetaphorical, unambiguous and dichotomous; and psychologically is rigid, fixed and linear." Most damaging in Shepard's view, it is an ideology which makes art and science into data-making enterprises instead of tools for myth and ritual.

For Shepard, the Protestants who founded the European experience in North America were the most fanatical, extreme version of Christian dualism and the denial of the sacred bonds with Earth.

However, Shepard reserves his strongest words for his description of the impact of the city experience on modern or contemporary consciousness. "Let us suppose, with some evidence, that the city is typically a sink of psychological problems. In the individual these are partly caused by city life, but in the long view they cause the city."

He is also especially critical of secular social science as taught in modern cultures. "A typical [social science] textbook does not deal with the nonhuman living world at all." In schools, the child sees Nature only as "data" in courses on geology or biology, and on the streets rarely, if ever, sees "free Nature."

Shepard admits that his theory is very tentative, especially the thesis of parallel development of culture in the West and the psychological development of individuals. Much further work is required by intellectuals, historians and social scientists, especially those using non-positivist methodology, to explore the cultural history of the West. The relation of monotheism and personal development, although studied by many thinkers from the time of Freud's seminal work, remains controversial.

... Careless of waste, wallowing in refuse, exterminating the enemies ... despising age, denying human natural history, fabricating pseudotraditions, swamped in the repeated personal crises of the aging preadolescent; all are familiar images of American society. They are signs of private nightmares of incoherence and disorder in broken climaxes where technologies in pursuit of mastery create ever-worsening problems — private nightmares expanded to a social level.
— Paul Shepard, *Nature and Madness* (1982)

The irony, Shepard remarks, is that our technocratic-industrial society "works" because many, if not most, of its members are "ontogenetically stuck," encouraged, if not outright condemned, to remain in the human developmental stage of early adolescence.

This phase of the natural life cycle and psychological development is marked by intense emotion, "masculine" characteristics (aggressiveness, striving to "show others" through outward action, playing "king of the mountain") rather than "feminine" (being more receptive, cooperative, introspective), and also by rapid alterations between regressive, infantile behavior and bold, striving behavior which is pseudomature. Phrases frequently repeated in advertisements and by many people in casual conversation illustrate this: "Me first," "I want . . . ," "Give me . . . ," "I don't give a damn," "All I know is my own preferences."

Advertisements appeal to this as narrow immediate ego gratification: "Do something special for yourself today, buy . . . ," "Our _____ is powerful. A real man feels its responsiveness when he challenges the wide open countryside," "Come to where the action is." Or the frank opening statement of a credit card advertisement: "Mastercharge, I'm bored. Take me away today to . . . ."

In terms of the dominant worldview and the dominant behaviors which flow from this worldview, large outdoor spaces, deserts, even officially designated wilderness areas, public beaches, parks and Nature reserves are seen by many people as places to have aggressive, egotistical fun, frequently by consuming large quantities of drugs and alco-

185

hol, racing huge congregations of vehicles (up to 5,000 at a time across parts of the fragile ecosystem of the southern California desert), using all-terrain vehicles to "master" delicate sand dunes and penetrate the swamps and everglades trying to capture rare animals. In the unrestrained human attitudes of extreme subjectivity, this approach to one's spare time can be summarized by a student who said, "Who the hell are you to tell me I can't ride my motorcycle on the sand dunes. That's *my* way of having fun!"

Many people devote much of their time participating in recreational, urban-based "scenes" in natural areas. These social encounters, sometimes involving millions of people in, say, the "surfing scene," or "skiing scene," or "recreational travel scene," are trendy and characterized by ever-changing wardrobes and equipment. Vehicles such as jet-skis, snowmobiles, and off-road three-wheelers have been invented only during the last decade or so and they often become "instant traditions." Heavily marketed and easily available, these noisy and destructive vehicles give participants motorized entry into natural areas previously protected because of their inherently difficult access to older, more cumbersome vehicles. The participants leave tracks and often trash in their wake, disturbing the serenity and destroying the ecology of delicate plant and wildlife habitats. [8]

This situation has made it difficult for reform environmentalists to get even the most fragile ecosystems officially closed to off-road vehicles. Some defenders of a place have spent most of their adult lives trying to protect the biological diversity and natural processes of some small valley or mountain. Mary DeDecker is an example of such a person. She lived near the Eureka Sand Dunes, northwest of Death Valley National Monument, for thirty years. Seeing the impact of off-road vehicle users on the valley, she began a one-woman campaign to ban off-road vehicles and "save the valley." In 1984, the Bureau of Land Management, the federal agency officially holding management responsibility for the area, declared the area a National Natural Landmark, a site deemed "nationally significant, possessing exceptional values as an illustration of nature's heritage." But off-road vehicle users continue to protest the closure and some threaten to ride their vehicles into the area anyway.

186

II. A WAY TO ENCOURAGE MATURITY

Paul Shepard, in *Nature and Madness,* suggests:

Perhaps we do not need new religious, economic, technological, ideological, aesthetic, or philosophical revolutions. We may not need to start at the top and uproot political systems, turn life-ways on their heads, emulate hunters and gatherers or naturalists, or try to live lives of austere privation or tribal organization. The civilized ways inconsistent with human maturity will themselves wither in a world where children move normally through their ontogeny.

Shepard states that if we let go of the efforts of the educational system, the mass media and the propaganda of egotistical cultural heroes, we can open the way to passage through the natural progression of stages to more mature persons in terms such as we have defined in this book. We urge people to really assess their vital needs and come to the understanding that these needs are connected to the vital needs of all other beings.

Until now, hunter/gatherer communities do seem the best model of the community which allows such passage to maturity and facilitates it, but the minority tradition generally contains many suggestions for such passage. Small-scale communities, living in but not commanding their bioregion, can understand the vital needs of the place and vital needs of the human members of the land community.

All suggestions will be less than pure, less than perfect, but they are at least possible, based on existing traditions in our own culture. For example, deep ecologists recognize the vital need for outdoor recreation, rather than the more artificial need for entertainment. But there are several criteria for outdoor recreation which are consistent with the goal of increasing psychological maturity and identification with all life.

First is the principle of taking care of the place. Minimum impact camping is now widely practiced by many wilderness users. No littering means taking care of the garbage you bring into parks, wilderness areas, beaches, sand dunes, deserts, mountains, rivers. Respect for the place itself and its nonhuman inhabitants is a basic attitude to take in approaching a park, river, mountain one wants to climb, an ocean beach, a desert.

Second, it means bringing an attitude of watchful attentiveness to one's recreation and one's responses to the environment, alert to possibilities which are different from the preconceptions one brought to the place. This can be summarized by the phrase "listening with the third ear."[9]

Third, it means a kind of psychological removal of self from the urban scene or the discussion and intense focus of technology that one brought to the place for recreational purposes. Instead of focusing on the social status of the four-wheel drive vehicle one brought to a fishing hole, or the brand name of one's fishing pole, there should be attention to the relationship between the person and the equipment and the environment in a more direct fashion. The goal of surfing, for example, is to keep the surfer and surfboard as one in a certain relationship to the incoming wave, knowing when to time the ascent and retreat from the wave. This is the "action." The rest is just the "surfing scene"— beach fashions, language, equipment-status watching.

Fourth, from this theory of growing maturity, we realize that the usual admonishment in our culture to "have fun" is somewhat shallow if not compulsive: "I must have fun or something is wrong with me." From the theory of naturalness and growing maturity, joyfulness is a deeper, celebratory emotion, an *affection,* as termed in Spinoza's theory of psychology.

Fifth, as indicated in our chapter on wilderness, the use of rituals and celebratory expressions of place—painting, dancing, expressive writing, poetry—drawn from the emotions and observations of persons who feel the rhythms of the place, are themselves direct action of the sort which further encourages ecological consciousness.

Some of the activities which are especially useful, in our estimation, if done with the proper attitude, include fishing, hunting, surfing, sun bathing, kayaking, canoeing, sailing, mountain climbing, hang gliding, skiing, running, bicycling and birdwatching. There is a very large body of literature coming from people who have participated in some of these activities, especially mountain climbing and fishing, which attest to possibilities for developing a sense of place and intuitive understanding of the connections between humans and nonhumans together with a respect for the principle of biocentric equality.

Indeed, fishing as a meditative exercise might be one of the most direct actions of all, as the ancient Chinese poet Li Po realized:

> *Since water still flows, though we cut it with swords*
> *And sorrow returns, though we drown it with wind,*
> *Since the world can in no way answer to our craving,*
> *I will loosen my hair tomorrow and take to a fishing boat.*

Besides suggestions for outdoor recreation, Dolores LaChapelle offers specific ways of letting the curiosity for Nature develop naturally during each stage of the physical life cycle, thus cultivating ecological consciousness and acceptance of the ultimate norms of deep ecology. LaChapelle explicitly uses a deep ecology context for her own teaching while drawing from Native American as well as Eastern traditions. She discusses four general physical phases of life. [10]

During the first phase of life, children would spend most of their time in untrammeled landscapes, stimulated by the body rhythms of swinging, watching, touching. LaChapelle gives a simple example from her own life:

During the first few years of my life I spent a great deal of time hanging in aspen trees. My father was allergic to certain types of pollen so my family spent considerable time in the mountains, where lowland weeds did not grow. I was put into a canvas seat, suspended from a spring, which was hooked onto a tree limb. In this way I was imprinted on aspen leaves. To this day, when autumn begins I have a compelling urge to be among the aspen and silently watch the play of golden light and shadow among the constantly flickering leaves.

Children around the age of nine or ten may be most receptive to initiation into the larger sense of organic wholeness through experiences of play in streams, rivers, mountains, oceans.

The second stage, adolescence, is a time for risk-taking and alternation between desire for solitude (to "think things out") and intensive play activity with one's own age group. Allowing what Paul Shepard calls the "karma of adolescence" to be expressed through ritual and long, close, intimate experiences in mountaineering, sailing, etc., is a natural way to allow development.

The third stage of life, LaChapelle says, is that time of growing responsibility in the sense of taking time to help one's kin, friends, community and understanding the vital needs of the larger community of nonhuman species.

The fourth stage, aging, reveals the advantage of mortality. LaChapelle provides a summary of what she means by this:

The advantage of mortality is that it permits ever new manifestations of Being to occur. For example, the components (atoms, cells, etc.) which go to make up the temporary organism which is my self at this moment, have been contained in many other beings in the past and will be part of many new, as yet unknown beings in the future. But the parts which go to make up my self have always been around and always will be as long as there is life on Earth. What changes is the relationships involved.

189

Pollution, defilement, squalor are words that never would have been created had man lived conformably to Nature. Birds, insects, bears die as cleanly and are disposed of as beautifully. . . . The woods are full of dead and dying trees, yet needed for their beauty to complete the beauty of the living. . . . How beautiful is all Death!

—John Muir, *John of the Mountains* (1938)

Rachel Carson provides advice to parents on awakening a sense of wonder in children in her essay "Sense of Wonder":

If I had influence with the good fairy who is supposed to preside over the christening of all children I should ask that her gift to each child in the world be a sense of wonder so indestructible that it would last throughout life, as an unfailing antidote against the boredom and disenchantments of later years, the sterile preoccupation with things that are artificial, the alienation from the sources of our strength.

If a child is to keep alive his inborn sense of wonder without any such gift from the fairies, he needs the companionship of at least one adult who can share it, rediscovering with him the joy, excitement and mystery of the world we live in. Parents often have a sense of inadequacy when confronted on the one hand with the eager, sensitive mind of a child and on the other with a world of complex physical nature, inhabited by a life so various and unfamiliar that it seems hopeless to reduce it to order and knowledge. In a mode of self-defeat, they exclaim, "How can I possibly teach my child about nature—why, I don't even know one bird from another!"

I sincerely believe that for the child, and for the parent seeking to guide him, it is not half so important to *know* as to *feel*. If facts are the seeds that later produce knowledge and wisdom, then the emotions and the impressions of the senses are the fertile soil in which the seeds must grow. The years of early childhood are the time to prepare the soil. Once the emotions have been aroused—a sense of the beautiful, the excitement of the new and the unknown, a feeling of sympathy, pity, admiration or love—then we wish for knowledge about the object of our emotional response. Once found, it has lasting meaning. It is more important to pave the way for the child to want to know than to put him on a diet of facts he is not ready to assimilate.

We have suggested that the minority tradition is an appropriate type of community, especially focused on bioregion, for cultivating maturity and ecological insights, and we encourage the belief that it is possible to develop toward more advanced stages of psychological and

190

emotional maturity, toward identification with all life, even within our technocratic-industrial society.

The Sacred Books of the East are nothing but words.
I looked through their covers one day sideways.
Kabir talks only about what he has lived through.
If you have not lived through something, it is not true.
    —Kabir

CHAPTER 11
•
ECOLOGICAL
RESISTING

I went to the woods because I wished to live deliberately, to front only the essential facts of life, and see if I could not learn what it had to teach, and not, when I came to die, discover that I had not lived. I did not wish to live what was not life, living is so dear; nor did I wish to practice resignation, unless it was quite necessary. I wanted to live deep and suck out all the marrow of life, to live so sturdily and Spartan-like as to put to rout all that was not life, to cut a broad swath and shave close, to drive life into a corner, and reduce it to its lowest terms, and, if it proved to be mean, why then to get the whole and genuine meanness of it, and publish its meanness to the world; or if it were sublime, to know it by experience, and be able to give a true account of it in my next excursion. For most men, it appears to me, are in a strange uncertainty about it, whether it is of the devil or of God, and have somewhat hastily concluded that it is the chief end of man here to "glorify God and enjoy Him forever."
—Henry David Thoreau, Walden

We began this book by suggesting a variety of specific actions which people can take directed at reforming public policy, developing bioregional communities, and cultivating ecological consciousness. We return in this concluding chapter to the theme of direct action. We have demonstrated that deep ecology is not just a game of abstract theorizing. As a perspective it is lived, danced, celebrated. It has resonance.

Cultivating ecological consciousness means, in part, cultivating what Theodore Roszak calls *rhapsodic intellect.* Rhapsodic intellect is engaged in the process of integrating intellect, body, and joyous emotion. [1]

Based on the insights, ultimate norms, principles and theories of deep ecology, the central practical question is how do we become more mature persons, given the constraints of this culture?

We suggest there is an interplay between outward direct action and inward direct action, between acting on one's self and acting in the world, with the result of further and deeper maturity in the deep ecological sense of identification with all life. There is no sharp break between inward and outward. People take direct action from deep ecological principles and they become more mature through direct action. The label we use for the type of direct action in its outward form is *ecological resisting.*

I. ACTING FROM DEEP PRINCIPLES

The central principle of Ecological Resistance is the conviction that diversity is natural, good, and threatened by the forces of monoculture. . . . If there is a base model it is that of the ecosystem. . . . The image of humanity in Ecological Resistance is more holistic and participatory, "Man" does not stand over against "his environment" as manager, sight-seer, or do-gooder; he is an integral part of the food chain . . . a microcosm of the cosmos who takes very personally the wounds inflicted on his/her androgynous body.
—John Rodman, "Theory and Practice in the Environmental Movement" (1978)

194

Perhaps we may now begin to see why men have an almost universal tendency to seek relief from their own kind among the trees and plants, the mountains and waters. There is an easy and rather cheap sophistication in mocking the love of nature, but there is always something profound and essential in the universal theme of poetry, however hackneyed. For hundreds of years the great poets of East and West have given expression to this basically human love of "communing with nature," a phrase which in present-day intellectual circles seems to have acquired a slightly ridiculous tone. Presumably it is regarded as one of those "escapes from reality" so much condemned by those who restrict reality to what one reads about in newspapers.

But perhaps the reason for this love of nonhuman nature is that communion with it restores to us a level of our own human nature at which we are still sane, free from humbug, and untouched by anxieties about the meaning and purpose of our lives. For what we call "nature" is free from a certain kind of scheming and self-importance. The birds and beasts indeed pursue their business of eating and breeding with the utmost devotion. But they do not justify it; they do not pretend that it serves higher ends, or that it makes a significant contribution to the progress of the world.

This is not meant to sound unkind to human beings, because the point is not so simple as that the birds are right and we are wrong. The point is that rapport with the marvelously purposeless world of nature gives us new eyes for ourselves—eyes in which our very self-importance is not condemned, but seen as something quite other than what it imagines itself to be. In this light all the weirdly abstract and pompous pursuits of men are suddenly transformed into natural marvels of the same order as the immense beaks of the toucans and hornbills, the fabulous tails of the birds of paradise, the towering necks of the giraffes, and the vividly polychromed posteriors of the baboons. Seen thus, neither as something to be condemned nor in its accustomed aspect of serious worth, the self-importance of man dissolves in laughter. His insistent purposefulness and his extraordinary preoccupation with abstractions are, while perfectly natural, overdone—like the vast bodies of the dinosaurs. As means of survival and adaptation they have been overplayed, producing a species too cunning and too practical for its own good, and which for this very reason stands in need of the "dead cat's head" philosophy. For this is the philosophy which, like nature, has no purpose or consequence other than itself.

—Alan W. Watts, *Nature, Man and Woman* (1958)

Ecological resisters do not accept that there are only narrow technical solutions to narrowly defined social problems (such as air pollution). These problems are seen only as symptoms of the larger issues.

There are three main dangers to technocratic solutions. First is the danger in believing there is a complete or acceptable solution using modern dominant ideologies and technology. The second danger is the presentation of an impression that something is being done when in fact the real problem continues. Tinkering distracts from the "real work." Finally, there is the danger of assuming there will be new experts—such as professional ecologists—who will provide the solution but who may in fact be constrained to be public relations spokespersons for the agenda of profit or power of some corporation or agency.

Ecological resistance is action from central principles of doing what is necessary, of witnessing nonviolently. It arises from a shift in consciousness. Ecological resisting is deeper, some would say more radical, than just reformism. Some of the reformist actions to mitigate some of the worst forms of air and water pollution (due to auto exhaust, for example) are motivated by concern only for human health and safety and not by the intrinsic values of the biosphere. But the limits of reformism are by now well known.

CATHEDRAL FOREST WILDERNESS DECLARATION

The last significant stands of Oregon's old growth cathedral forests are being destroyed. The so-called 1984 Oregon Forest Wilderness Bill not only fails to protect the major remaining forested wilderness in Oregon, but opens it to accelerated development by removing even the flimsy protection of the RARE II planning process: therefore, we offer our own protection for these lands.

We believe that all things are connected, that whatever we do to the earth, we do to ourselves. If we destroy our remaining wild places, we will ultimately destroy our identity with the earth: wilderness has values for humankind which no scientist can synthesize, no economist can price, and no technological distraction can replace.

We believe that we should protect in perpetuity these wild places, not only for our own sake, but for the sake of the plants and animals and for the good of the sustaining earth. The forests, like us, are living things: wilderness should exist intact solely for its own sake; no human justification, rationale, or excuse is needed.

We perceive the earth is dying. We pledge ourselves to turning this process around, to stopping the destruction, so that the earth can become alive, clean, and healthy once again.

We call on the United States government to preserve the forests of the Pacific Northwest as some of many irreplaceable treasures of our great continent.

On behalf of all citizens of the earth community, we declare the Oregon Cathedral Forest—all that which remains of Oregon's old-growth ecosystems—an inviolable wilderness for all time.

*The Cathedral Forest Action Group was formed in 1984 to make a stand in the Santiam Cathedral Forest, an 80,000 acre wilderness which includes both the Middle Santiam and the Old Cascades Wilderness proposals in the central Oregon Cascade mountains. The land is managed by the United States Forest Service. Group members placed themselves in front of logging trucks and bulldozers sent by the Forest Service to clear-cut the wilderness area. Several resisters were arrested. Their statement refers to attempts to work with the Forest Service in the Roadless Area Review and Evaluation (RARE II) process.

———

Deeply committed persons in the ecology movement sense the vulnerability of natural processes to human intervention, and the fundamental necessity of maintaining biological diversity. Affirmation of the integrity of ecosystems frequently involves a campaign to save from development some river or canyon or wilderness area.

In a real sense, ecological resistance involves becoming friends with another species or a river or a mountain, for example. In general, the resister takes up the burden of responsibility, the burden of witnessing for the other as Self. The hero of Romain Gary's novel *The Roots of Heaven* (1958) takes up responsibility for the elephant herds of Central Africa. He urges tribes, nations, and the United Nations to take up the burden of responsibility to protect these creatures in their habitat from poaching and destruction of habitat by humans. This process of befriending may be based on Aristotle's criteria for friendship: the promotion of the other's good for the other's own sake. Or friendship can be the extension of self. When Gandhi was asked if his good deeds in a village expressed his humanitarianism, he replied he worked "to serve no one else but myself. . . ." Gandhi's statement defines maturity. Altruism was unnecessary because his self embraced the whole village.

Patterns of defending a place are illustrated by Sigurd Olson's defense of the north woods of Minnesota, Pete Gunter's defense of the Big Thicket of Texas, David Brower's defense of the Grand Canyon, and Edward Abbey's defense of the American southwest. John Muir's prototypical defense of Hetch Hetchy has been called a "spiritual watershed" in American history, much like the spiritual watershed the nation faces in the 1980s.[2]

197

There are many different tactics of individuals and organizations in political campaigns which seek to "save the river" or "save the Earth," but there is one overriding or basic norm of ecological resisting: non-violence.

Sailing in small boats, but supported by the good cheer and donations of large numbers of people in Canada and the United States in the 1960s and 1970s, volunteers for Greenpeace sailed to the South Pacific to protest atmospheric testing of nuclear devices by the French, to Alaskan water (from Vancouver, B.C.) to protest proposed nuclear testing by the U.S. Department of Defense, and to many waters to place themselves between whalers and endangered whales.

Many people are beginning to witness and affirm a sane society of humans in balance with the Earth. The Greenpeace philosophy summarizes many of the major points of witnessing as a tactic of ecological resisting:

We are ecologists, actively working to protect our fragile world. We have fought nuclear testing in French Polynesia, and won. We have confronted the Russian whaling industry at sea, and driven them from North American waters. We have helped to publicize the slaughter of dolphins by tuna fishermen. And we have helped to expose the brutality of baby seal hunting in Newfoundland. In the name of ecology.

Ecology teaches us that mankind is not the center of life on the planet. Ecology has taught us that the whole earth is part of our "body" and that we must learn to respect it as we respect ourselves. As we feel for ourselves, we must feel for all forms of life—the whales, the seals, the forests, the seas. The tremendous beauty of ecological thought is that it shows us a pathway back to an understanding and an appreciation of life itself—an understanding and appreciation that is imperative to that very way of life.

As with the whales and the seals, life must be saved by nonviolent confrontations, by what the Quakers call "bearing witness." A person bearing witness must accept responsibility for being aware of an injustice. The person may then choose to do something or stand by, but he may not turn away in ignorance. The Greenpeace ethic is not only to personally bear witness to atrocities against life; it is to take direct action to prevent them. While action must be direct, it must also be non-violent. We must obstruct a wrong without offering personal violence to its perpetrators. We must know that our greatest strength is life itself, and the commitment to direct our lives to protect others.

In Australia, ecological resisters protested attempts by government agencies to build dams on free-flowing rivers of Tasmania, blockaded logging trucks which were removing logs from some of the last sub-tropical rain forests in New South Wales, and repeatedly petitioned the federal government to cease exporting uranium used in building nuclear bombs.

John Seed founded the Rainforest Information Centre and began a worldwide campaign to alert all people to the intrinsic value and worth of rain forests. In an interview he explained his own psychological development from passive observer to participant. "I am protecting the rain forest,'" he said, "develops into 'I am part of the rain forest protecting myself.' I am that part of the rain forest recently emerged into thinking." What a relief, he said. "The thousands of years of (imagined) separation are over and we begin to recall our true nature. That is, the change is a spiritual one, thinking like a mountain, sometimes referred to as 'deep ecology.'"

During one action to protect the Nightcap Rainforest in New South Wales, Seed and many others were arrested on charges of trespassing and "obstruction." When he was brought to trial on these charges, Seed read the following statement to the Court:

I respectfully submit, your Worship, that the defendants in front of this court were a key to saving rain forests. In the light of the ecological evidence, and the expressed desire of the people of this state, I suggest we should be receiving medals, not the maximum penalty under the law!

I was arrested while attempting to show the police evidence of crimes committed by the Forestry Commission and the loggers. These crimes included the removal of unmarked trees, failure to follow the Standard Erosion Mitigation Conditions and logging without an Environmental Impact Statement. The latter charge has since been proved by the Supreme Court. Not only did the loggers lose the case, the costs were awarded against them. I was arrested while attempting to show the police evidence of these crimes. When they refused to investigate, I allowed them to arrest me in protest. [3]

II. EMBRACING YOUR OPPONENT

Ecological resisting could be defined as keeping the peace of the neighborhood. Rarely are vandals or violent neighbors welcome in the neighborhood. When the neighbors include rivers and mountains, seashores and prairie, then the integrity of the ecosystem is maintained.

Sometimes even witnessing with one's life for a place may arouse undesired actions in opponents. Mark Dubois chained himself in a section of the Stanislaus River of California scheduled to be flooded behind the New Melones Dam. He said he would stay until drowned or until the Corps of Engineers agreed to halt the filling of the reservoir. When the Corps agreed to halt filling until a court hearing could be held, he came out of the canyon, but some persons in the Central Valley of California on irrigated farms were outraged by Dubois's action. Dubois tried to talk to the farmers and explain his motives on a speaking tour of the farmers' groups.

In his explication of Gandhi's theory of nonviolence, Arne Naess lists several norms for nonviolent political campaigns. These include:

1. Announce your case and the goal of your campaign explicitly and clearly, distinguishing essentials from nonessentials.

2. Seek personal contact with your opponent and be available to him. Bring conflicting groups into personal contact.

3. Turn your opponent into a believer in and supporter of your case, but do not coerce or exploit him.

4. You provoke your opponent if you deliberately or carelessly destroy his property. [4]

Empirical studies of specific political campaigns of ecological resisting could determine which norms are followed by resisters. While nonviolent campaigns have been studied by some social scientists, few have applied these theories to the ecology movements. One study of the antinuclear movements did include some discussion of the dilemmas of nonviolent witnessing and confrontations at nuclear power plants. Sociologist Steve Barkan suggests that messages such as the random violence that frequently accompanies mass demonstrations are frequently given top billing by media, rather than the intended message of questioning technology or the decision to build the nuclear power plant. [5]

Case studies of specific campaigns, such as Greenpeace's campaigns to save the whales, would generate more explication of the premises of nonviolent action. For example, are whalers led to questioning of the companies for which they work? Do the resisters clearly articulate who the primary decision makers are and who is accountable for continued whaling? Do ecological resisters clarify their understanding of their resistance through group processes and through meditation? Allen Ginsberg, arrested while meditating on a railroad track leading to the plutonium facility at Rocky Flat, Colorado, said to reporters:

*My contention is, if done with the proper human dignity and lightness, meditation can be appropriate in a protest situation. But are you really being mindful of your breath while sitting there, or are you sitting there thinking of what you look like on the television camera? Buddhist practice doesn't lead to inactivity and passivity. It leads to more open minded activity, where you're fighting your illusions less. To the extent that protest against evil is anger at your father, or anger at the universe itself, or resentment of being born, then it would be dissolved by meditation. (*San Francisco Chronicle, *September 18, 1979)*

Leading theorists of ecological resisting denounce violence versus nonviolence as tactics. But as Robert Aitken Roshi wrote:

Non-violence is not just a tactic for people who make it a practice. . . . The end is the means, in other words. Look at political history or at the history of any movements. When we work for certain goals, those goals tend to betray us. We defeated L. B. Johnson only to get Richard Nixon. We got rid of the B-1 Bomber (temporarily) and the Cruise Missile appeared. We have to make our action the goal. Our action must itself be the truth. Our action must be its own defense, its own proclamation, its own purpose. (Letter to the author, June 1982)

Both on practical and ethical grounds, violence is rejected as a mode of ecological resistance. Terrorist attacks on nuclear plants or missile sites could cause "red" alerts and violent responses from government agencies.

Placing one's own life at risk, such as sitting in front of bulldozers or police cars at a demonstration to protest destruction of the rain forest, may be illegal but not violent. And spontaneous acts such as the decommissioning of a power generator or bulldozer may dramatize the continuing destruction of a special ecosystem.

Ecological resistance also means defending natural diversity through education, public speaking, and use of lawsuits; trying to convert public opinion to the cause; and informing politicians and decision makers. Resistance is another name for affirmation — joyful affirmation of the integrity of Nature, natural diversity, and minimum human impact on place.

Frequently there are alliances between ecological resisters and native peoples working for traditional sacred places. An excellent example is the Native Hawaiian Movement and the attempt to reclaim Kaho'olawe Island from the U.S. Navy, which has used it for bombing practice. Kaho'olawe was important, historically, for sweet potato cultivation and as a sacred site where the gods were brought from Tahiti.

In his paper on the Native Hawaiian Movement, Robert Aitken Roshi describes the meeting of a U.S. Navy officer and representatives of the Hawaiian group visiting Kaho'olawe. "Don't ask me what I think about Kaho'olawe," the officer said, "I am here as a representative of the Navy, carrying out American policy."

Aitken concludes:

Confronted with people with profound religious convictions, the bureaucrat can only give way. On Kaho'olawe the Navy is fighting a losing battle because it lacks the armament of truth.

Along with the process of finding the truth and of becoming Hawaiian again goes a deep rejection of all the values, if they can be called values, which brought the people to their present state of personal and social disorganization. [6]

Thus the process of ecological resistance is both personal and collective. Changing the foundations of our minds and seeking help from others of like mind as well as understanding from natural processes is the challenge of living.

One of the outcomes of this process is modesty. This modesty is a virtue nearly lost in the dominant technocratic-industrial society. It is personal modesty which finds no reward in egotistical domination over other people or some aspect of wild Nature. It is the collective modesty of the species or the nation. As Arne Naess concludes:

As I see it, modesty is of little value if it is not a natural consequence of much deeper feelings, and even more important in our special context, a consequence of a way of understanding ourselves as part of nature in the wide sense of the term. This way is such that the smaller we come to feel ourselves compared to the mountain, the nearer we come to participating in its greatness. I do not know why this is so. [7]

III. JOHN MUIR: AN EXAMPLE OF RESISTANCE, LEADERSHIP AND CHARACTER

Muir's theory of leadership seems best described by the following quote from the *Tao Te Ching:* "Rivers and seas dominate the landscape because, by being good at seeking the lowest places, they fill and occupy and spread over everything. Likewise the intelligent man is superior to others because he admits that he is inferior, and he is a leader of others because he is willing to be a follower. Thus, although he is actually superior to others, they do not feel that they are being forced to obey. So all are happy to give him their support. Since he competes with no one, no one competes with him."[8]

Muir had faith that others could appreciate beauty as he did. Bringing flowers back to San Francisco after a hike in Marin County, he encountered a group of children and saw the delight in their faces when he gave them the flowers. ". . . Their dirty faces fairly glowed with enthusiasm while they gazed at them and fondled them reverently as if looking into the faces of angels from heaven. It was a hopeful sign and made me say: 'No matter into what depths of degradation humanity may sink, I will never despair while the lowest love the pure and beautiful and know it when they see it.'"[9]

Muir cultivated friendships with diverse people, men and women, who encouraged him and whom he encouraged in his political campaigns. Some of these friends were politically powerful, such as President Roosevelt and the railroad baron Edward Henry Harriman. Muir needed all the friends he could get to wrestle the mountains away from the miners, loggers, and other resource developers. Certainly his friend Harriman was able to intervene both with the California state legislature and with the federal Congress at crucial times during various political debates over the future of the national parks, and Muir remained his friend until Harriman's death in 1909.

Muir was never enthusiastic about abstract political causes or campaigns. He was specific and personal. In his early adulthood, Muir was concerned with the suffering of victims of the Civil War. But he was also a pacifist and decided to go to medical school to help those who were suffering. The delay in the mails due to the war prevented his letter of acceptance to medical school from reaching him, and he left his home to travel in Canada. Muir was never a misanthrope. His friendships with Jeanne Carr, with Harriman, and with others he met on his travels attest to that. He was gracious even in his most bitter defeat over Hetch Hetchy. He understood why some opposed him and said, after the Hetch Hetchy vote in congress, "They will see what I meant in time. There must be places for human beings to satisfy their souls. Food and drink is not enough. There is the spiritual. In some it is only a germ, of course, but the germ will grow!"

The issue of damming the Hetch Hetchy valley involved many subissues: public versus private water development in California, the integrity of the new national park system, the national interest versus regional interests, the "greatest good for the greatest number in the long run," and most important, for Muir, right livelihood, the way we should live, relating to places beyond civilization. If Hetch Hetchy was dammed, Muir realized, all the rivers in California were open to scientific management, to economic development to serve the perceived needs of some humans rather than letting the river be.

In William Everson's perceptive theory, Hetch Hetchy became:

. . . One of the main turning points in the spiritual life of the nation, perhaps the chief turning point, as far as the future was concerned. It marked the real closing of the concept of unlimited expansion, and insisted on the point that man was going to have to think of depriving himself rather than abusing his environment. But more than that, it marked the moment when the implicit religious attitudes of the people gained explicit status, and though by a kind of reflex America violated its conscience, dammed the Hetch Hetchy, opted for the norms of the past rather than those of the future, a blow that sent Muir to his grave, nevertheless the corner was in fact turned. [10]

Although it could be concluded that Muir lost Hetch Hetchy to what some people *thought* was the vital need to provide water to the city of San Francisco with its rapidly increasing human population, the larger context is more sanguine. Muir was resisting, or in more positive language, he was affirming the integrity of Hetch Hetchy. He had touched the Earth. He was experiencing his own self beyond the narrow social self and his style of resistance, his persistence, and even his personal expressions of frustration and inadequacy in the face of the overriding concerns of political leaders and developers, inspires us to seek a way for our own ecological consciousness to develop.

IV. CONCLUSION

From a deep, long-range ecology perspective, whatever is to be done, we are the people to do it; the only people to do it.

Direct action means giving active voice to deep ecological intuitions, encouraging more intuitive insights, as well as acquiring more knowledge and understanding of our bioregion, homeland, Nature and ourselves.

Much of the process of direct action means attuning our rhapsodic intellect and physical bodies more fully to Heidegger's "round dance of appropriation," that quality of living fully in the space between Earth, sky, gods and our own mortal flesh, realizing the danger, in our technocratic-industrial society, that acting in such a way is risking our socially-defined self. But we provide an opening to being, to receiving answers to questions we have not yet begun to ask.

From a deep ecology perspective there is a fascination, a deep engagement with living, and yet a simplicity and joy in this serious undertaking. Muir, near the end of his very active life, once said, "I only went out for a walk and finally concluded to stay until sundown, for going out, I discovered, was actually going in."

Inward and outward direction, two aspects of the same process. We are not alone. We are part and parcel of the larger community, the land community. Each life in its own sense is heroic and connected. In the words of the Bodhisativa, "No one is saved until we are all saved."

This perspective encompasses all notions of saving anything, whether it be an endangered species, the community, or your own self. Each life is a heroic quest. It is a journey of the spirit during which we discover our purpose. We have only to embark, to set out in our own hearts, on this journey we began so long ago, to start on the "real work" of becoming real and of doing what is real. Nothing is labored, nothing forced.

The process of developing maturity is simpler than many think. Like water flowing through the canyons, always yielding, always finding its way back, simple in means, rich in ends.

In this book we have looked at many aspects of the ultimate norms of deep ecology, self-realization and biocentric equality. We have seen how these norms can apply to our individual lives, to the development of maturity, and to public policy. We have presented a tentative platform or set of basic principles of deep ecology derived from these norms which applies to our predicament in technocratic-industrial society. We have discussed various paths to better public policy from a deep ecology perspective to the development of bioregional communities as we reinhabit the land, and various ways to greater maturity in the individual. And we have suggested that we need more ecotopian visions of living in mixed communities of humans, rivers, deer, wolves, insects and trees.

A final suggestion comes from Arne Naess: "In the long run, in order to joyfully and wholeheartedly participate in the deep ecology movement, you have to take your own life very seriously. People who successfully maintain a low material standard of living and successfully cultivate a deep, intense inner life are much better able to consistently maintain a deep ecological view and to act on behalf of it. And I sit down and breathe deeply and just feel where I am."

Ah to be alive
  on a mid-September morn
  fording a stream
  barefoot, pants rolled up,
  holding boots, pack on,
  sunshine, ice in the shallows,
  northern rockies.

Rustle and shimmer of icy creek waters
stones turn underfoot, small and hard on toes
  cold nose dripping
  singing inside
  creek music, heart music,
  smell of sun on gravel.

  I pledge allegiance.

I pledge allegiance to the soil
  of Turtle Island
  one ecosystem
  in diversity
  under the sun—
With joyful interpenetration for all.
  —Gary Snyder from Axe Handles *(1983)*

EPILOGUE

The Ohlone people, people living simply in means, rich in ends, on the shores of San Francisco Bay and Monterey Bay in what is now California, were "discovered" by the Spanish in the 1770s. Within fifty years of this discovery, the Ohlone were almost gone—dead of European diseases, murdered and raped by white men, deprived of their best hunting and fishing areas. We know little of the richness of their myths, rituals, and lifestyles, but one haunting line is enough to call us, in the present generation, into awareness: "Dancing on the brink of the world."

The line may refer to dancing on the edge of the continent with the great western ocean, the western spirit gate to many Indian peoples, stretching onward from their dancing grounds. It may refer to a particularly painful pessimism that some commentators say overwhelmed them after contact with Europeans. It may refer to the dance of living beings in that land between existence and being.

It may mean all that and more. For us, living under the shadow of nuclear holocaust and the relentless conversion of Nature into commodities and managed tree farms, it has an evocative calling, a feeling.

We are dancing on the brink of our little world of which we know so little; we are dancing the dance of life, of death; dancing the moon up in celebration of dimly remembered connections with our ancestors; dancing to keep the cold and darkness of a nuclear winter from chilling our bones; dancing on the brink of ecological awareness; dancing for the sake of dancing without analyzing and rationalizing and articulating; without consciously probing for meaning but allowing meaning in being to emerge into our living space.

Dancing has always been part of living for primal peoples. For us, the dance may be a Ghost Dance for all that is lost: condor, bison, redwood, watershed, wolf, whale, and passenger pigeon. Or it may be the dance of a new revelation of Being, of modesty and Earth wisdom on the turning point.

NOTES

CHAPTER 1
NOTHING CAN BE DONE,
EVERYTHING IS POSSIBLE

1. The most informative recent book on reformist environmentalism in the context of British society is Philip Lowe and Jane Goyder's *Environmental Groups in Politics* (London: George Allen, 1983). Sociological explanations of the environmental movement in North America are found in Craig R. Humphrey and Frederick R. Butell's *Environment, Energy and Society* (Belmont, Ca.: Wadsworth, 1983); Allan Schnaiberg's *The Environment: From Surplus to Scarcity* (New York: Oxford, 1980); Lester Milbrath's *Environmentalists* (Albany: State University of New York Press, 1984); "Sociology of the Environment," *Sociological Inquiry* 53 (Spring 1983); Jonathon Porritt, *Green: The Politics of Ecology Explained* (New York: Basil Blackwell, 1985).

2. Peter Berg, editorial, *Raise the Stakes* (Fall 1983).

3. Murray Bookchin, "Open Letter to the Ecology Movement," *Rain* (April 1980), as well as other publications.

4. James Lovelock, *Gaia: A New Look At Life On Earth* (New York: Oxford, 1979), p. 127.

5. Ibid.

6. John Baden and Richard Stroup, "Saving the Wilderness," *Reason* (July 1981).

7. Theodore Roszak, *Person/Planet* (Garden City, N.Y.: Doubleday, 1978), p. 99.

8. Fritjof Capra and Charlene Spretnak, *Green Politics* (New York: E. P. Dutton, 1984).

9. Alan Watts, *Psychotherapy East and West* (New York: Vintage, 1975), p. 184.

10. _____, *Nature, Man and Woman* (New York: Vintage, 1970), p. 178.

11. Roszak, p. 296.

12. Gary Snyder, *The Real Work* (New York: New Directions, 1980), p. 81.

13. Stephen Bodian, "Simple in Means, Rich in Ends: A Conversation with Arne Naess," *Ten Directions* (California: Institute for Transcultural Studies, Zen Center of Los Angeles, Summer/Fall 1982).

14. Po-Keung Ip, "Taoism and the Foundations of Environmental Ethics," *Environmental Ethics* 5 (Winter 1983), pp. 335-344.

CHAPTER 2
THE MINORITY TRADITION AND DIRECT ACTION

1. Murray Bookchin, *The Ecology of Freedom* (Palo Alto: Cheshire, 1982), p. 43.

2. Pierre Clastres, *Society Against the State: The Leader as Servant and the Humane Uses of Power Among the Indians of the Americas* (New York: Urizen Books, 1977).

208

3. Stanley Diamond, *In Search of the Primitive: A Critique of Civilization* (New Brunswick, N.J.: Transaction, 1974), p. 172.

4. Jack Forbes, "The Native American Experience in California History," *California Historical Quarterly* 50, 3 (1971), p. 236. Restated in Jack D. Forbes, *A World Ruled By Cannibals: The Wetiko Disease of Aggression, Violence and Imperialism* (Davis, Ca.: D-Q University Press, 1979). See also Jamake Highwater, *The Primal Mind: Vision and Reality in Indian America* (New York: New American Library, 1981).

5. Jim Dodge, "Living By Life," *CoEvolution Quarterly* 32 (Winter 1981), pp. 6-12; see also Peter Berg, ed., *Reinhabiting a Separate Country, A Bioregional Anthology of Northern California* (San Francisco: Planet Drum, 1978); on self-reliance in India with applications for North America, see Mark Shepard, *Since Gandhi: India's Sarvodaya Movement* (Weare, N.H.: Greenleaf Books, 1984); Joel Garreau, *The Nine Nations of North America* (Boston: Houghton Mifflin, 1981).

6. *CoEvolution Quarterly* 34 (Winter 1981). Some changes have been made for this book from the original version of the "test" as created by Jim Dodge.

7. Byron Kennard, *Nothing Can Be Done, Everything Is Possible* (Andover, Ma.: Brick, 1982).

8. Duane Elgin, *Voluntary Simplicity: Toward A Way of Life That Is Outwardly Simple, Inwardly Rich* (New York: Morrow, 1981).

9. A. Westbrook and O. Ratti, *Aikido and the Dynamic Sphere* (Rutland, Vt.: Charles E. Tuttle, 1970), p. 363.

10. William Greider, "Fines Aren't Enough: Send Corporate Polluters to Jail," *Rolling Stone* (29 March 1984).

11. John Carmody, *Ecology and Religion: Toward a New Christian Theology of Nature* (New York: Paulist Press, 1983). In Chapter 7, after reviewing the references to Nature in Church fathers and Protestant theologians from the sixteenth to the twentieth century, Carmody concludes, "My impression is that ecological convictions now have a widespread general following, but that they have yet to penetrate the churches' doctrinal assumptions sufficiently to make the churches effective exponents of an ecological ethics or worldview. . . . It is not hard to make the argument that the Catholic church needs a new theology of nature."

12. Vincent Rossi, *The Eleventh Commandment Fellowship Newsletter* (Forestville, Ca., Spring 1984).

13. Langdon Winner, *Autonomous Technology* (Cambridge, Ma.: MIT Press, 1977), p. 325.

14. Carl Sagan et al., *The Cold and the Dark: The World After Nuclear War* (New York: Norton, 1984).

15. G. Tyler Miller, Jr., *Living in the Environment*, 3d ed. (Belmont, Ca.: Wadsworth, 1983), pp. 465-466.

CHAPTER 3
THE DOMINANT, MODERN WORLDVIEW
AND ITS CRITICS

1. Dennis Pirages and Paul R. Ehrlich, *Ark II: Social Response to Environmental Imperatives* (San Francisco: Freeman, 1974), p. 43.

2. Thomas Kuhn, *The Structure of Scientific Revolutions,* 2d ed. (Chicago: University of Chicago Press, 1970).

3. William Catton, Jr. and Riley Dunlap, "New Ecological Paradigm for Post-Exuberant Sociology," *American Behavioral Scientist* 24 (September 1980), pp. 15-48.

4. David Ehrenfeld, *The Arrogance of Humanism* (New York: Oxford, 1978), p. 16-17.

5. William Catton, Jr., *Overshoot: The Ecological Basis of Revolutionary Change* (Urbana: University of Illinois Press, 1980), p. 239.

6. Robin Williams, *American Society,* 3d ed. (New York: Knopf, 1970).

7. Morris Berman, *The Reenchantment of the World* (Ithaca, N.Y.: Cornell University Press, 1981), p. 50.

8. See as references: William Leiss, *The Domination of Nature* (New York: G. Braziller, 1972); Eugene C. Hargrove, "Anglo-American Land Use Attitudes," *Environmental Ethics* 2, 2 (1980), pp. 121-148; Carolyn Merchant, *The Death of Nature: Women, Ecology and the Scientific Revolution* (San Francisco: Harper & Row, 1980); Elizabeth Dodson Gray, *Patriarchy as a Conceptual Trap* (Wellesley, Ma.: Roundtable Press, 1982); Roderick Nash, *Wilderness and the American Mind,* 3d ed. (New Haven, Ct.: Yale University Press, 1983); Richard Routley, *Roles and Limits of Paradigms in Environmental Thought and Action* (Research School of Social Sciences, Australian National University, 1982); Karl Polyani, *The Great Transformation* (Boston: Beacon, 1944); John Passmore, *Man's Responsibility for Nature* (New York: Scribner's, 1974). See also works by Martin Heidegger cited in Chapter 6 of this book.

9. Catton, *Overshoot.*

10. George Santayana, "The Genteel Tradition in American Philosophy," *Winds of Doctrine* (New York: Scribner's, 1926), pp. 186-215.

11. Harvey Cox, *The Secular City: Secularization and Urbanization in Theoretical Perspective* (New York: Macmillan, 1966); quoted in Frederick Elder, *Crisis in Eden: A Religious Study of Man and the Environment* (Boston: Abingdon Press, 1970).

12. Neil Everndon, "Beyond Ecology," *North American Review* 263 (1978), pp. 16-20.

CHAPTER 4
THE REFORMIST RESPONSE

1. John Passmore, "Attitudes Toward Nature," *Nature and Conduct,* ed. by R. S. Peters (New York: Macmillan, 1975), pp. 251-264. See also John Passmore, *Man's Responsibility for Nature* (New York: Scribner's, 1974).

2. Garrett Hardin, *Exploring New Ethics for Survival: The Voyage of Spaceship Beagle* (New York: Viking, 1972). Hardin and John Baden, eds., *Managing the Commons* (San Francisco: Freeman, 1977).

3. John Rodman, "Resource Conservation: Economics and After" (Unpublished, Pitzer College, Claremont, Ca., 1977).

4. Pete Gunter, "Man-Infinite and Nature-Infinite: A Mirror-Image Dialectic" (Unpublished paper, Texas: North Texas State University, 1980).

5. Theodore Roszak, *Where the Wasteland Ends* (New York: Anchor, 1972).

6. Russell, Bertrand, ed., *History of Western Philosophy* (New York: Simon and Schuster, 1945), pp. 788-789, 827-828.

7. Rodman, "The Liberation of Nature?" *Inquiry* 20 (Oslo, 1977).

8. Jay Forrester, *World Dynamics* (Cambridge, Ma.: Wright-Allen, 1971).

9. Gerald O. Barney, director, *The Global 2000 Report to the President* (New York: Penguin, 1981), Part II, "Analysis of the Projection of Tools: Other Global Models." See also Donella H. and Dennis L. Meadows, et al., *The Limits to Growth* (Washington, D.C.: Potomac Associates, 1972). See Craig R. Humphrey and Frederick R. Buttell's *Environment, Energy and Society* (Belmont, Ca.: Wadsworth, 1983).

10. John Livingston, *The Fallacy of Wildlife Conservation* (Toronto: McClelland and Steward, 1981).

11. Passmore, *Man's Responsibility for Nature.*

12. Vine Deloria, *God is Red* (New York: Grossett, 1973), p. 298.

13. Joseph Sax, *Mountains Without Handrails: Reflections on the National Parks* (Ann Arbor, Mi.: University of Michigan Press, 1980).

14. Stephen Fox, *John Muir and His Legacy* (Boston: Little, Brown and Co., 1981), chapter 5.

15. Frank Graham, *Since Silent Spring* (Boston: Houghton Mifflin, 1970); Carol Van Strum, *A Bitter Fog: Herbicides and Human Rights* (San Francisco: Sierra Club, 1983); Robert Van Den Bosch, *The Pesticide Conspiracy* (Garden City, N.Y.: Doubleday, 1978); Dorothy Nelkin and Michael S. Brown, *Workers at Risk* (Chicago: University of Chicago Press, 1984); Fred Wilcox, *Waiting for an Army to Die: The Tragedy of Agent Orange* (New York: Vintage, 1983); Jon Luoma, *Troubled Skies, Troubled Waters* (New York: Viking, 1984); John Sheaffer and Leonard Stevens, *Future Water* (New York: William Morrow, 1983); Edward C. Fritz, *Sterile Forest: The Case Against Clearcutting* (Austin, Tx.: Eakin Press, 1983).

16. Stewart Udall, *The Quiet Crisis* (New York: Holt, Rinehart, and Winston, 1963).

17. John Quarles, *Cleaning Up America: An Insider's View of the Environmental Protection Agency* (Boston: Houghton Mifflin, 1976).

18. Eugenia Horstman Connally, ed., *National Parks in Crisis* (Washington, D.C.: National Parks and Recreation Association, 1982).

19. Jonathan Lash, Katherine Gillman and David Sheridan, *A Season of Spoils:*

The Story of the Reagan Administration's Attack on the Environment (New York: Pantheon Books, 1984). See also Harold Koopowitz and Hilary Kay, *Plant Extinction; A Global Crisis* (Washington, D.C.: Stone Wall Press, 1983); M. W. Holdgate, M. Kassas and G. F. White, eds., *The World Environment, 1972-1982* (London: Tycooly International Publishing, 1983); *Changing Climate* (Washington, D.C.: National Academy of Sciences, 1983); *Acid Deposition: Atmospheric Processes in Eastern North America: A Review of Current Scientific Understanding* (Washington, D.C.: National Academy Press, 1983); Stephen Seideal and Dale Keyes, et al., *Can We Delay A Greenhouse Warming?* (Washington, D.C.: U.S.A. Environmental Protection Agency, 1983); Paul Ehrlich, "The Nuclear Winter: Discovering the Ecology of Nuclear War," *The Amicus Journal* (Winter 1984), pp. 20-37.

20. Examples of the search for appropriate environmental philosophy include many articles annotated in Mary Anglemyer's *A Search for Environmental Ethics: An Initial Bibliography* (Washington, D.C.: Smithsonian Institution, 1980); Don Mannison, Michael McRobbie, and Richard Routley, eds., *Environmental Philosophy,* Monograph Series No. 2 (Dept. of Philosophy, Research School of Social Sciences, the Australian National University, Canberra, A.C.T., 1980); Robert Cahn, *Footprints on the Planet: A Search for an Environmental Ethic* (New York: Universe, 1978); Rice Odell, *Environmental Awakening: The New Revolution to Protect the Earth* (Cambridge, Ma.: Ballinger, 1980); Robin Attfield, *The Ethics of Environmental Concern* (New York: Columbia University Press, 1983).

CHAPTER 5
DEEP ECOLOGY

1. Arne Naess, "The Shallow and The Deep, Long-Range Ecology Movements: A Summary," *Inquiry* 16 (Oslo, 1973), pp. 95-100.

2. Theodore Roszak, *Where the Wasteland Ends* (New York: Anchor, 1972).

3. Warwick Fox, "Deep Ecology: A New Philosophy of Our Time?" *The Ecologist,* v. 14, 5-6, 1984, pp. 194-200. Arnie Naess replies, "Intuition, Intrinsic Value and Deep Ecology," *The Ecologist,* v. 14, 5-6, 1984, pp. 201-204.

4. Tom Regan, *The Case for Animal Rights* (New York: Random House, 1983). For excellent critiques of the animal rights movement, see John Rodman, "The Liberation of Nature?" *Inquiry* 20 (Oslo, 1977). J. Baird Callicott, "Animal Liberation," *Environmental Ethics* 2, 4, (1980); see also John Rodman, "Four Forms of Ecological Consciousness Reconsidered" in T. Attig and D. Scherer, eds., *Ethics and the Environment* (Englewood Cliffs, N.J.: Prentice-Hall, 1983).

5. Tom Regan, "The Nature and Possibility of an Environmental Ethic," *Environmental Ethics* 3 (1981), pp. 19-34.

6. Stephen Bodian, "Simple in Means, Rich in Ends: A Conversation with Arne Naess," *Ten Directions* (California: Institute for Transcultural Studies, Zen Center of Los Angeles, Summer/Fall 1982).

CHAPTER 6
SOME SOURCES OF THE
DEEP ECOLOGY PERSPECTIVE

1. For criticism of modern philosophy and psychology from this perspective, see Henryk Skolimowski, *Eco-Philosophy* (New York: Marion Boyars, 1981), chapters 1 and 2 (the rest of Skolimowski's book tends to be anthropocentric); Alan Watts, *Psychotherapy East and West* (New York: Vintage Books, 1961); Jacob Needleman, *A Sense of the Cosmos: The Encounter of Ancient Wisdom and Modern Science* (Garden City, N.Y.: Doubleday, 1975).

2. Leo Marx, "American Institutions and Ecological Ideals," *Science* 170 (1970). Reprinted in Carroll Pursell, *From Conservation to Ecology: The Development of Environmental Concern* (New York: T. Y. L. Crowell, 1973).

3. For an ecological discussion of the writings of D. H. Lawrence, Aldous Huxley, Robinson Jeffers, and Gary Snyder, see Del Ivan Janik, "Environmental Consciousness in Modern Literature," in J. D. Hughes and R. C. Schultz, eds., *Ecological Consciousness* (Washington, D.C.: University Press of America, 1981); see also John Alcorn, *The Nature Novel* (New York: Columbia University Press, 1977); Paul Brooks, *Speaking for Nature* (Boston: Houghton Mifflin, 1980).

4. E. McDonald, ed., *Phoenix* (New York: Macmillan, 1936). "Pan in America" was published as "The Death of Pan" in a wonderful literary/ecophilosophical collection of papers: L. Forstner and J. Todd, eds., *The Everlasting Universe: Readings on the Ecological Revolution* (Lexington, Ma.: Heath and Co., 1971).

5. L. Edwin Folsom, "Gary Snyder's Descent to Turtle Island: Searching for Fossil Love," *Western American Literature* 15 (Summer 1980), pp. 103-121. See also C. Molesworth, *Gary Snyder's Vision* (Columbia: University of Missouri Press, 1983). For further references to deep ecology and Eastern thought, see George Sessions, "Shallow and Deep Ecology: A Review of the Philosophical Literature," in Hughes and Schultz, *Ecological Consciousness*.

6. For a bibliography and references to these early ecologists, see George Sessions, "Shallow and Deep Ecology," in Hughes and Schultz, *Ecological Consciousness*, pp. 391-462.

7. In addition to *A Sand County Almanac*, see Susan Flader, *Thinking Like a Mountain: Aldo Leopold and the Evolution of an Ecological Attitude Toward Deer, Wolves, and Forests* (Columbia: University of Missouri Press, 1974), and the excellent chapter on Leopold in Nash, *Wilderness and the American Mind*, 3d ed. (New Haven, Ct.: Yale University Press, 1983).

8. Frank Egler, *The Way of Science: Toward a Philosophy of Ecology for the Layman* (New York: Hafner, 1970).

9. A special issue of the *American Behavioral Scientist* 24, 1 (Sept./Oct. 1980) is devoted to an ecological paradigm change for the social sciences.

10. For a discussion of Thoreau's participatory science, see Donald Worster, *Nature's Economy* (San Francisco: Sierra Club Books, 1977); for Muir, see Michael Cohen, *The Pathless Way* (Madison: University of Wisconsin Press, 1984).

11. For more discussion of holistic medicine and the human body as an ecosystem, see Lewis Thomas, *The Lives of a Cell* (New York: Viking, 1974); Needleman, *A Sense of the Cosmos*; and Capra, *The Turning Point: Science, Society and the Rising Culture* (New York: Simon and Schuster, 1982). See also Ashis Nandy, "The Pathology of Objectivity," *Ecologist* 1, 3, 6 (1983), pp. 202-207.

12. Morris Berman, "The Cybernetic Dream of the 21st Century" (Unpublished, 1984).

13. Lynn White, Jr., "Historical Roots of Our Ecologic Crisis," *Science* 155 (1967). Widely reprinted in ecological anthologies of the early 1970s.

14. Dorothy Dinnerstein, *The Mermaid and the Minotaur* (New York: Harper & Row, 1976); Carolyn Merchant, *The Death of Nature: Women, Ecology, and the Scientific Revolution* (San Francisco: Harper & Row, 1980) and "Women of the Progressive Conservation Movement, 1900-1915," *Environmental Review* 8, 1 (1984); Susan Griffin, *Women and Nature: The Roaring Inside Her* (San Francisco: Harper & Row, 1978) and *Pornography and Silence: Culture's Revolt Against Nature* (New York: Harper & Row, 1982); Patricia Mische, "Women and Power," *New Age* 4, 6 (November 1978), pp. 38-40.

15. Augusta Fink, *I-Mary: A Biography of Mary Austin* (Tucson: University of Arizona Press, 1983).

16. Vera L. Norwood, "Heroines of Nature: Four Women Respond to the American Landscape," *Environmental Review* 8, 1 (Spring 1984).

17. Dolores LaChapelle, *Earth Wisdom* (Los Angeles: L.A. Guild of Tudor Press, 1978).

18. Calvin Martin, *Keepers of the Game* (Berkeley: University of California Press, 1978); Paul Shepard, *The Tender Carnivore and the Sacred Game* (New York: Scribner's, 1973); Richard Leakey, Roger Lewin, *Origins: What New Discoveries Reveal About the Emergence of Our Species and Its Possible Future* (New York: Dutton, 1977); Vine Deloria, *God is Red;* (New York: Grossett, 1973); *Touch the Earth: A Self-Portrait of Indian Existence,* compiled by T. C. McLuhan (New York: Pocket Books, 1971); J. Donald Hughes, *American Indian Ecology* (El Paso: Texas Western Press, 1983); Richard Nelson, *Make Prayers to the Raven: A Koyukon View of the Northern Forest* (Chicago: University of Chicago Press, 1983). See also J. Baird Callicott, "Traditional American Indian and Western European Attitudes Toward Nature: An Overview," *Environmental Ethics* 4 (Winter 1982), pp. 293-318.

19. Richard Nelson, *Make Prayers to the Raven.*

20. Stan Steiner, *The Vanishing White Man* (New York: Harper & Row, 1976), p. 113.

21. An outstanding work on Heidegger and deep ecology is Michael Zimmerman's "Toward a Heideggerian Ethos for Radical Environmentalism," *Environmental Ethics* 5 (1983).

22. William LaFleur, "Sattva: Enlightenment for Plants and Trees in Buddhism," *CoEvolution Quarterly* 19 (Fall 1978), pp. 47-52.

23. For further references to Jeffers's thought, see George Sessions, "Spinoza and Jeffers on Man in Nature," *Inquiry* 20 (Oslo, 1977).

214

24. Stephen Fox, *John Muir and His Legacy* (Boston: Little, Brown, 1981); Linnie Marsh Wolfe, *Son of the Wilderness: The Life of John Muir* (New York: Knopf, 1945); Edwin Way Teale, *The Wilderness World of John Muir, Selections of His Writings* (Boston: Houghton Mifflin, 1954); Tom Lyons, "A Mountain Mind," in Michael Tobias, ed., *The Mountain Spirit* (Woodstock, N.Y.: Overlook Press, 1979), pp. 22-28.

25. Quoted in Fox, *John Muir and His Legacy.*

26. Cohen, *The Pathless Way.*

27. See Part Four, "Visionary Science (1871-1872)" in *John Muir: To Yosemite and Beyond,* Robert Engberg and Donald Wesling, eds. (Madison: University of Wisconsin Press, 1980), p. 162.

28. David Brower, ed., *Wilderness: America's Living Heritage* (San Francisco: Sierra Club Books, 1961).

29. Mark Evanoff, "Boondoggle at Diablo: The 18-Year Saga of Greed, Deception, Ineptitude—And Opposition," *Not Man Apart* (September 1981), D1-D16.

CHAPTER 7
WHY WILDERNESS IN THE NUCLEAR AGE

1. Charles R. Anderson, ed., *Thoreau's Vision: The Major Essays* (Englewood Cliffs, N.J.: Prentice-Hall, 1973). Essay on "Walking." Later in life, Thoreau revised this essay, according to Roderick Nash, and concentrated his message into eight words: "In Wildness is the preservation of the World." Nash, *Wilderness and the American Mind,* 3d ed. (1982), p. 84.

2. "Editorial: Wilderness and the Biosphere," *Environmental Conservation* 10, 4 (Winter 1983), pp. 281-82.

3. William Devall, "John Muir as Deep Ecologist," *Environmental Review* 6, 1 (1982).

4. Cohen, *The Pathless Way* (Madison: University of Wisconsin Press, 1984). Tom Lyon, "John Muir's Enlightenment," *The World of John Muir* (California: University of the Pacific, 1981).

5. Devall, "John Muir as Deep Ecologist."

6. Alan Gussow, *A Sense of Place* (San Francisco: Friends of the Earth, 1971).

7. Shepard, "A Sense of Place in American Culture," *North American Review* 262 (1977), pp. 22-32.

8. Dōgen, "Treasury of the True Dharma Eye: Book XXIX, the Mountains and Rivers Sutra," *The Mountain Spirit,* Michael Tobias, ed. (Woodstock, N.Y.: Overlook, 1979), pp. 41-50.

9. Dolores LaChapelle, *Earth Wisdom,* (Los Angeles: L.A. Guild of Tudor Press, 1978) chapter 9.

10. David Brower, ed., *Gentle Wilderness* (San Francisco: Sierra Club Books, 1968).

11. The literature on American encounters with the richness of wilderness is

extensive. As an introduction, see Frank Bergon, ed., *The Wilderness Reader* (New York: New American Library, 1980).

12. John Rodman, "Resource Conservation—Economics and After" (Unpublished paper, Claremont, Ca.: Pitzer College, 1976).

13. John V. Krutilla and Anthony C. Fisher, *The Economics of Natural Environments: Studies in the Valuation of Commodity and Amenity Resources* (Baltimore: Johns Hopkins Press, 1975). Some resource economists understand their dilemma. Stephen Kellert, a member of the School of Forestry and Environmental Studies at Yale University, writes, ". . . we are confronted by the dilemma of generating prices for the priceless, of quantifying the unquantifiable, of creating commensurable units for things apparently unequatable. Yet what are the alternatives? Our society tends to be governed by a tyranny of numbers, both in custom and mandated by legal requirement. To ignore the challenge of empirical measurement is to engender, by default, decisions inherently biased toward the quantifiable." Kellert proceeds to develop a system of value not based on dollars but "units of value." He believes he can do so for all human uses except spiritual meaning of place. This is of course a frankly and honestly anthropocentric form of argument but this kind of argumentation may win converts to 'saving' some important areas and other species. See Stephen R. Kellert, "Assessing Wildlife and Environmental Values in Cost-benefit Analysis," *Journal of Environmental Management* 18 (1984), pp. 355-363.

14. Martin H. Krieger, "What's Wrong With Plastic Trees?" *Science* 179 (2 Feb. 1973), p. 451.

15. Roderick Nash, *Wilderness and the American Mind*, chapter 16.

16. E. F. Schumacher, *Small Is Beautiful: Economics as if People Mattered* (New York: Perennial Library, Harper & Row, 1975), p. 53.

17. Gwen Bell, ed., *Strategies for Human Settlements: Habitat and Environment* (Honolulu: University Press of Hawaii, 1976).

18. Mark Sagoff, "On Preserving the Natural Environment," *The Yale Law Journal* 84, 2 (Dec. 1974), p. 228. See also Sagoff, "Do We Need a Land Use Ethic?" *Environmental Ethics* 3, 4 (Winter 1981) pp. 293-308. In the latter article Sagoff criticizes the remedies and stratagems by which economists have tried to defend market-based and property-based solutions to environmental problems. He says the "last refuge of the liberal mind" is the attempt to make "shadow pricing" of "intangible" or "soft" variables. "This is the attempt to price not only our interests but our principles and beliefs as market externalities. It may be understood, in the context of the Lockean tradition, as the last effort to interpret political issues in economic terms. It is a way of representing contradiction as competition." (p. 306)

19. Krieger, "What's Wrong With Plastic Trees?" p. 453.

20. Michael Harrington, "To the Disney Station," *Harpers* (Jan. 1979), pp. 35-44; see also R. Schickel, *The Disney Version* (New York: Simon and Schuster, 1968).

21. On the general ethical question of present generations' responsibility to far future generations of humans, see R. and V. Routley, "Nuclear Energy and Obligations to the Future," *Inquiry* 21, 2 (Summer 1978), pp. 133-179.

22. David Brower, ed., *Galápagos: The Flow of Wildness* (San Francisco: Sierra Club Books, 1968).

23. Wendell Berry, *The Unsettling of America* (San Francisco: Sierra Club Books, 1977).

24. Jeremy Rifkin, *Entropy: A New World View* (New York: Viking, 1981), p. 239.

25. James Lovelock, *Gaia: A New Look at Life on Earth* (New York: Oxford, 1979).

26. Ibid., p. 121.

27. Roy Silen, "The Care and Handling of the Forest Gene Pool," *Pacific Search* (June 1976), pp. 7-9; Alastair S. Gunn, "Why Should We Care About Rare Species?" *Environmental Ethics* 2, 1 (Fall 1980), pp. 17-38; R. Michael McGonigle, "The 'Economizing' of Ecology: Why Big Rare Whales Still Die," *Ecology Law Review* 9, 1 (1980), pp. 119-238; David Ehrenfeld, "The Conservation of Non-Resources," *American Scientist* 64 (1976), pp. 648-656; Paul and Anne Ehrlich, *Extinction: The Causes and Consequences of the Disappearance of Species* (New York: Random House, 1983); Norman Myers, *The Sinking Ark* (Oxford: Pergamon Press, 1979); G. M. Woodewell, et al., "Global Deforestation Contribution to Atmospheric Carbon Dioxide," *Science* (9 Dec. 1983), pp. 1081-1086.

28. Hugh H. Iltis, "Tropical Forests: What Will Be Their Fate?" *Environment* 25, 10 (Dec. 1983); Val Plumwood and Richard Routley, "World Rainforest Destruction: The Social Factors," *Ecologist* 12, 1 (Jan. 1982), pp. 4-22. See also *The Tenth Annual Report of the Council on Environmental Quality* (1979), chapter 11; Ira Rubinoff, "Tropical Forests: Can We Afford Not to Give Them a Future?" *The Ecologist* 12, 6 (1982). Forty years ago the visionary ecologist Richard St. Barbe Baker was calling for conservation of the world's forests, including the Redwoods of northwest California. It seems to be difficult to remember these lessons. See his *Green Glory: The Forests of the World* (New York: A. A. Wyn, 1949).

29. *The Eleventh Annual Environmental Report to the President* (Washington, D.C., 1980), p. 7.

30. Cheryl E. Holdren and Anne E. Ehrlich, "The Virunga Volcanoes: Last Redoubt of the Mountain Gorilla," *Not Man Apart* (June 1984), pp. 8-9. Their concluding paragraphs summarize the situation in many Third World nations:

Although the Pac des Volcans *has been reduced to a tiny fraction of the country's land area—about 0.5 percent—those still forested high slopes are critically important to the hydrological regime of the entire country, serving as the principal watershed. The reductions of forest area that have occurred in recent decades have led to the drying up of streams and irregularities of rainfall. Further losses would cause serious problems with floods and droughts. The small gain in cropland would be more than offset by losses in productivity elsewhere. Rwanda thus stands to gain much more than a profitable tourist industry by protecting the* Pac des Volcans.

But whether a nation so poor can successfully defend the park in the face of the intensifying local pressures for more farmland remains to be seen. Rwanda

217

must grapple with the whole array of population-resource problems: rapid population growth, agricultural development, land use, resource management, and social and economic development. On its success in meeting this enormous challenge hang the fates of the Rwandese population and their endangered cousins, the mountain gorillas.

31. *The Whale Manual* (San Francisco: Friends of the Earth, 1978).

32. For example, Gwen Struik, "Commercial Fishing in New Zealand: An Industry Bent on Extinction," *Ecologist* 1, 3, 6 (1983), pp. 213-221. See also the *International Union for the Conservation of Nature Bulletin* 15, 4-6 (April-June 1984), pp. 42-457.

33. Judieth Wright et al., eds., *Reef, Rainforest, Mangroves, Man* (Brisbane: Wildlife Preservation Society of Queensland, 1980); *Australia's Wilderness* (Australian Conservation Foundation, 1978).

34. E. D. Suten, *World Law and the Last Wilderness* 2d ed. (Sydney: Friends of the Earth, 1980); Richard Laws, "Antarctica: A Convergence of Life," *New Scientist* 99, 1373, (1 Sept. 1983), pp. 608-616; Roger Wilson, "Antarctica: The Last Continent Faces Exploitation," *Ecologist* 13, 2/3 (1983), pp. 74-83; William Y. Brown, "The Conservation of Antarctica Marine Living Resources," *Environmental Conservation* 10, 3 (1983), pp. 187-196.

CHAPTER 8
NATURAL RESOURCE CONSERVATION OR PROTECTION OF THE INTEGRITY OF NATURE: CONTRASTING VIEWS OF MANAGEMENT

1. Gifford Pinchot, *Breaking New Ground* (New York: Harcourt, Brace and Co., 1947).

2. Ibid., p. 261.

3. Stephen Fox, *John Muir and His Legacy,* (Boston: Little, Brown and Co., 1981), chapter four.

4. Theodore Roszak, *Where the Wasteland Ends* (New York: Anchor, 1972), pp. 26-67.

5. John Rodman, "Resource Conservation: Economics and Beyond" (Unpublished paper, Claremont, Ca.: Pitzer College, 1976).

6. Remarks by Robert Broadbent, Commissioner of Reclamation, U.S. Department of the Interior, National Cotton Outlook Conference, South Padre Island, Texas (16 June 1982).

7. See J. P. Milton and M. T. Favor, *The Careless Technology* (New York: Natural History Press, 1971).

8. William Burch, Jr., *Daydreams and Nightmares* (New York: Harper & Row, 1971), p. 154.

9. Karl Polyani, *The Great Transformation* (Boston: Beacon, 1944), p. 72.

10. Terry Daniel and Ron Boster, "Measuring Landscape Esthetics: The Scenic

Beauty Estimation Method," USFS Research Paper RM-167 (Rocky Mountain Experimental Station, May 1976).

11. René Dubos, *The Wooing of the Earth* (New York: Scribner's, 1980), p. 79.

12. W. D. Hagenstein, "The Old Forest Maketh Way for the New," *Environmental Law* 8 (Summer 1978), p. 485.

13. Marilyn Ferguson, *The Aquarian Conspiracy: Personal and Social Transformation in the 1980s* (New York: St. Martin's, 1980).

14. Jeremy Rifkin, *Algeny* (New York: Viking, 1983).

15. Dick Russell, "The Tree of Knowledge Grows on Wall Street," *The Amicus Journal* (Summer 1983).

16. J. Peter Vayk, *Doomsday Has Been Cancelled* (Menlo Park, Ca.: Peace Publishers, 1978), p. 61.

17. Dubos, *The Wooing of the Earth.*

18. Thomas Berry, *Teilhard in the Ecological Age* (Chambersburg, Pa.: Anima Books, 1982), pp. 9-25.

19. James Christian, *Philosophy,* 3d ed. (New York: Holt, Rinehart & Winston, 1981), pp. 357, 375, 381-382.

20. For a discussion of "hands-on" versus "hands-off" wildlife management, see David Phillips and Hugh Nash, eds., *The Condor Question* (San Francisco: Friends of the Earth, 1982); John Livingston, *The Fallacy of Wildlife Conservation;* A. Larkin, "Maybe You Can't Get There from Here: A Foreshortened History of Research in Relation to Management of Pacific Salmon," *Journal of Fisheries Board, Canada,* 36 (1979), pp. 98-106; R. McGonigle, "The 'Economizing' of Ecology: Why Big Rare Whales Still Die"; for an account of the sorry state of wildlife management in Africa, see Peter Matthiessen, *Sand Rivers* (New York: Viking Press, 1981); for the National Parks crisis, see Eugenia Connally, ed., *National Parks in Crisis;* Joseph Sax, *Mountains without Handrails* (Michigan: University of Michigan Press, 1980); for the Taoist view of management, see Russell Goodman, "Taoism and Ecology," *Environmental Ethics* 2 (Spring 1980), pp. 37-80.

21. "The San Joaquin Valley," *The Eleventh Annual Report of the Council on Environmental Quality,* (Washington, D.C., 1980), pp. 352-359.

22. Arne Naess, "Self Realization in Mixed Communities of Humans, Bears, Sheep and Wolves," *Inquiry* 22 (1979), pp. 231-242.

23. Richard Conviser, "Toward an Agriculture of Context," *Environmental Ethics* 6, 1 (Spring 1984), pp. 71-86.

24. Masanobu Fukuoka, *The One-Straw Revolution: An Introduction to Natural Farming* (Emmaus, Pa.: Rodale Press, 1978).

25. Denzel and Nancy Ferguson, *Sacred Cows at the Public Trough* (Bend, Or.: Maverick Publications, 1983).

26. Wendell Berry, *The Unsettling of America* (San Francisco: Sierra Club Books, 1977), p. 9.

27. J. Baird Callicott, "Traditional American Indian and Western European Attitudes Toward Nature."

28. Paul Shepard, "A Sense of Place in American Culture," *North American Review* 262 (1977), pp. 22-32.

29. John Cairns, Jr., ed., *The Recovery Process of Damaged Ecosystems* (Ann Arbor, Mi.: Ann Arbor Science, 1981), p. 2.

30. Ibid., p. 9.

31. *Watershed Rehabilitation in Redwood National Park and Other Pacific Coastal Areas* (Washington, D.C.: National Park Service, 1981), p. 1.

32. Robert Lake, *Chilula* (Washington, D.C.: University Press of America, 1982).

33. Public Law 95-250, Sec. 01 (a) (b).

34. *Watershed Rehabilitation,* pp. 24-28.

35. Phillips and Nash, *The Condor Question,* p. 275.

36. Stan Croner, *An Introduction to the World Conservation Strategy* (San Francisco: Friends of the Earth, 1983).

37. These citations are a representative sample of the articles and books which have appeared during the last decade. Erik Eckholm, "Wild Species vs. Man: The Losing Struggle for Survival," *Living Wilderness* 42 (1978), pp. 11-22; Anne and Paul Ehrlich, *Extinction*; "Nature Conservancy," *The Preservation of Natural Diversity: A Survey and Recommendations,* prepared for the U.S. Department of the Interior (1975); Barney, study director, *The Global 2000 Report,* pp. 150-153; C. de Klemm, "Species and Habitat Preservation: An International Task," *Environmental Policy and Law* 1, 1 (1975), pp. 10-15; David Ehrenfeld, *Conserving Life on Earth* (New York: Oxford, 1972).

On international efforts at species and habitat preservation, see Robert Boardman, *International Organization and the Conservation of Nature* (Bloomington: Indiana University Press, 1981). On the efforts of one Third World nation to establish a system of "nature preserves" in a heavily-populated continent, see Huen-pu Wang, "Nature Conservation in China," *Parks* 5, 1 (April 1980), pp. 1-10.

38. See Ray Raphael, *Tree Talk: The People and Politics of Timber* (Covelo, Ca.: Island Press, 1981).

39. Gary Snyder, "Good, Wild, and Sacred," *CoEvolution Quarterly* 39 (Fall 1983), p. 17.

CHAPTER 9
ECOTOPIA: THE VISION DEFINED

1. For a historical discussion on utopian thinking, see Mulford Sibley, *Nature and Civilization: Some Implications for Politics* (Itasca, Il.: F. E. Peacock, 1977).

2. Loren Eiseley, *The Invisible Pyramid: A Naturalist Analyzes the Rocket Century* (New York: Scribner's, 1970).

3. Baker Brownell, *The Human Community* (New York: Harper & Row, 1950).

4. Thomas Colwell, Jr., "Baker Brownell's Ecological Naturalism and Its Educational Significance," *Journal of Educational Thought* 9, 1 (1973), pp. 29-40.

5. Ibid., pp. 36-38.

6. Aldous Huxley, *Island* (New York: Harper & Row, 1962).

7. Gary Snyder, "Four 'Changes,'" in *Environmental Handbook,* G. Debell, ed. (New York: Ballantine, 1970), pp. 323-333. Revised in Snyder's *Turtle Island* (New York: New Directions, 1974).

8. Paul Shepard, *The Tender Carnivore and the Sacred Game* (New York: Scribner's, 1973).

9. Ibid., p. 237.

10. Ibid., p. 260.

11. Ibid., p. 266.

12. Ibid., p. 273.

13. Ibid., pp. 260-264.

14. Ibid., pp. 177, 233, 267, 273.

15. Ibid., p. 229.

16. Roderick Nash, *Wilderness and the American Mind,* 2d ed. (New Haven: Yale University Press, 1973), p. 94.

17. Shepard, *The Tender Carnivore,* p. 273.

18. Ibid., pp. 275-278.

19. Another bioregional vision is expressed in Peter Berg, ed., *Reinhabiting A Separate Country* (San Francisco: Planet Drum Foundation, 1978). See also Raymond Dasmann, "National Parks, Nature Conservation and 'Future Primitive,'" *The Ecologist* 6, 5 (1976). Dasmann, *Environmental Conservaton,* 4th ed. (Wiley and Sons, 1979). chs. 16-17.

CHAPTER 10
CHARACTER AND CULTURE

1. Edith Cobb, *The Ecology of Imagination in Childhood* (New York: Columbia University Press, 1977); Joseph Pearce, *The Crack in the Cosmic Egg* (New York: Julian Press, 1971); and *Magical Child* (New York: E. P. Dutton, 1977).

2. Susan Griffin, *Woman and Nature: The Roaring Inside Her* (San Francisco: Harper & Row, 1978), and *Pornography and Silence* (New York: Harper & Row, 1982).

3. Irwin Altman and Jaochim F. Wohlwill, eds., *Behavior and the Natural Environment,* v. 6 of *Human Behavior and the Environment* (New York: Plenum Press, 1983). These social scientists find it "surprising that so many people still respond positively to Nature." Roger Ulrich in "Aesthetic and Affective Response to Natural Environment," for example, concluded: "One of the most clear-cut and potentially important findings to date is the consistent tendency for North Americans and European groups to prefer even unspectacular natural scenes over the vast majority of urban views. This pattern of differential responsiveness appears to extend well beyond aesthetic preference to include other emotions such as interest, and it is probably also expressed in differences in neurophysiological activity. The theoretical view here is that both unlearned and learned factors are responsible for these differences."

Rachel Kaplan in "The Role of Nature in the Urban Context," uses the convoluted and dehumanizing language of Resource Conservation ideology. But she concludes that, "We recognize humans as a resource that is integrally related to the natural resource. In reversing the denaturing of the urban environment, by preserving and enhancing the bits and pieces of nature that exist there, perhaps we can restore the people as well."

Stephen Kaplan and Janet Talbot in "Psychological Benefits of a Wilderness Experience" comment, "We had not expected the wilderness experience to be quite so powerful or pervasive in its impact. And we were impressed by the durability of that residue in the human makeup that still resonates so strongly to those remote, uncivilized places."

4. Paul Shepard, *Thinking Animals: Animals and the Development of Human Intelligence* (New York: Viking, 1978), and *Nature and Madness* (San Francisco: Sierra Club Books, 1983).

5. John C. Sawhill, "The Unlettered University," *Harper's* 258, 1545 (Feb. 1979), pp. 35-40; Alston Chase, "Skipping Through College: Reflections on the Decline of Liberal Arts Education," *Atlantic* (Sept. 1978), pp. 33-40.

6. Aldo Leopold, *A Sand County Almanac* (New York: Oxford, 1949).

7. Shepard seemed particularly influenced in writing *Nature and Madness* by Erik Erikson's *Childhood and Society* (New York: W. W. Norton, 1950).

8. David Sheridan, *Off Road Vehicles on the Public Lands: A Report to the Council on Environmental Quality* (Washington, D.C.: E.E.Q., 1979); Stuart W. Watson, Michael H. Legg and Joy B. Reeves, "The Endoro Dirt-Bike Rider: An Empirical Investigation," *Leisure Sciences* 3, 3 (1980), pp. 241-256; William Leitch, "Backpacking in 2078," *Sierra* (Jan. 1978), pp. 25-27; Christopher Lasch, *The Culture of Narcissism: American Life in an Age of Diminishing Expectations* (New York: W. W. Norton, 1978), see especially chapters 4 and 5.

For comment on "industrial tourism" and its impact on participants and national parks, see Edward Abbey, *Desert Solitaire: A Season in the Wilderness* (New York: McGraw-Hill, 1968), pp. 46-67; Lane Jennings, "Future Fun: Tomorrow's Sports and Games," *The Futurist* (Dec. 1979), pp. 18-431; Lawrence Hamilton, "Modern American Rock Climbing: Some Aspects of Social Change," *Pacific Sociological Review* 22, 3 (July 1980), pp. 285-308.

9. Robert Bly, *News of the Universe: Poems of Twofold Consciousness* (San Francisco: Sierra Club Books, 1980). Bly says that some poets living within modern Western civilization have attempted to do what primal peoples did for a millennia — really *see. Seeing,* the ability to observe, means paying attention to something beyond one's own subjectivity and introspection. This "second stage" of understanding is crudely rejected by many in modern technocratic society.

"It is possible," Bly writes, "that mass culture traps people in the first stage, or even the pre-stage, a pre-introspective state. We develop a 'culture of narcissism.' Advertisements on television encourage the human being to follow his body's whims, and finally one believes that the Montana hills were created to provide oil for central heating. Mass culture encourages the comfort of not-seeing. So when an artist moves into the second stage, the audience trained on mass culture often becomes upset. . . ."

10. Dolores LaChapelle, *Earth Wisdom* (Los Angeles: L.A. Guild of Tudor Press, 1978), Part III, pp. 99-133. See also Michael J. Cohen, *Prejudice Against Nature: A Guidebook for the Liberation of Self and Planet* (National Audubon Society Expedition Institute, 1983).

CHAPTER 11
ECOLOGICAL RESISTING

1. Roszak, *Where the Wasteland Ends* (New York: Anchor, 1972), chapter 11.

2. Case studies of ecological resistance are found in the following books and articles: Robert Hunter, *Warriors of the Rainbow: A Chronicle of the Greenpeace Movement* (New York: Holt, Rinehart & Winston, 1979); Sigurd Olson, *Open Horizons* (New York: Knopf, 1969); Don Rawlings, "Abbey's Essays: One Man's Quest for Solid Ground," *The Living Wilderness* (June 1980), pp. 44-46; Pete Gunter, "The Big Thicket: A Case Study in Attitudes Toward Environment," *Philosophy and Environmental Crisis,* William T. Blackstone, ed. (Univ. of Georgia Press, 1974), pp. 117-137; Dea Z. Mallin, "Fighting the Crane Drain, A Portrait of George Archibald," *American Way* (Jan. 1984); Ruth Eisenberg, "The Lady Who Saved Volcanoes," *University of Chicago Alumni Magazine* 121, 3 (Spring 1979); Michael Robertson, "Dian Fossey: The Great Champion of Mountain Gorillas," *San Francisco Chronicle* (26 Sept. 1983), p. 10; Michael Helm, "On Surviving the '80s: A Conversation with David Brower, the Environmental Movement's Iconoclastic Elder Statesman," *Express: The East Bay's Free Weekly* (16 Jan. 1981); "The Tide Turned: Mark Dubois and the Defense of the Stanislaus River," *Greenpeace Chronicles, California Edition* (July 1979). Also various issues of *Earth First!* in 1983, 1984 on the Bald Mountain Road blockage and Middle Santiam projects, both in defense of Oregon wilderness.

3. Bill Devall, "The Edge: The Ecology Movement in Australia," *Ecophilosophy Newsletter* VI (Spring 1984).

4. Arne Naess, *Gandhi and Group Conflict: An Exploration of Satyagaraha, Theoretical Background* (Norway: Universitetsforlaget, 1974).

5. Steven Barkan, "Strategic, Tactical and Organizational Dilemmas of the Protest Movement Against Nuclear Power," *Social Problems* 27, 1 (Oct. 1979), pp. 38-61; S. T. Bruyn and Paula M. Mayman, *Nonviolent Action and Social Change* (New York: Irvington, 1979).

6. Robert Aitken Roshi, "Koho'olawe and the Native Hawaiian Movement" (Unpublished manuscript, Honolulu, 1982). See also Peter Matthiessen, *Indian Country* (New York: Viking, 1984).

7. Arne Naess, "Modesty and the Conquest of Mountains," *The Mountain Spirit,* Michael Tobias, ed. (Woodstock, N.Y.: Overlook Press, 1979).

8. Lao Tzu, *Tao Te Ching,* translated by Archie Bahn (New York: Frederic Ungar, 1958), p. 59.

9. Edwin Way Teale, *The Wilderness World of John Muir.* (Boston: Houghton Mifflin, 1954).

10. William Everson, *Archetype West: The Pacific Coast as a Literary Region* (Berkeley: Oyez, 1976), pp. 49-60.

APPENDIX A
ECOSOPHY T
Arne Naess

Arne Naess is a Norwegian, born in 1912. He has been a major source of inspiration in Scandinavian social science and philosophy. He was a professor of philosophy at the University of Oslo from 1939 until 1970, when he resigned to devote himself more fully to the urgent environmental problems facing mankind.

Naess was founder and editor of the interdisciplinary journal in social science and philosophy, *Inquiry*, and has published widely on the philosophy of science, empirical semantics, and Gandhi's theory of nonviolence. He engaged in a major reevaluation of Spinoza's theory of freedom and ethics and wrote on the parallels between certain aspects of Buddhist thinking and Spinoza's philosophy. His work on the philosophy of ecology, or *ecosophy*, developed out of his work on Spinoza and Gandhi and his relationship with the mountains of Norway.

Apart from his career in academia, Naess has been an active mountaineer. He has visited the Himalayas several times and led successful expeditions to Tirich Mir in 1950 and 1964. A bibliography of selected writings by Naess is included at the end of this essay.

On the occasion of his seventieth birthday, former colleagues and students published a *Festschrift* containing fifteen papers inquiring into various aspects of his philosophy together with nine replies from Naess himself, in a volume entitled *In Sceptical Wonder*.

In discussing the relationship between deep ecology and major traditions such as Buddhism and Christianity, Naess stresses that people can agree broadly on a set of principles and disagree greatly on other aspects of ideology or logical derivations. He states the relationship between deep ecology and other traditions thusly:

In order to facilitate discussion it may be helpful to distinguish a common platform (basic principles) of deep ecology from the fundamental features of philosophies and religions from which that platform (basic principles) is derived, if the platform is formulated as a set of norms and hypotheses (factual assumptions). The fundamentals, if verbalized, are Buddhist, Taoist, Christian or of other religious persuasions, or philosophic with affinities to the basic views of Spinoza, Whitehead, Heidegger, or others. The fundamentals are mutually more or less incompatible or at least difficult to compare in terms of cognitive contents. The incompatibility does not affect the deep ecology principles adversely.

The basic principles within the deep ecology movement are grounded in religion or philosophy. In a loose sense, it may be said to be derived from the fundamentals. Because these are different, the situation only reminds us that very similar or even identical conclusions may be drawn from divergent premises. The principles (or platform) are the same, the fundamental premises differ.

In order to clarify the discussion one must avoid looking for one definite philosophy or religion among the supporters of the deep ecological movement.

Fortunately there is a rich manifold of kinds of consequences derived from the principles.

The discussion has four levels to take into account: verbalized fundamental philosophical and religious ideas and intuitions, the deep ecology basic principles, the more or less general consequences derived from the platform — lifestyles and general policies of every kind — and lastly, descriptions of concrete situations and decisions made in them.

From the point of view of derivation one may use the following diagram, the direction of derivation proceeding down the page:

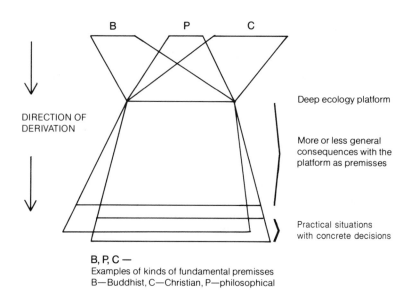

B, P, C —
Examples of kinds of fundamental premisses
B—Buddhist, C—Christian, P—philosophical

In this figure, B, P, and C are not made largely overlapping, chiefly because of the difficulties of formulating agreements and disagreements in relation to texts written in religious language.

It is a characteristic feature of deep ecological literature that it contains positive reference to a formidable number of authors belonging to different traditions and cultures. [1]

As an expert in the areas of philosophical semantics, logic and the methodology of science, Arne Naess has attempted to provide a logical diagram or systematization of his own version of deep ecology or ecosophy which he calls "Ecosophy T." He calls this a normative system which includes both norms (or basic values) and factual hypotheses. The lower norms or action statements are derived from the top norms in a loosely logical sense. The top or most basic norms are arrived at by the deep questioning intuitive process.

226

It is also crucial to remember that his top norm or *ultimate norm,* Self-realization, is meant not in the sense of narrow ego realization nor in the sense often used by Abraham Maslow and other Western humanistic psychologists, but in the sense of *universal self* as described in the perennial philosophy; a self with a capital "S" that identifies not only with the ecosphere but even with the entire universe. The diagram for Ecosophy T appears below.

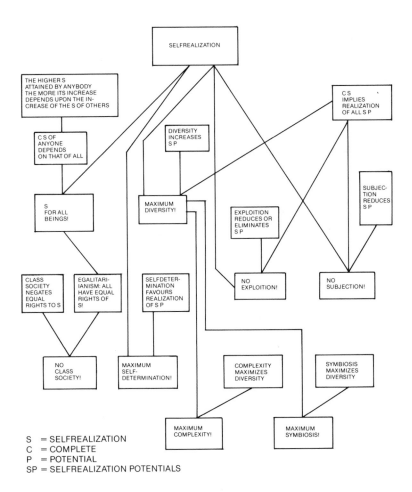

Naess stresses that Ecosophy T is only *his* version of deep ecology, and that many versions need to be worked out. Some people might be critical that many of the norms of deep ecology are held on an intuitive basis, but Naess points out all theories begin somewhere beyond logical constructions.

1. Cp. the 70-page review by George Sessions in R. C. Schultz and J. D. Hughes, eds., *Ecological Consciousness,* University Press of America, 1981.

NAESS, ARNE:
    − *Gandhi and the Nuclear Age* (Totowa, N.J., 1965).
    − "The Shallow and the Deep, Long-Range Ecology Movement," *Inquiry 16* (1973), pp. 95-100.
    − *Gandhi and Group Conflict: An Exploration of Satyagraha—Theoretical Background* (Oslo, 1974).
    − "Notes on the Methodology of Normative Systems," *Methodology and Science 10* (1977), pp. 64-79.
    − "Spinoza and Ecology," in S. Hessing, ed., *Speculum Spinozanum 1677-1977* (London, 1978).
    − "Through Spinoza to Mahayana Buddhism, or through Mahayana Buddhism to Spinoza?" in J. Wetlesen, ed., *Spinoza's Philosophy of Man; Proceedings of the Scandinavian Spinoza Symposium 1977* (Oslo, 1978).
    − "Self-realization in Mixed Communities of Humans, Bears, Sheep and Wolves," *Inquiry 22* (1979), pp. 231-241.
    − "Defense of the Deep Ecology Movement," *Environmental Ethics 6, 3* (1984).
    − "Some Philosophical Implications of the Deep Ecology Movement," *Philosophical Inquiry* (forthcoming).
    − "Identification as a Source of Deep Ecological Attitudes" in Michael Tobias, ed., *Deep Ecology* (San Diego: Avant Books, 1985).

228

APPENDIX B

FEMINISM AND ECOLOGY
Carolyn Merchant

The simultaneous emergence of the women's and environmental movements over the past two decades raises additional questions about the relationships between feminism and ecology. Is there a set of assumptions basic to the science of ecology that also holds implications for the status of women? Is there an ecological ethic that is also a feminist ethic?

The structures and functions of the natural world and of human society interact through a language common to both. Ethics in the form of description, symbol, religion, and myth help to mediate between humans and their world. Choices are implied in the words used to describe nature: choices of ways in which to view the world and ethical choices that influence human behavior toward it. Ecology and feminism have interacting languages that imply certain common policy goals. These linkages might be described as follows:

1. All parts of a system have equal value.

Ecology assigns equal importance to all organic and inorganic components in the structure of an ecosystem. Healthy air, water, and soil—the abiotic components of the system—are as essential as the entire diverse range of biotic parts—plants, animals, and bacteria and fungi. Without each element in the structure, the system as a whole cannot function properly. Remove an element, reduce the number of individuals or species, and erratic oscillations may appear in the larger system.

Similarly, feminism asserts the equality of men and women. Intellectual differences are human differences rather than gender- or race-specific. The lower position of women stems from culture rather than nature. Thus policy goals should be directed toward achieving educational, economic, and political equity for all.

Ecologists and feminists alike will therefore assign value to all parts of the human-nature system and take care to examine the long- and short-range consequences of decisions affecting an individual, group, or species. In cases of ethical conflict, each case must be discussed from the perspective of the interconnectedness of all parts and the good of the whole.

2. The Earth is a home.

The Earth is a habitat for living organisms; houses are habitats for groups of humans. Each ecological niche is a position in a community, a hole in the energy continuum through which materials and energy enter and leave. Ecology is the study of the Earth's household. Human houses, whether sodhouses, igloos, or bungalows, are structures in an environment. Most are places wherein life is sustained—shelters where food is prepared, clothes are repaired, and human beings cared for.

For ecologists and feminists the Earth's house and the human house are habitats to be cherished. Energy flows in and out; molecules and atoms enter and leave. Some chemicals and forms of energy are life-sustaining; others are life-defeating. Those that lead to sickness on the planet or in the home cannot be tolerated. Radioactive wastes or potential radioactive hazards are present in some people's environments. Hazardous chemicals permeate some back-yards and basements. Microwaves, nitrite preservatives, and cleaning chemicals have invaded the kitchen.

The home, where in fact women and children spend much of their time, is no longer a haven. The soil over which the house is built or the rocks used in its construction may emit radon (a radioactive decay product of radium), potentially a source of lung cancer. The walls, furniture, floor coverings, and insulation may contain urea formaldehyde, a nasal, throat, and eye irritant. Leaky gas stoves and furnaces can produce nitrogen dioxide and carbon monoxide, resulting in nausea, headaches, and respiratory illnesses. An underground garage in an apartment building can be an additional source of indoor carbon monoxide. The home's faucets may be piping in carcinogenic drinking water, formed by the action of chlorine on organic compounds in reservoir supplies.

Disinfectants sprayed where people eat or children play may contain phenols, creosols, or ammonium chlorides that can produce toxic effects on the lungs, liver, and kidneys, or act as nervous system depressants. Oven cleaners may contain caustic alkalis.

The bathroom and bedroom may feature cosmetics and shampoos that can produce headaches, eye-makeup contaminated by bacteria and fungi, deodorants laced with hexachlorophene, and hairdyes containing aromatic amines that have been linked to cancer.

The kitchen may have a microwave oven and the living room a color television emitting low-level radiation when in use. The refrigerator may be stocked with food containing nitrite preservatives, food dyes, and saccharin-filled "low-cal" drinks suspected as potential carcinogens. In the cupboards pewter pitchers or dishes containing lead glazes can slowly contribute to lead poisoning, especially when in contact with acidic foods. The indoor atmosphere may be filled with smoke, containing particles that remain in the air and accumulate even in the lungs of non-smokers. For ecologists and feminists alike, the goal must be the reversal of these life-defeating intrusions and the restoration of healthy indoor and outdoor environments.

3. Process is primary.

The first law of thermodynamics, which is also the first law of ecology, asserts the conservation of energy in an ecosystem as energy is changed and exchanged in its continual flow through the interconnected parts. The total amount of energy entering and leaving the Earth is the same. The science of ecology studies the energy flow through the system of living and non-living parts on the Earth. All components are parts of a steady-state process of growth and development, death and decay. The world is active and dynamic; its natural processes are cyclical, balanced by cybernetic, stabilizing, feedback mechanisms.

The stress on dynamic processes in nature has implications for change and process in human societies. The exchange and flow of information through the human community is the basis for decision making. Open discussion of all alternatives in which ecologists and technologists, lawyers and workers, women and men participate as equals is an appropriate goal for both environmentalists and feminists. Each individual has experience and knowledge that is of value to the human-nature community.

4. There is no free lunch.

"No free lunch" is the essence of the laws of thermodynamics. To produce organized matter, energy in the form of work is needed. But each step up the ladder of organized life, each material object produced, each commodity manufactured increases entropy in its surroundings, and hence increases the reservoir of energy unavailable for work.

Although underpaid environmentalists are said to accept free lunches, nature cannot continue to provide free goods and services for profit-hungry humans, because the ultimate costs are too great. Thus, whenever and wherever possible, that which is taken from nature must be given back through the recycling of goods and the sharing of services.

For feminists, reciprocity and cooperation rather than free lunches and household services are a desirable goal. Housewives frequently spend much of their waking time struggling to undo the effects of the second law of thermodynamics. Continually trying to create order out of disorder is energy consumptive and spiritually costly. Thus the dualism of separate public and private spheres should be severed and male and female roles in both the household and the workplace merged. Cooperation between men and women in each specific context — childrearing, day-care centers, household work, productive work, sexual relations, etc. — rather than separate gender roles could create emotional rewards. Men and women would engage together in the production of use-values and would work together to scale down the production of commodities that are costly to nature. Technologies appropriate to the task, technologies having a low impact on the environment, would be chosen whenever possible.

APPENDIX C
GANDHI, DOGEN AND DEEP ECOLOGY
Robert Aitken Roshi

A friend once inquired if Gandhi's aims in settling in the village and serving the villagers as best he could were purely humanitarian. Gandhi replied . . . "I am here to serve no one else but myself, to find my own self-realization through the service of these village folk."[1]

This remarkable conversation reveals Gandhi's stature as a world teacher. It is a true *mondo,* with the enlightened one responding to the fixed attitude of the questioner, turning the question around and using it as a vehicle for showing the truth that the question in its original form actually obscured.

The question was asked, not without malice, from the conventional suspicion of generosity: Isn't everything you do for others really a way of aggrandizing yourself? Is there really such a thing as pure generosity? Is it possible to live just for others? Aren't you serving your own psychological needs by living with poor people like this?

Gandhi replied from a point of view that is not conventional. He omits the word "humanitarian" entirely from his reply, and indeed I wonder if it is found anywhere in his writings or speeches. For the questioner, humanitarianism seems unrealistic, and in effect, Gandhi acknowledges this, agreeing in order to make a deeper point.

Like a judo expert, Gandhi uses the energy and thrust of the other. Challenged to deny that he is just serving himself, he does not deny it at all, but takes the challenge a step further, and states clearly that the villagers are serving him.

This is not self-aggrandizement, but the way of self-realization, as Gandhi says. Ego-concerns vanish, and the true nature of the one who observes and takes action becomes clear. It is none other than all beings and all things. Thomas Merton observes that Gandhi's practice was the awakening of India and of the world within himself[2] — or, I would say, as himself. Merton obviously felt this was an existential awakening, but whether it was existential or merely political, the truth remains: the other is no other than myself.

The conventional view that serving others is a means for self-aggrandizement is the view that accepts exploitation of people and the environment, wars between nations, and conflicts within the family. As Yasutani Hakuun Roshi used to say, the fundamental delusion of humanity is to suppose that I am here and you are out there.

Gandhi's view is traditionally Eastern, and is found with differing emphases in Hinduism, Taoism, and in Theravada and Mahayana Buddhism. For Dōgen Zenji and for Zen Buddhists generally, the way is openness to all beings, all things. Each being confirms my self nature, but if I seek to control the other, I fall into delusion.

That the self advances and confirms the myriad things is called delusion.
That the myriad things advance and confirm the self is enlightenment.[3]
— Genjōkōan

The self imposing upon the other is not only something called delusion, it is the ruination of our planet and all of its creatures. But enlightenment is not just a matter of learning from another human being. When the self is forgotten, it is recreated again and again, ever more richly, by the myriad things and beings of the universe:

The wild deer, wand'ring here & there
Keeps the Human Soul from Care. [4]

This is not just a matter of sensing the oneness of the universe. Stars of a tropical sky spread across the ceiling of my mind, and the cool wind unlocks my car.

Such experiences are not philosophy, and are not confined to the traditional East, but in the past two hundred years, East or West, we must look to the periphery of culture, rather than to the mainstream, to find anything similar. The mainstream follows a utilitarian interpretation of God's instructions to Noah:

And the fear of you and the dread of you shall be upon every beast of the earth, and upon every fowl of the air, and upon all that moveth on the earth, and upon all the fishes of the sea; into your hand they are delivered. [5]

It is only a very few, relatively isolated geniuses in the West, such as Wordsworth and Thoreau, who have taught confirmation of the human self by nature, and the crime of confirming nature by the self. For example, here Wordsworth echoes Dōgen:

Think you, 'mid all this mighty sum
Of things for ever speaking,
That nothing of itself will come,
But we must still be seeking? [6]

Openness to the myriad things follows what George Sessions, in his discussion of deep ecology, calls conversion:

The forester ecologist Aldo Leopold underwent a dramatic conversion from the "stewardship" shallow ecology resource-management mentality of man-over-nature to announce that humans should see themselves realistically as "plain members" of the biotic community. After the conversion, Leopold saw steadily and with "shining clarity" as he broke through the anthropocentric illusions of his time and began "thinking like a mountain." [7]

Man-over-nature is the self advancing and confirming the myriad things, an anthropocentric delusion. It is the same mind-set as Americans over Vietnamese, or men over women, or managers over workers, or whites over blacks.

The Deep Ecology movement has grown out of the despair of ecologists over the conventional resource-management mentality which is rapidly depleting our minerals, razing our forests, and poisoning our rivers and lakes. It is precisely the same as the welfare society mentality that manages human resources for the short-term benefit of the managers themselves.

Readers of the conventional media have more awareness of the dangers of war and nuclear poison than they have of the biological holocaust involved in clearing jungles, strip-mining mountains, disrupting the balance of life in oceans, and draining coastal swamps. One must read the journals and bulletins of ecological societies to gain a perspective of the accelerating global disaster that our luxurious way of life is bringing down upon us all.

233

But even with knowledge, I wonder if it would be possible to reverse the machine of death and destruction. We in the peace movement have sought to levitate the Pentagon, falling into the same delusion that Dōgen Zenji warns us about. When we stopped the B-1 Bomber, we got the Cruise Missile. When we stopped the Omnibus Crime Bill, we got another Omnibus Crime Bill. When we stopped LBJ, we got Richard Nixon.

The point is that, with all our good intentions, we are still seeking to advance and control the myriad things. The alternative is not just to respond passively or to run away. Once one thinks like a mountain, the whole world is converted. All things confirm me. Then I sit on dōjō cushions which do not move. There is no controller and no one to control.

I think again of Gandhi, urging each of us to follow our own light. Erik H. Erikson suggests that Gandhi held fast to his values to the exclusion of human needs in his family and even in his nation. [8] Probably so. We need not venerate him blindly. With all his flaws, he was surely a forerunner of a New Reformation that seeks to encourage self-sufficiency and personal responsibility for all beings and all things.

In the Buddhist world we have in the past generation seen the development of Sarvodaya Shramana in Sri Lanka, the Coordination Group for Religion in Society in Thailand, the School of Youth for Social Service in South Vietnam, and Ittōen in Japan. These movements developed in the modern zeitgeist of social consciousness, and have found guidance in the Buddhist doctrine of non-ego and in the Buddhist precepts, just as Gandhi could find guidance for the Indian independence movement in the ancient Hindu doctrine of self-reliance.

In the Christian world, we have seen the rise of similar movements, notably the Catholic Worker, an anarchist network of communal houses in dozens of American cities, set up by families of laymen and laywomen to feed the poor, clothe them, and shelter them, just as Jesus taught: "Inasmuch as you have done it to one of the least of these my brothers and sisters, you have done it to me."

These movements grew from their roots with the understanding that confirmation by the myriad things is not just an esoteric experience confined within monastery walls. Swaraj, or independence, was for Gandhi the self-reliance of individuals who practiced the way of realization by complete openness to the British, the ultimate "other" for colonial India. It is also, as Gandhi indicated to the one who questioned his humanitarianism, the practice of being with the poor, the handicapped, the oppressed, thinking as they do, drawing water and digging the earth as they do. It is the practice of realization through their service—and through the service of all others, including police and politicians.

The practice of "being with them" converts the third person, *they, it, she, he,* into the first person, *I* and *we.* For Dōgen Zenji, the others who are "none other than myself" include mountains, rivers, and the great earth. When one thinks like a mountain, one thinks also like the black bear, and this is a step beyond Gandhi's usual concerns to deep ecology, which requires openness to the black bear, becoming truly intimate with him.

This is compassion, suffering with others. "Dwell nowhere, and bring forth that mind." [10] "Nowhere" is the zero of purest experience, known inwardly as peace and rest. To "come forth" is to stand firmly and contain the myriad things. For the peace or ecology worker, the message of the *Diamond Sutra* would be: "From that place of fundamental peace, come forth as a man or woman of peace, presenting peace in the inmost community of those who would destroy it."

NOTES

Thanks to George Sessions, whose paper, "Spinoza, Perennial Philosophy, and Deep Ecology," was a direct inspiration for this essay. (Mimeo., Sierra College, Rocklin, Calif., 1979). I was told that Arne Naess, the Norwegian ecophilosopher who coined the term "deep ecology," is now using the expression "New Philosophy of Nature" as something less divisive and invidious.

1. Jag Parvesh Chander, *Teachings of Mahatma Gandhi* (Lahore: The India Book Works, 1945), p. 375. (Tähtinen, *Non-violence as an Ethical Principle,* p. 83.)

2. Thomas Merton, *Gandhi on Non-violence* (New York: New Directions, 1965), p. 5.

3. Cf. Maezumi, *The Way of Everyday Life* (Los Angeles: Center Publications, 1978), n.p.

4. William Blake, "Auguries of Innocence," *Poetry and Prose of William Blake,* Geoffrey Keynes, ed. (London: Nonesuch Library, 1961), p. 118.

5. Genesis 9:2.

6. William Wordsworth, "Expostulation and Reply," *Lyrical Ballads,* W. J. B. Owens, ed. (New York: Oxford University Press, 1967), p. 104.

7. Sessions, "Spinoza, Perennial Philosophy, and Deep Ecology," p. 15. Space is too limited for a complete discussion of deep ecology, which naturally must include provision for agriculture and other kinds of environmental management. It is the mind-set which would exploit the future and exterminate species which the ecophilosophers wish to see turned around.

8. Erik H. Erikson, *Gandhi's Truth: On the Origins of Militant Nonviolence* (New York: Norton, 1969), especially p. 251.

9. Matthew 24:40.

10. See A. F. Price, trans., "The Diamond Sutra," Book One of *The Diamond Sutra and the Sutra of Hui Hong* (Boulder: Shambhala, 1969), p. 74.

APPENDIX D
WESTERN PROCESS METAPHYSICS
(HERACLITUS, WHITEHEAD,
AND SPINOZA)
George Sessions

Since the demise of logical positivism in the 195Cs, a number of philosophers in the West have begun the search for a new metaphysical synthesis for Western society. The first new metaphysics to gain considerable acceptance was a sophisticated mechanistic materialism in the late 1950s in the form of the mind-brain identity theory of J. J. C. Smart and others, having its historical roots in Hobbes and ultimately Democritus. But there has also been a minor process metaphysical tradition in the West which is now seen to be more compatible with recent developments in theoretical physics, ecology, and with Eastern metaphysics.

The process metaphysics of the Presocratic pantheist, Heraclitus, has been mentioned by several theorists as a possible basis for an ecological metaphysics for the West. The Presocratics, especially Anaxamander, Pythagoras, Heraclitus, and Empedocles, developed perennial philosophies which were pantheistic and surprisingly ecological, as they both engaged in theoretical scientific specula-tion and attempted to reconcile the emerging science with spiritual develop-ment and nature mysticism. The parallels between these systems and Eastern philosophy/religion is startling, including a rejection of the ideas of historical progress in favor of a cyclical conception of time which accorded the natural seasons and the growth cycles of organisms, together with theories of the har-mony resulting from the conflict of opposites. Unfortunately, our knowledge of these systems is quite fragmentary and often conjectural.

There have been contemporary philosophers who, for a number of years, have advocated the panpsychistic process "philosophy of organicism" of twentieth-century theorist Alfred North Whitehead. Philosophers such as Charles Hartshorne and John Cobb, Jr., have recently argued its relevance as a basis for the New Philosophy of Nature. But many of these theorists, who also happen to be Christian theists, when applying Whiteheadian process metaphysics to the problems of environmental ethics, argue that, in their esti-mation, humans have the greatest degree and highest quality of sentience, or consciousness, hence humans have the highest value and the most rights in Nature. In a manner similar to the attempt to "extend" humanistic ethical theory to the nonhuman, there is what Rodman points to as a "pecking order in this moral barnyard." This attempt to apply Whiteheadian panpsychism, while positing various degrees of intrinsic value to the rest of Nature, nonetheless merely reinforces existing Western anthropocentrism, and thus fails to meet the deep ecology norm of "ecological egalitarianism in principle."

Philosopher Ervin Laszlo has made a major effort to develop a Whitehead-ian metaphysical synthesis which results in a nonanthropocentric ethic. He calls this a "neo-Whiteheadianism" supplemented by the general systems the-ory of Ludwig von Bertalanffy, which results in a moral attitude of "reverence for natural systems"—an attitude which, he claims, "already pervades the minds of today's younger generation." Reverence for natural systems is a kind of ecosystem ethics:

... a reverence for our own kind when our vision is wide enough to see ourselves not only in our children, family and compatriots, and not even in all human beings and all living things, but in all self-maintaining and self-evolving organizations brought forth on this good earth and, if not perturbed by man, existing here in complex but supremely balanced hierarchical inter-dependencies. [1]

The ecological view of Nature as a vast hierarchy of interrelated systems brings us to the great pantheistic process metaphysics of seventeenth-century Dutch philosopher Baruch Spinoza. Stuart Hampshire, who has long been an advocate of Spinoza's theory of mind and concepts of human freedom and ethics, points out that Spinoza's metaphysics provides us with a "model of systems within systems each with its own characteristic equilibrium of forces (of individuals within individuals, of increasing power and complexity, each type of individual differentiated by its characteristic activity in self maintenance)." [2]

While philosophers of a materialist persuasion have been increasingly drawn to Spinoza's system, the most radical developments in Spinoza scholarship have come about through the work of Arne Naess and Paul Wienpahl. Naess worked with the Vienna Circle of positivists in the 1930s and has described his drift away from "scientism" to the philosophy of Spinoza. Paul Wienpahl also found himself a "philosopher without a position" in the 1950s and set about to study Buddhism by spending time in a Zen monastery in Japan in 1959. This experience and continued meditation gave him fresh insight into Spinoza, whereupon he recently completed a totally new translation of the complete works of Spinoza which results in a very "Eastern" process metaphysics. Wienpahl also argues, contrary to conventional interpretations, that true *understanding* occurs only at the intuitive mystical level; all forms of conceptualization are levels of *imagination,* under the Spinozistic system. As Wienpahl describes Spinozistic metaphysics, given the new translations: "You find that you can view your world as a kind of fluidity. The ocean is a suitable simile. There is BEING and the modes of being, constantly rising up from it, and just as constantly subsiding into it. . . . Perceived clearly and distinctly, God is Being." [3]

As a result of this recent fruitful Spinoza scholarship, a number of philosophers are looking to Spinoza's system as a unique Western basis for deep ecology. Arne Naess recently had some very strong positive things to say about Spinoza:

The increased interest in meditation and Mahayana Buddhism has resulted in a search for a philosophy that might be understandable in the West and takes care of basic insights of the East. A philosophy inspired by Spinoza may be the answer or one answer. . . . Part Five of [Spinoza's] Ethics *represents, as far as I can understand, Middle East wisdom par excellence. Spinoza fits in with Eastern traditions in a way that makes it highly unlikely that he can be completely absorbed in any of the major Western trends . . . the system of Spinoza is highly precarious: its pretension is extreme in so far as it tries to take care of everything of lasting value in every major tradition, East and West, even when the values seem mutually utterly inconsistent . . . [and in addition] no great philosopher has so much to offer in the way of clarification and articulation of basic ecological attitudes as Baruch Spinoza.* [4]

Historically, Spinoza's system has had a major influence on those thinkers who have been most influential in resisting the development of the modern homocentric technological worldview and society. Some of the leading figures of the European Romantic movement (Goethe, Coleridge, Wordsworth, and Shelley) read Spinoza and were impressed with his religious vision of the unity and divinity of Nature. And, indirectly, then, the American Transcendentalists (Emerson, Thoreau, and Muir) also felt the impress of Spinoza, although Muir was probably the only one to overcome the idealistic subjectivism of Romanticism and return to the more objective nonanthropocentrism of Spinoza. Spinoza had a strong formative influence on George Santayana, Bertrand Russell, Albert Einstein, and Robinson Jeffers. And Wittgenstein's pantheism has been compared with Spinozism. Spinoza's system is very similar to Eastern religions, and Norwegian philosopher Jon Wetlesen has just finished a meticulous academic comparison of Spinozism and the ways of enlightenment of Mahayana Buddhism. [5]

Spinozism is clearly a modern version of perennial philosophy. Stuart Hampshire once pointed out that Spinoza's "metaphysics and dependent theory of knowledge are designed to show man's place in nature as a thinking being. Spinoza always argued that, until this is understood, nothing can be said about the nature and possibility of human happiness and freedom. Ethics without metaphysics must be nonsense; we must first know what our potentialities are and what our situation is as parts of Nature."

Spinoza's metaphysics is a conceptualization of the idea of unity; there can be only one Substance or non-dualism which is infinite, and this Substance is also God or Nature. What we experience as the mental and the physical have no separate metaphysical reality, but rather are aspects or attributes of this one Substance. Individual things, such as Mt. Everest, humans, trees, and chipmunks, are temporary expressions of the continual flux of God/Nature/Substance, and he calls them modifications or modes. Spinozism can be thought of as a kind of panpsychism; there is sentience throughout Nature, but there is also matter throughout Nature. But Spinoza is not a materialist, an idealist, or a dualist; in this respect he is metaphysically neutral.

Spinoza's epistemology/psychology is the key to his idea of spiritual development and ethics. He tells us in the *Treatise on the Improvement of the Understanding* that the attempt to find lasting happiness by catering to ego desires is doomed to defeat. We must break free from the bonds of desire and ignorance which captivate and frustrate most humans, and attain a higher Self ("a human nature much more stable") which is aligned with a correct understanding of God/Nature. And Spinoza thought that the theoretical sciences can play an important role in the attainment of this higher Self. Unlike his contemporaries, Bacon, Descartes, and Leibniz, who saw the role of science primarily in terms of the egoistic technological domination and mastery of Nature, Spinoza claimed that "I want to direct all the sciences to a single field and goal, this being the attainment of the supreme human perfection which we have described. Thus anything that belongs to the sciences and does not advance us toward our goal will have to be dismissed out of hand; for to put it in a word, all our thoughts and deeds have got to be directed to this one end."

238

Spinoza's account of how humans can acquire true and adequate ideas of God/Nature and themselves (and thus achieve spiritual emancipation) is similar to the Platonic path to wisdom, and to many of the perennial philosophies in the West and East. Most people are like the slaves in Plato's cave; they have mostly *opinion* about causal sequences in Nature in that their perceptions and thoughts are colored by their ego desires. They are essentially helpless and *passive,* moved by emotions, fears, and desires based on ignorance and imagination, and living life largely by reacting to *external* causes and situations. A rational scientific knowledge of the world, however, can raise a human to a higher level of knowing and being, according to Spinoza, where one can at least begin the process of psychic rearrangement which is a prelude to transcending one's narrowly egoistic subjectivity. As Jacob Needleman describes this:

Surely every serious student of modern science knows those moments when the intellectual grasp of a lawful pattern in nature freed him from his own subjective perceptions of what is before him, embroiled as these perceptions are in the tormented machinations of the ego. This brief release from ordinary thought, which is a foretaste of inner freedom, occurs when the mind is touched by a relatively objective idea. Why then did modern man forget that so much of the value of apprehending scientific law lies just in this quality of direct self-knowledge which such apprehending brings? How did he not see that if a general law of nature is objective it is also a law of man's own nature?[6]

But the highest level of knowledge, for Spinoza, is direct intuitive knowledge of individual things (modes) and this is clearly a mystical kind of knowing. The subject/object distinction disappears — actually, one goes beyond all conceptual knowledge, and experiences the "union that the mind has with the whole of Nature." And only at this level is there *understanding;* all lesser forms of "knowing" consist of increasingly inadequate ideas based on the *imagination.* As Paul Wienpahl describes this:

The first characteristic, then, that sets understanding off from imagination is that it is affective as well as cognitive (one sees the idea of unity at work here). A second is that understanding concerns singular things directly; whereas imagination always does so by means of some kind of images, whereby "images" is to be meant any means of representing a thing. Thus images include words, ideas insofar as they are like "mute pictures on a tablet," and what Spinoza calls "universal notions," such as Human Being, Dog, Horse, etc. A good way of seeing this difference between imagination and understanding is in terms of a metaphor that occurs throughout Spinoza's writings: dreaming with our eyes open as contrasted with being awake. In imagination individual things are always seen, as if in a dream, with some image between us and the thing. With understanding the thing itself or the being of the thing is present to a Mind.[7]

Spinoza's system is sometimes thought of as being "too rationalistic," but one can see that it was meant to lead from the passive slave to active freedom for humans, by grasping God as manifested in individual beings via direct intuitive awareness with one's *whole* being (what Wienpahl translates as "God's understanding love"). This is very similar to certain forms of Buddhist mysticism, and to what Henri Bergson called "a true empiricism": direct unmediated perception which eliminates all conceptualization to grasp the absolute uniqueness of each individual thing.

While scientific knowledge is a kind of "seeing things under the aspect of eternity," it ultimately is only a higher and more objective form of imagination than mere opinion, but it can lead to direct understanding. Given that all rational conceptualization is a form of imagination, what would Spinoza have to say of his own rational-logical metaphysical system? Like theoretical science, it too is a higher form of imagination which can help guide one to intuitive understanding. Wittgenstein seemed to understand his metaphysical system in the *Tractatus* in a similar way (6.54): "My propositions serve as elucidation in the following way: anyone who understands me eventually recognizes them as nonsensical, when one has used them — as steps — to climb up beyond them. (He must, so to speak, throw away the ladder after he has climbed up it.) He must transcend these propositions, and then he will see the world aright. What we cannot speak about we must pass over in silence."

As one passes from a state of slavery to one of active internal freedom, one experiences joy in one's whole being.

Some Spinoza scholars have recently claimed that an ecological interpretation of Spinozism is not justified.[8] There are notes in the *Ethics* where Spinoza says that we can treat other animals in any way which best suits us. Professors E. M. Curley and Genevieve Lloyd have argued that although the metaphysics is nonanthropocentric, the ethics is rightfully anthropocentric. Schopenhauer, who was steeped in Eastern philosophy, was quick to pick up on the anomolous attitude of Spinoza toward other animals: "Spinoza's contempt for animals, as mere things for our use, and declared by him to be without rights, is thoroughly Jewish, and in conjunction with pantheism is at the same time absurd and abominable." Arne Naess and I agree that Schopenhauer was correct in his criticism of Spinoza. Naess admits that although Spinoza himself was what we would now call a "speciesist," his system is not speciesist. Naess claims:

[For Spinoza] all particular things are expressions of God; through all of them God acts. There is no hierarchy. There is no purpose, no final causes such that one can say that the "lower" exist for the sake of the "higher." There is an ontological democracy or equalitarianism which, incidentally, greatly offended his contemporaries, but of which ecology makes us more tolerant today.[9]

Spinoza's system does not result in a moral or ethical theory in the usual sense of the term. Spinoza does not speak of moral "rights" or "duties," rather it is an ethics of what we would now call "self realization." We can continue to speak of the "rights" of other beings, but only in the metaphorical sense of allowing human and nonhuman individuals "to live and blossom" and arrive at their own unique forms of self-realization and completion.

Some have also thought that mysticism and the contemplative life in both its Eastern and Western forms necessarily leads to a "do nothing" inward withdrawal from the world and its problems. There would be little or no basis or motivation to act on the behalf of other people, other species, or the protection of ecosystems. But, on the contrary, Naess sees the Spinozistic free person as a very active, powerful individual, as a sort of *karmayogi* in the tradition of Buddha or Gandhi:

The supremely free human being according to Wetlesen's Spinoza is one of introvert tranquility. The foregoing comments favor an activist interpretation: The free human being is a wise human being permanently and with increasing

240

momentum on the road to still higher levels of freedom. The supremely free person shows perfect equanimity, forceful, rich and deep affects, and is active in a great variety of ways corresponding to the many "parts of the body," and all of them bound up with increasing understanding—and certainly including social and political acts. . . . This image of the sage has in common with (a certain variety of) Mahayana Buddhism the idea that the higher level of freedom reached by an individual, the more difficult it gets to increase the level without increasing that of all other beings, human and nonhuman. . . . It again rests on identification with all beings. [10]

As our understanding of God increases with our understanding of individuals in this intuitive mystical sense, and our identification with all beings increases with our increase in internal power and freedom, does this expanded identification with God/Nature eventually coalesce with an ecosystem or environmental ethics? An answer to this question depends largely on what can count as an "individual." For Spinoza, the most obvious (paradigm) case of an individual was a human being and, since the nature of individual humans is more similar to each other than to other animals, we can come to know ourselves and perhaps certain selected other humans in this direct way, after long years of intense hard work. But can this way of understanding extend to other animals, domestic and wild, and, for example, to individual trees? Ethologists such as Jane Goodall seem to begin to understand in this way chimpanzees and other animals with which they have worked and lived for many years. And Paul Shepard has argued that we all need to understand large wild animals in this way to model ourselves after and become fully human. [11]

Can our identification extend still further, can we begin to "think like a mountain" and come to understand El Capitan and Mt. Everest after long, intimate acquaintance and interaction? Spinozistic understanding involves a way of being and living with the other. Paul Wienpahl has claimed that he has come to understand his mate, his dog, and a particular hillside near his home in this intuitive way. One suspects that John Muir understood Yosemite and other parts of the Sierra with "God's understanding love," as did Thoreau of Walden Pond, Jeffers of parts of the Big Sur coast, and Ed Abbey of the desert country of Utah and Arizona.

It seems clear that many individuals and societies throughout history have developed an intuitive mystical sense of interpenetration with the landscape and an abiding and all-pervading "sense of place." Some field ecologists may, on occasion, rise above their professionally scientific approach to Nature (e. g., the quantitative measurement of energy transfers of biomass) and begin to apprehend ecosystems intuitively. Rachel Carson and Loren Eiseley seem to have been good examples of this. And if the Gaia hypothesis, recently advanced by two professional ecologists, is true ("the system of the Earth's biosphere seems to exhibit the behavior of a single organism, even a living creature"), then the whole biosphere would count as a Spinozistic individual and would thus be at least theoretically understandable on the level of "God's understanding love." Of course, Taoists/Buddhists have long held that to overcome society-produced ego and find Self, one must at least temporarily get away from society and other humans and align one's Self with the Tao (the *way* of God/Nature) in wilderness.

NOTES

1. Ervin Laszlo, *Introduction to Systems Theory,* chapter 14 (New York: Gordon and Breach, 1972).

2. S. Hampshire, *Spinoza* (New York: Penguin Books, 1951), pp. 17-81; *Freedom of the Mind and Other Essays* (New Jersey: Princeton University Press, 1971), and *Two Theories of Morality* (New York: Oxford University Press, 1977).

3. Arne Naess, *Freedom, Emotion, and Self-Subsistence: The Structure of a Central Part of Spinoza's Ethics* (Oslo: University of Oslo Press, 1975); Paul Wienpahl, *The Radical Spinoza* (New York: New York University Press, 1979).

4. Naess, "Through Spinoza to Mahayana Buddhism, or Through Mahayana Buddhism to Spinoza?" in Jon Wetlesen, ed., *Spinoza's Philosophy of Man* (Oslo: University Press of Oslo, 1978).

5. Jon Wetlesen, *The Sage and the Way: Spinoza's Ethics of Freedom* (Oslo: University of Oslo Press, 1978).

6. Jacob Needleman, *A Sense of the Cosmos* (New York: Doubleday, 1975), p. 35.

7. Paul Wienpahl, "Spinoza's Mysticism," in Wetlesen, *Spinoza's Philosophy of Man,* op. cit.

8. E. M. Curley, "Man and Nature in Spinoza," in Wetlesen, *Spinoza's Philosophy of Man,* op. cit., and Genevieve Lloyd, "Spinoza's Environmental Ethics," together with Naess's reply to Lloyd, in *Inquiry, 23, 3* (Oslo, 1980).

9. Naess, *Freedom, Emotion and Self-Subsistance,* pp. 118-119, and *Ecology, Community, and Lifestyle, A Philosophical Approach* (Oslo: University of Oslo Press, 1977).

10. Naess, "Through Spinoza to Mahayana Buddhism," op. cit.; "Spinoza and Ecology," in S. Hessing, ed., *Speculum Spinozanum* (Massachusetts: Routledge & Kegan Paul, 1978), and "Reply to Richard Watson's Critique of Deep Ecology," *Environmental Ethics,* 6, 3 (Fall 1984).

11. Paul Shepard, *Thinking Animals* (New York: Viking, 1978).

APPENDIX E
ANTHROPOCENTRISM
John Seed

But the time is not a strong prison either.
A little scraping the walls of dishonest contractor's concrete
Through a shower of chips and sand makes freedom.
Shake the dust from your hair. This mountain sea-coast is real
For it reaches out far into the past and future;
It is part of the great and timeless excellence of things. [1]

"Anthropocentrism" or "homocentrism" means human chauvinism. Similar to sexism, but substitute "human race" for "man" and "all other species" for "woman."

Human chauvinism, the idea that humans are the crown of creation, the source of all value, the measure of all things, is deeply embedded in our culture and consciousness.

And the fear of you and the dread of you shall be upon every beast of the earth, and upon every fowl of the air, and upon all that moveth on the earth, and upon all the fishes of the sea; into your hands they are delivered. [2]

When humans investigate and see through their layers of anthropocentric self-cherishing, a most profound change in consciousness begins to take place.

Alienation subsides. The human is no longer an outsider, apart. Your humanness is then recognized as being merely the most recent stage of your existence . . . you start to get in touch with yourself as mammal, as vertebrate, as a species only recently emerged from the rain forest. As the fog of amnesia disperses, there is a transformation in your relationship to other species, and in your commitment to them.

What is described here should not be seen as merely intellectual. The intellect is one entry point to the process outlined, and the easiest one to communicate. For some people, however, this change of perspective follows from actions on behalf of mother Earth.

"I am protecting the rain forest" develops to "I am part of the rain forest protecting myself. I am that part of the rain forest recently emerged into thinking."

What a relief then! The thousands of years of imagined separation are over and we begin to recall our true nature. That is, the change is a spiritual one, thinking like a mountain, [3] sometimes referred to as "deep ecology."

As your memory improves, as the implications of evolution and ecology are internalized and replace the outmoded anthropocentric structures in your mind, there is an identification with all life. Then follows the realization that the distinction between "life" and "lifeless" is a human construct. Every atom in this body existed before organic life emerged 4,000 million years ago. Remember our childhood as minerals, as lava, as rocks?

Rocks contain the potentiality to weave themselves into such stuff as this. We are the rocks dancing. Why do we look down on them with such a condescending air? It is they that are the immortal part of us. [4]

243

If we embark upon such an inner voyage, we may find, upon returning to 1983 consensus reality, that our actions on behalf of the environment are purified and strengthened by the experience.

We have found here a level of our being that moth, rust, nuclear holocaust or destruction of the rain forest genepool do not corrupt. The commitment to save the world is not decreased by the new perspective, although the fear and anxiety which were part of our motivation start to dissipate and are replaced by a certain disinterestedness. We act because life is the only game in town, but actions from a disinterested, less attached consciousness may be more effective.

Activists often don't have much time for meditation. The disinterested space we find here may be similar to meditation. Some teachers of meditation are embracing deep ecology[5] and vice versa[6].

Of all the species that have ever existed, it is estimated that less than one in a hundred exist today. The rest are extinct.

As environment changes, any species that is unable to adapt, to change, to evolve, is extinguished. All evolution takes place in this fashion. In this way an oxygen-starved fish, ancestor of yours and mine, commenced to colonize the land. Threat of extinction is the potter's hand that moulds all the forms of life.

The human species is one of millions threatened by imminent extinction through nuclear war and other environmental changes. And while it is true that "human nature" revealed by 12,000 years of written history does not offer much hope that we can change our warlike, greedy, ignorant ways, the vastly longer fossil history assures us that we *can* change. We *are* that fish, and the myriad other death-defying feats of flexibility which a study of evo-lution reveals to us. A certain confidence (in spite of our recent "humanity") is warranted.

From this point of view, the threat of extinction appears as the invitation to change, to evolve. After a brief respite from the potter's hand, here we are back on the wheel again.

The change that is required of us is not some new resistance to radiation, but a change in consciousness. Deep ecology is the search for a viable con-sciousness.

Surely consciousness emerged and evolved according to the same laws as everything else—moulded by environmental pressures. In the recent past, when faced with intolerable environmental pressures, the mind of our ancestors must time and again have been forced to transcend itself.

To survive our current environmental pressures, we must consciously remem-ber our evolutionary and ecological inheritance. We must learn to think like a mountain.

If we are to be open to evolving a new consciousness, we must fully face up to our impending extinction (the ultimate environmental pressure). This means acknowledging that part of us which shies away from the truth, hides in intoxication or busyness from the despair of the human, whose 4,000 mil-lion year race is run, whose organic life is a mere hair's-breadth from finished.[7]

A biocentric perspective, the realization that rocks *will* dance, and that roots go deeper than 4,000 million years, may give us the courage to face despair and break through to a more viable consciousness, one that is sustainable and in harmony with life again.

Protecting something as wide as this planet is still an abstraction for many. Yet I see the day in our lifetime that reverence for the natural systems—the oceans, the rain forests, the soil, the grasslands, and all other living things—will be so strong that no narrow ideology based upon politics or economics will overcome it. (Jerry Brown, Governor of California)[8]

NOTES

1. From the poem "A Little Scraping," *The Selected Poetry of Robinson Jeffers* (New York: Random House, 1933, out of print).

2. Genesis 9:2.

3. "The forester ecologist Aldo Leopold underwent a dramatic conversion from the 'stewardship' shallow ecology resource-management mentality of man-over-nature to announce that humans should see themselves as 'plain members' of the biotic community. After the conversion, Leopold saw steadily, and with 'shining clarity' as he broke through the anthropocentric illusions of his time and began 'thinking like a mountain.'" George Sessions, "Spinoza, Perennial Philosophy and Deep Ecology" (photostat, Sierra College, Rocklin, California, 1979). See also Aldo Leopold, *A Sand County Almanac* (London: O.U.P., 1949).

4. Prominent physicists such as David Bohm (*Wholeness and the Implicate Order,* Routledge, 1980), and biologists and philosophers such as Charles Birch and John Cobb, Jr. (*The Liberation of Life,* Cambridge, 1981) would agree with Alfred North Whitehead that "A thoroughgoing evolutionary philosophy is inconsistent with materialism. The aboriginal stuff, or material from which a materialistic philosophy starts, is incapable of evolution." (*Science and the Modern World,* Fontana, 1975 [first published 1926], p. 133). Similar views to those of these authors on the interpenetration of all "matter" (better conceived of as "events") are developed in Fritjof Capra's *The Tao of Physics* (Fontana, 1976), while the sixth-century B.C. *Tao Te Ching* itself tells us that "Tao" or "the implicate order," as Bohm might say, "is the source of the ten thousand things" (translated by G. Feng and J. English, New York: Vintage, 1972).

5. "For Dōgen Zenji, the others who are 'none other than myself' include mountains, rivers and the great earth. When one thinks like a mountain, one thinks also like the black bear, and this is a step . . . to deep ecology, which requires openness to the black bear, becoming truly intimate with the black bear, so that honey dribbles down your fur as you catch the bus to work." Robert Aitken Roshi, Zen Buddhist teacher, "Gandhi, Dōgen and Deep Ecology," *Zero,* 4 (1980).

6. Theodore Roszak, for example, has written in *Person/Planet* (Victor Gollanz, 1979, p. 296): "I sometimes think there could be no keener criterion to measure our readiness for an economics of permanence than silence." Roszak has argued eloquently in another context that, if ecology is to work in the service of transforming consciousness, it will be because its students recognize the truth contained in a single line of poetry by Kathleen Raine: "It is not birds that speak, but men learn silence." (*Where the Wasteland Ends,* Massachusetts: Faber and Faber, 1974, p. 404).

7. For the creative uses of despair, see Joanna Macy, "Despair Work," *Evolutionary Blues* 1 (1981). For a long look at our impending extinction, see Jonathan Schell, *The Fate of the Earth* (Pan Books, 1982).

8. "Not Man Apart," Friends of the Earth newsletter, 9, 9 (August 1979).

APPENDIX F
RITUAL IS ESSENTIAL
Dolores LaChapelle

Most native societies around the world had three common characteristics: they had an intimate, conscious relationship with their place; they were stable "sustainable" cultures, often lasting for thousands of years; and they had a rich ceremonial and ritual life. They saw these three as intimately connected. Out of the hundreds of examples of this, consider the following:

1. The Tukano Indians of the Northwest Amazon River basin, guided by their shamans who are conscious ecologists, make use of various myths and rituals that prevent over-hunting or over-fishing. They view their universe as a circuit of energy in which the entire cosmos participates. The basic circuit of energy consists of "a limited quantity of procreative energy that flows continually between man and animals, between society and nature." Reichel-Dolmatoff, the Columbian anthropologist, notes that the Tukano have very little interest in exploiting natural resources more effectively but are greatly interested in "accumulating more factual knowledge about biological reality and, above all, about knowing what the physical world requires from men."

2. The Kung people of the Kalahari desert have been living in exactly the same place for 11,000 years! They have very few material belongings but their ritual life is one of the most sophisticated of any group.

3. Roy Rappaport has shown that the rituals of the Tsembaga of New Guinea allocate scarce protein for the humans who need it without causing irreversible damage to the land.

4. The longest inhabited place in the United States is the Hopi village of Oraibi. At certain times of the year they may spend up to half their time in ritual activity.

5. Upon the death of their old *cacique,* Santa Ana Pueblo in New Mexico recently elected a young man to take over as the new *cacique.* For the rest of his life he will do nothing else whatsoever but take care of the ritual life of the Pueblo. *All* his personal needs will be taken care of by the tribe. But he cannot travel any further than sixty miles or one hour distance. The distance has grown further with the use of cars but the time remains the same — one hour away from the Pueblo — his presence is that important to the ongoing life of the Pueblo. They know that it is ritual which embodies the people.

Our Western European industrial culture provides a striking contrast to all these examples. We have idolized ideals, rationality and a limited kind of "practicality," and have regarded the conscious rituals of these other cultures as at best frivolous curiosities. The results are all too evident. We've only been here a few hundred years and already we have done irreparable damage to vast areas of this country now called the U.S. As Gregory Bateson notes, "mere purposive rationality is necessarily pathogenic and destructive of life."

We have tried to relate to the world around us through only the left side of our brain, and we are clearly failing. If we are to re-establish a viable relationship, we will need to rediscover the wisdom of these other cultures who knew that their relationship to the land and to the natural world required the whole of their being. What we call their "ritual and ceremony" was a sophisticated social and spiritual technology, refined through many thousands of years of experience, that maintained their relationship much more successfully than we are.

The human race has forgotten so much in the last 200 years that we hardly know where to begin. But it helps to begin remembering. In the first place, *all* traditional cultures, even our own long-ago Western European cultural ancestors, had seasonal festivals and rituals.

The true origin of most of our modern major holidays dates back to these seasonal festivals. There are four major festivals: winter and summer solstice (when the sun reverses its travels) and spring and autumn equinox (when night and day are equal). But in between each of these major holidays are the "cross quarter days." For example, spring equinox comes around March 21 or 22 but spring is only barely beginning at that time in Europe. True spring—warm reliable spring—doesn't come until later. This is the cross quarter day—May 1—which Europe celebrated with maypoles, gathering flowers, and fertility rites. May became the month of Mary after the Christian church took over and May crownings and processions were devoted to Mary instead of the old "earth goddesses." Summer solstice comes on June 21. The next cross quarter day is Lammas Day in early August. This is the only festival that our country does not celebrate in any way. The Church put the Feast of the Assumption on this day to honor Mary. Fall equinox comes on Sept. 21—the cross quarter day is Hallowe'en, the ancient Samhain of the Celts. Then comes winter solstice—the sun's turn-around point from darkness to light. The cross quarter day between the solstice and spring equinox is in early February—now celebrated in the church as Candlemas.

The purpose of seasonal festivals is periodically to revive the *topocosm*. Gaster coined this word from the Greek— *topo* for place and *cosmos* for world order. Topocosm means "the world order of a particular place." The topocosm is the entire complex of any given locality conceived as a living organism—not just the human community but the total community—the plants, animals, and soils of the place. The topocosm is not only the actual and present living community, but also that continuous entity of which the present community is but the current manifestation.

Seasonal festivals make use of myths, art, dance and games. All of these aspects of ritual serve to connect—to keep open the essential connections within ourselves. Festivals connect the conscious with the unconscious, the right and left hemispheres of the brain, the cortex with the older three brains (this includes the Oriental *tan tien* four fingers below the navel), as well as connecting the human with the non-human—the earth, the sky, the animals and plants.

The next step after seasonal rituals is to acknowledge the non-human co-inhabitants of your place. You can begin by looking into the records of the tribes of Indians who lived there and see what their totem was. Look into the accounts of the early explorers and very early settlers. Barry Lopez relates that the Eskimo told him that their totem animal was always the one who could teach them something they needed to learn.

Beginning in the Northwest, because *In Context* is published in the Northwest, it is fitting that we talk of Salmon. Salmon is the totem animal for the North Pacific Rim. "Only Salmon, as a species, informs us humans, as a species, of the vastness and unity of the North Pacific Ocean and its rim. . . .

248

Totemism is a method of perceiving power, goodness and mutuality in locale through the recognition of and respect for the vitality, spirit and interdependence of other species," as Linn House explains. For at least 20,000 years the Yurok, Chinook, Salish, Kwakiutl, Haida, and Aleut on this side of the rim, and on the other rim of the Pacific, the Ainu (the primitives of Japan) ordered their daily lives according to the timing of the Salmon population.

Several years ago I did some in-depth study of Celtic myth and discovered that Salmon was the totem animal for the Celts, too. According to their myth, there was a sacred well situated under the sea where the sacred Salmon acquired their supernatural wisdom. The famous Celtic hero, Finn, traditionally obtained his wisdom when he sucked on the thumb he had just burnt when picking up the Salmon he cooked. It is not suprising that Salmon links all these areas. The North Pacific Rim and the British Isles are maritime climates in the northern half of the earth. Here is the perfect way to ritualize the link between planetary villagers around the earth — through their totem animal.

How can we learn from Salmon? One specific way is to reclaim our waterways so that Salmon can again flourish. If we reclaim the water so that Salmon can flourish we have reclaimed the soil, the plants and the other species of the ecosystem — restored them to aboriginal health. In so doing we would be restoring full health to our children as well.

Linn House feels that the people who live in or near the spawning ground of Salmon should form associations, not as law enforcement agencies such as the State Fish and Game Department, but as educational groups and providers of ritual and ceremony which would celebrate the interdependence of species. Linn was a Salmon fisherman on Guemes Island; he now lives in Northern California where he is restocking Salmon rivers.

What relevance does this kind of ritual have for people who live in the city? All of us need seasonal and nature rituals wherever we live, but let me give you a specifically urban example.

Siena, Italy, with a population of about 59,000, has the lowest crime rate of any Western city of a comparable size. Delinquency, drug addiction and violence are virtually unknown. Class is not pitted against class nor young against old.

Why? Because it is a tribal, ritualized city organized around the *contrada* (clans) — with names such as Chiocciola, the Snail, Tartule, the Turtle, etc. — and the *Palio* (the annual horse race). The *contrada* function as independent city states. Each has its own flag, its own territorial boundaries, its own discrete identity, church songs, patron saint and rituals. Particular topographical features of each *contrada's* area are ritualized and mythologized. The ritualized city customs extend clear back to the worship of Diana, the Roman goddess of the moon. Her attributes were taken over by the worship of Mary when Christianity came in.

Many famous writers such as Henry James, Ezra Pound and Aldous Huxley sensed the energy of the city and its events and tried to write about it, but none of them even faintly grasped the year-long ritualized life behind it. About one week before the day of the *Palio* race, workmen from the city of Siena begin to bring yellow earth (*la terra* from the fields outside Siena) and spread it over the great central square, the Campo, thus linking the city with its origins in the earth of its *place*. In fact, anytime during the course of the year when someone needs to be cheered up, the sad person is told not to worry because there will be "la terra in piazza" (soon there will be earth in the square).

The horse race serves two main purposes. In the intense rivalry surrounding the race, each *contrada* "rekindles its own sense of identity." The *Palio* also provides the Sienese with an outlet for their aggression and as such is a ritual war. The horse race grew out of games which were actually mimic battles and were used to mark the ends of religious festivals.

The *Palio* is truly a religious event. On this one day of the year the *contrada's* horse is brought into the church of its patron saint. In the act of blessing the horse, the *contrada* itself is blessed. This horse race is the community's greatest rite. "In the *Palio*, all the flames of Hell are transformed into the lights of Paradise," according to a local priest, Don Vittorio.

If we want to build a sustainable culture, it is not enough to "go back to the land." That's exactly where our pioneering ancestors lived and, as the famous Western painter Charles Russell said, "A pioneer is a man who comes to virgin country, traps off all the fur, kills off the wild meat, plows the roots up. . . . A pioneer destroys things and calls it civilization."

If we are to truly re-connect with the land, we need to change our perceptions and approach more than our location. As long as we limit ourselves to rationality and its limited sense of "practicality," we will be disconnected from the "deep ecology" of our place. As Heidegger explains: "Dwelling is not primarily inhabiting but taking care of and creating that space within which something comes into its own and flourishes." It takes both time and ritual for real dwelling. Likewise, as Roy Rappaport observes, "Knowledge will never replace respect in man's dealings with ecological systems, for the ecological systems in which man participates are likely to be so complex that he may never have sufficient comprehension of their content and structure to permit him to predict the outcome of many of his own acts." Ritual is the focused way in which we both experience and express that respect.

Ritual is essential because it is truly the pattern that connects. It provides communication at all levels — communication among all the systems within the individual human organism; between people within groups; between one group and another in a city and throughout all these levels between the human and the non-human in the natural environment. Ritual provides us with a tool for learning to think logically, analogically and ecologically as we move toward a sustainable culture. Most important of all, perhaps, during rituals we have the experience, unique in our culture, of neither *opposing* nature or *trying* to be in communion with nature; but of *finding* ourselves within nature, and that is the key to sustainable culture.

APPENDIX G
BUDDHISM AND THE POSSIBILITIES
OF A PLANETARY CULTURE[1]
Gary Snyder

Buddhism holds that the universe and all creatures in it are intrinsically in a state of complete wisdom, love and compassion, acting in natural response and mutual interdependence. The personal realization of this from-the-beginning state cannot be had for and by one"self" — because it is not fully realized unless one has given the self up and away.

In the Buddhist view, that which obstructs the effortless manifestation of this is Ignorance, which projects into fear and needless craving. Historically, Buddhist philosophers have failed to analyze out the degree to which ignorance and suffering are caused or encouraged by social factors, considering fear and desire to be given facts of the human condition. Consequently, the major concern of Buddhist philosophy is epistemology and "psychology" with no attention paid to historical or sociological problems. Although Mahayana Buddhism has a grand vision of universal salvation, the actual achievement of Buddhism has been the development of practical systems of meditation toward the end of liberating a few dedicated individuals from psychological hangups and cultural conditionings. Institutional Buddhism has been conspicuously ready to accept or ignore the inequalities and tyrannies of whatever political system it found itself under. This can be death to Buddhism, because it is death to any meaningful function of compassion. Wisdom without compassion feels no pain.

No one today can afford to be innocent, or to indulge himself in ignorance of the nature of contemporary governments, politics and social orders. The national politics of the modern world are "states" which maintain their existence by deliberately-fostered craving and fear: monstrous protection rackets. The "free world" has become economically dependent on a fantastic system of stimulation of greed which cannot be fulfilled, sexual desire which cannot be satiated and hatred which has no outlet except against oneself, the persons one is supposed to love, or the revolutionary aspirations of pitiful, poverty-stricken marginal societies. The conditions of the Cold War have turned most modern societies — both Soviet and capitalist — into vicious distorters of true human potential. They try to create populations of "preta" — hungry ghosts, with giant appetites and throats no bigger than needles. The soil, the forests and all animal life are being consumed by these cancerous collectivities; the air and water of the planet is being fouled by them.

There is nothing in human nature or the requirements of human social organization which intrinsically requires that a society be contradictory, repressive and productive of violent and frustrated personalities. Findings in anthropology and psychology make this more and more evident. One can prove it for oneself by taking a good look at Original Nature through meditation. Once a person has this much faith and insight, one will be led to a deep concern with the need for radical social change through a variety of nonviolent means.

The joyous and voluntary poverty of Buddhism becomes a positive force. The traditional harmlessness and avoidance of taking life in any form has nation-shaking implications. The practice of meditation, for which one needs only "the ground beneath one's feet" wipes out mountains of junk being pumped into the mind by the mass media and supermarket universities. The belief in a serene and generous fulfillment of natural loving desires destroys ideologies which blind, maim and repress—and points the way to a kind of community which would amaze "moralists" and transform armies of men who are fighters because they cannot be lovers.

Avatamsaka (Kegon or Hua-yen) Buddhist philosophy sees the world as a vast interrelated network in which all objects and creatures are necessary and illuminated. From one standpoint, governments, wars, or all that we consider "evil" are uncompromisingly contained in this totalistic realm. The hawk, the swoop and the hare are one. From the "human" standpoint we cannot live in those terms unless all beings see with the same enlightened eye. The Bodhisattva lives by the sufferer's standard, and he or she must be effective in aiding those who suffer.

The mercy of the West has been social revolution; the mercy of the East has been individual insight into the basic self/void. We need both. They are both contained in the traditional three aspects of the Dharma path: wisdom (prajña), meditation (dhyāna), and morality (sila). Wisdom is intuitive knowledge of the mind of love and clarity that lies beneath one's ego-driven anxieties and aggressions. Meditation is going into the mind to see this for yourself—over and over again, until it becomes the mind you live in. Morality is bringing it back out in the way you live, through personal example and responsible action, ultimately toward the true community (sangha) of "all beings." This last aspect means, for me, supporting any cultural and economic revolution that moves clearly toward a truly free world. It means using such means as civil disobedience, outspoken criticism, protest, pacifism, voluntary poverty and even gentle violence if it comes to a matter of restraining some impetuous crazy. It means affirming the widest possible spectrum of nonharmful individual behavior—defending the right of individuals to smoke hemp, eat peyote, be polygamous, polyandrous or homosexual. Worlds of behavior and custom long banned by the Judaeo-Capitalist-Marxist West. It means respecting intelligence and learning, but not as greed or means to personal power. Working on one's own responsibility, but willing to work with a group. "Forming the new society within the shell of the old"— the I.W.W. slogan of seventy years ago.

The traditional, vernacular, primitive, and village cultures may appear to be doomed. We must defend and support them as we would the diversity of ecosystems; they are all manifestations of Mind. Some of the elder societies accomplished a condition of Sangha, with not a little of Buddha and Dharma as well. We touch base with the deep mind of peoples of all times and places in our meditation practice, and this is an amazing revolutionary aspect of the Buddhadharma. By a "planetary culture" I mean the kind of societies that would follow on a new understanding of that relatively recent institution, the National State, an understanding that might enable us to leave it behind. The State is disorderly, natural societies are orderly. The State is greed made legal, with a monopoly on violence; a natural society is familial and cautionary. A natural society is one which "Follows the Way," imperfectly but authentically.

Such an understanding will close the circle and link us in many ways with the most creative aspects of our archaic past. If we are lucky we may eventually arrive at a world of relatively mutually tolerant small societies attuned to their local natural region, and united overrall by a profound respect and love for the mind and nature of the universe.

I can imagine further virtues in a world sponsoring societies with matrilineal descent, free-form marriage, "natural credit" economics, far less population, and much more wilderness.

1. 1984 version, to be re-published soon. Earlier version in Gary Snyder's "Buddhism and the Coming Revolution," *Earth Household* (New York: New Directions Press, 1969).

APPENDIX H
1984
A POSTSCRIPT
George Sessions

Several philosophers concerned with ecological philosophy, beginning with John Passmore and including Richard Watson and animal rights theorist Tom Regan, have expressed concern that a "holistic" ecological ethic (such as Leopold's land ethic) results in a kind of totalitarianism or "ecological fascism." They seem to hold that any interference with, or challenge to, the Western metaphysics of the absolute reality of the discrete individual, and to the modern liberal doctrine of individual human rights, will help lead to an Orwellian totalitarian nightmare. The doctrine of the rights of human individuals stands as the only bulwark between the integrity and freedom of humans and the totalitarianism of the State.

A contemporary reading of Orwell's *1984* is not only timely, but instructive in this regard. In the closing pages of his novel, Orwell makes it plain that his supreme value is the importance of the human individual as against the power and intrusions of the State. The totalitarian State (Big Brother), however, has as its ultimate value *Power,* including total power over all human individuals. Orwell's analysis of how this power is achieved is interesting. According to Orwell, one of the major ways in which the State gains power over the individual is by defining reality. Reality becomes a totally human invention to be created and manipulated to serve the ends of the State. Language is warped into Newspeak to further create this reality. For Orwell, the danger is what he refers to as a kind of collective human *solipsism* in which reality exists strictly in our minds; the reality and independent existence of the "external" (nonhuman) world is denied. Similarly, on this totally subjective view of reality, humans are totally malleable and open to manipulation and conditioning by the social environment (in this case the totalitarian State). There is no human nature to resist total manipulation.

Like Bertrand Russell before him, Orwell thought that a crucial antidote for the dangers of this total anthropocentric subjectivity was the awareness of an objective reality which has an existence independent of the human mind. Universal solipsism is thus denied. Science describes the structure of this reality together with objective laws of nature which cannot be tampered with, or manipulated by, humans. Reality is therefore not a human invention to be manipulated and changed by the State to suit its purposes and to enslave the individual human.

Given Orwell's analysis, it seems ironic that theologian John Cobb, while admitting the role of anthropocentric Christianity in the environmental crisis, also implicated the development of modern Western philosophy. Cobb claimed that Western philosophy, beginning with Descartes and continuing with Berkeley, Hume, and Kant, to the modern phenomenologists and existentialists, resulted in a worldview that "explicitly or implicitly, presents the vision of the human mind alone with itself [solipsism]." The reality of an independently existing world is dissolved and thus cannot be an object of intrinsic value.[1] Thus in Orwell's analysis, the dominant trend of modern Western philosophy has played into the hands of the totalitarian State. But while the "hard" sciences such as physics, astronomy, geology, and biology have been helpful in providing a nonanthropocentric perspective, the dominant trend of the academic social sciences (especially psychology and sociology) have by-and-large both reinforced anthropocentrism and promoted a view of humans as being malleable and totally conditioned by the social environment.[2] To the extent to which contemporary academic philosophy remains highly specialized, narrowly language-oriented, or implicitly committed to an earlier positivist orientation, it has done little to resist or counteract this anthropocentric subjectivist world picture.

In retrospect, Orwell should have welcomed the recent studies in ethology and genetics which posit a basic human and primate nature, together with studies such as Paul Shepard's which argue for a normal psycho-genesis for humans. Would Orwell also have welcomed the emerging holistic science exemplified by the "new physics" and ecology, which sees everything as totally interrelated and which denies the absolute independence of the "individual"? Would he have recoiled from this view of reality as playing into the hands of totalitarianism or would he have embraced it as further denying the anthropocentrism of subjective solipsism? Aldous Huxley, who was equally concerned with the drift toward totalitarianism, outlived Orwell and was one of the first to recognize the dangers of human overpopulation. And, by 1960, he was advocating the ecological perspective.

It is, of course, one thing for us to recognize our ontological biological status as totally immersed in the ecological web of relationships and quite another thing to discuss totalitarian social structures and policies. It is not always obvious that the philosophers who speak of "ecological fascism" are careful to distinguish these two issues. The seriousness of the problem of human overpopulation of the planet together with its role in the destruction of natural systems and species cannot be overestimated. The challenge of stabilizing and then reducing the human population to ecologically sustainable levels by humane non-totalitarian means is one of the most crucial tasks facing humanity. All philosophers concerned with ecological philosophy need to immerse themselves in the principles of ecological science, including the study of population dynamics and the concept of "carrying capacity" and then work toward realistic non-totalitarian solutions to the problems of environmental crisis.[3] In all likelihood, this will require some kind of holistic ecological ethic in which the integrity of all individuals (human and nonhuman) is respected. The dualism between humans and the rest of Nature will need to be rejected.

Supporters of deep ecology have consistently called for decentralized, non-hierarchical, fully democratic social structures.[4] Deep ecology writings are mainly concerned with how the utmost respect for the individual can be reconciled with supportive human communities which are integrated with natural systems. Much can be learned along these lines by studying Taoism and the social structures and value systems of traditional American Indians and other primal societies.

NOTES

1. John B. Cobb, Jr., "The Population Explosion and the Rights of the Subhuman World," in R. T. Roelofs and J. N. Crowley, eds., *Environment and Society* (London: Prentice-Hall, 1974). For a discussion of Cobb's analysis, see George Sessions, "Anthropocentrism and the Environmental Crisis," *Humboldt Journal of Social Relations*, 2, 1 (Fall/Winter, 1974), pp. 71-81.

2. For criticism of modern psychology from the standpoint of self-realization, see Jacob Needleman, *A Sense of the Cosmos* (New York: Doubleday, 1975), chapter 5; Alan Watts, *Psychotherapy East and West* (New York: Random House, 1961); see also the description of Spinoza's psychology in appendix D.

3. For an excellent account of the principles of ecology and population dynamics, see G. Tyler Miller, *Living in the Environment*, 3d ed. (Wadsworth, 1983). For an account of "carrying capacity," see William Catton, *Overshoot: The Ecological Basis of Revolutionary Change* (University of Illinois Press, 1980).

4. See e.g., Val and Richard Routley, "Social Theories, Self Management and Environmental Problems," in Mannison, McRobbie, and Routley, eds., *Environmental Philosophy* (Australian National University, 1980). See also chapter 9 in this book on ecological utopias.

DEEP ECOLOGY ACTION GROUPS

There are no deep ecology groups or organizations. The following organizations and publications, however, provide information and suggestions for action which are relevant to many supporters of the deep, long range ecology movement.

• *Deep ecology contacts in Australia:*
Buddhist Peace Fellowship
P.O. Box 368
Lismore, 2480, N.S.W. Australia
Rainforest Information Centre
P.O. Box 368
Lismore, 2480, N.S.W. Australia

The Deep Ecologist
10 Alamein Avenue
Warracknabeal,
Victoria, 3393, Australia

• *Deep ecology direct action group in the United States:*
Earth First!
P.O. Box 5871
Tucson, AZ 85703

• *Environmental Publication (published by Friends of the Earth) to keep abreast of political happenings:*
Not Man Apart
1045 Sansome Street
San Francisco, CA 94111

• *Philosophical journal providing continuing intellectual debate on the development of environmental ethics and ecophilosophy:*
Environmental Ethics
Department of Philosophy
University of Georgia
Athens, GA 30602

• *Bioregional networking facilitated by Planet Drum Foundation (published by Planet Drum Foundation):*
Raise the Stakes
P.O. Box 31251
San Francisco, CA 94131

• *Regional journal (published by Northcoast Environmental Center) for Northwest California showing the interplay between reform and deep ecology:*
Econews
879 9th St.
Arcata, CA 95521

257

• *Center for Earth bonding rituals and experiential deep ecology:*
Way of the Mountain Center
P.O. Box 542
Silverton, CO 81433

• *Journal of the Environmental History Society:*
Environmental Review
Department of History
University of Denver
Denver, CO 80208-0184

• *Deep ecology contact for Japan:*
Earth First!
Chikyu Yusen
612 Kyoto-shi, Fushimi-ku
Fukakusa, Sanoyashiki-cho, 21-1
Kyoto, Japan

• *Deep ecology perspective in Canada:*
The Trumpeter
1138 Richardson St.
Victoria, B.C., Canada V8V 3C8

• *Continuing lively discussion of the post-industrial age:*
The Ecologist
Worthyvale Manor Farm
Camelford, Cornwell, PL32 9TT, United Kingdom

• *A journal devoted to helping create a cultural shift to a sustainable society:*
In Context
P.O. Box 215
Sequim, WA 98382

ANNOTATED BIBLIOGRAPHY

• Anglemyer, Mary and Seagraves, Eleanor R. *The Natural Environment: An Annotated Bibliography of Attitudes and Values.* Washington: Smithsonian Institution Press, 1984.

This is a bibliography containing 857 annotated statements. It is the most comprehensive listing of books and articles on deep ecology, ecophilosophy and environmental ethics available in the United States. Very useful for scholars and students.

• Berman, Morris. *The Reenchantment of the World.* Ithaca: Cornell, 1981.

A study of the emergence of our modern scientific consciousness and a challenge to its supremacy. Berman traces the rise of science as philosophy and political ideology. In his chapter on Isaac Newton he shows Newton to be a transitional figure, part in the world of the participatory science of the middle ages, part mechanist.

The concluding sections of the book are devoted to "tomorrow's metaphysics" and the "politics of consciousness." Berman sees Gregory Bateson's epistemology as a possible alternative to mechanism. The subject/object merger, found in ecology, has some pitfalls, according to Berman, but is the most important vision for post-modern society.

• Berry, Wendell. *The Unsettling of America.* San Francisco: Sierra Club, 1977.

An excellent critique of the exploitative industrial society and an articulate defense of small-scale organic farming and "living in place." The main shortcoming of this otherwise powerful book is that it is based on the "stewardship" model and Berry fails to reach an ecological consciousness in his lack of understanding of the importance of protecting wilderness and wild species.

• Birch, Charles, and Cobb, John B. *The Liberation of Life: From the Cell to the Community.* Cambridge: Cambridge University Press, 1983.

This is a work of extraordinary breadth. The authors are interested in nothing less than the liberation of life in both theory and practice: theory because they are concerned with invigorating the ways in which we think about life from the molecular to the cosmic level; and practice because they are urgently concerned with the liberation of social structure and human behavior that would flow from and encourage such a changed way of thinking. They maintain a graded hierarchy of value, however, and base their position on Alfred North Whitehead's process philosophy.

• Bookchin, Murray. *The Ecology of Freedom: The Emergence and Dissolution of Hierarchy.* Palo Alto, Ca.: Cheshire Books, 1982.

The most extensive statement by this seminal thinker on communalism and hierarchy. He contrasts the outlook of organic society with that of mechanical societies. "The great project of our time," he writes, "must be to open the other eye; to see all-sidedly and wholly, to heal and transcend the cleavage between humanity and nature that came with early wisdom." Bookchin's style of writing is sometimes turgid, but his analysis of communal traditions in the West shows some cultural roots to which we can turn for cultural forms neccessary for bioregional living.

• Capra, Fritjof, and Spretnak, Charlene. *Green Politics: The Global Promise.* New York: Dutton, 1984.

The German Greens see politics as only part of the transformation of consciousness. Their program is based on ecological wisdom, social responsibility, grassroots democracy, sexual equality and nonviolence. This book is both a description of the German Greens, their origins, leadership policies and strategy, and a critical assessment of the applications of Green politics to the U.S.A. and other nations. Green politics, thus far, has not clearly articulated a nonanthropocentric philosophy, but provides the most important approach to changing consciousness currently found in Western nations.

• Capra, Fritjof. *The Turning Point: Science, Society and the Rising Culture.* New York: Simon and Schuster, 1982.

Capra is a physicist who challenged conventional wisdom in *The Tao of Physics* by demonstrating the striking parallels between ancient mystical traditions and the discoveries of twentieth-century physics. In *The Turning Point,* he shows how the revolution in modern physics foreshadows an imminent revolution in all the sciences and a transformation of our worldview and values.

• Carson, Rachel. *The Sea Around Us.* New York: New American Library, 1961.

The oceans are among the most human-threatened areas of the planet. Rachel Carson's scientifically accurate and poetic book on ocean ecosystems and the human connection to them was first published in 1951, over a decade before her more famous book, *Silent Spring.* This book shows a woman naturalist's deep ecology intuition.

• Catton, William R., Jr. *Overshoot: The Ecological Basis of Revolutionary Change.* Urbana: University of Illinois Press, 1980.

The only book on this list by a sociologist. Catton presents one of the clearest expositions in print of the meaning of "carrying capacity" as applied to human populations. Catton recounts the fate of other species and population groups in circumstances which parallel our present crisis. His last chapter, "Facing the Future Wisely," presents no ecotopian vision but shows some policy changes which are necessary to deal with the predicament.

• Cohen, Michael. *The Pathless Way.* Madison: University of Wisconsin Press, 1984.

The first serious scholarly study of John Muir to clearly display his deep ecology orientation. Cohen's chapters on Muir's enlightenment and Muir's "stormy sermons" bring to life the founder of the American conservation/ecology movement.

• Colinvaux, Paul. *Why Big Fierce Animals Are Rare: An Ecologist's Perspective.* Princeton, N.J.: Princeton University Press, 1978.

While not a supporter of deep ecology, Colinvaux provides understandable explanations of the major theories of ecology— stability-change, species diversity, succession theory, ecological niches, and humanity's place on this Earth as one species among many.

• Diamond, Stanley. *In Search of the Primitive: A Critique of Civilization.* New Brunswick, N.J.: Transaction Books, 1974.

Diamond demystifies civilization and explicates *being* in primitive societies. By so doing, he has written a prolegomena for a Marxist ethnology and an existential anthropology. The first chapter on "Civilization and Progress" is a fundamental critique of civilization as based on imperialism and never-ending progress.

• Drengson, Alan. *Shifting Paradigms: From Technocrat to Planetary Person.* 1138 Richardson St., Victoria, B.C. V8W 3C8, Lightstar Press, 1983.
A Canadian philosopher provides a technical exposition of deep ecology.

• Ehrenfeld, David. *The Arrogance of Humanism.* New York: Oxford, 1978.
Humanism is the "religion of humanity," a supreme belief in our ability to rearrange the world of Nature and engineer our own future any way we see fit. Ehrenfeld, an ecologist, dissects the false assumptions of humanism and the reality of the dangerous actions of the technocrats. He calls for a union of emotion and reason and in his concluding chapter, "Beyond Humanism," makes tentative suggestions for "enduring somehow the unavoidable sadness."

• Ehrlich, Paul and Anne. *Extinction: The Causes and Consequences of the Disappearance of Species.* New York: Ballantine, 1981.
Paul Ehrlich is an ecologist and coauthor of a major textbook on *Ecoscience.* In this book, he describes the interplay of plants, animals, and lower organisms and dramatically illustrates the catastrophic consequences of humanity's interference in natural processes. The social and economic causes of the rising species extinction rate can be addressed and the concluding chapters discuss the strategies of conservation.

• Evernden, Neil. *The Natural Alien: Humankind and the Environment.* Toronto: University of Toronto Press, 1985.
The relation between mind and nature is the central concern of human ecology. Evernden draws from phenomenology and biology to present an alternative approach to that of modern science. We can see ourselves in nature. Evernden says "phenomenology requires a return to the things themselves, to a world that precedes knowledge and yet is basic to it, as countryside is to geography and blossoms to botany. This seems initially confusing, for we think of knowledge as something achieved through observation and analysis, not as something which precedes it. Yet this notion presupposes an observer who surveys the world and questions it."(p.57) Evernden suggests that the human species is a rootless, homeless "natural alien." But there is hope for this "natural alien" to develop into a mature person-in-nature.

• Fox, Stephen. *John Muir and His Legacy: The American Conservation Movement.* Boston: Little, Brown, 1981.
The first part of this book is a biography of Muir in which Fox uses previously unavailable material to show Muir's deep ecology insights. Fox then chronicles the development of the major conservation groups, highlighting the careers of the "radical amateurs" who repeatedly revitalized the movement. His last chapter on "Lord Man: The Religion of Conservation" illustrates the continuing tensions between Christians and ecologists.

• Gray, Elizabeth Dodson. *Green Paradise Lost.* Wellesley, Mass.: Roundtable Press, 1982.
Gray is a feminist, a Christian theologian, and a person who understands ecology. She provides an excellent explication of the impact of patriarchal

261

society and the domination of Nature. She calls for biocentric equality and a deep ecology perspective.

• Hughes, J. Donald. *American Indian Ecology*. El Paso: Texas Western Press, 1983.

Hughes's essay demonstrates the reverence for the land and animals of Native Americans and the kind of social structure which kept Native American societies in harmony with the rest of Nature. Hughes implies that the cosmology of Native Americans has no racial or temporal bounds but beckons to us today and provides us with inspiration and ideas for a post-modern cosmology of the "future primal mind."

• LaChapelle, Dolores. *Earth Wisdom*. Silverton, Colo.: Way of the Mountain Center (First published by Guild of Tudor Press, 1978).

LaChapelle is a climber, skier, student of Tai Chi, scholar and deep ecologist. *Earth Wisdom,* she says, is a beginning step toward restoring the lost communication with the Earth that primal peoples knew for a millenia. Part I includes particular experiences in the author's life which crystallized her feelings toward the Earth and led to an intuitive understanding of the relationship of mountains and mind in the beginnings of modern religions. Part II investigates the nature and boundaries of mind in relation to Nature as a whole. Part III delineates the practical results of healing the split between human consciousness and Nature. Part IV provides immediate help for those who want to live as Nature intended us to live.

• Leopold, Aldo. *Sand County Almanac*. New York: Oxford, 1968.

This environmental classic, first published in 1949, includes Leopold's essays on his own experiences in wilderness and the importance of land health and ecological diversity. Essays include poetic recounts of his experiences in the American southwest, Mexico, and the sand counties of Wisconsin. In the foreword he wrote, "There are some who can live without wild things, and some who cannot. These essays are the delights and dilemmas of one who cannot." It concludes with his famous statement of the "land ethic."

• Miller, George Tyler. *Living in the Environment,* 3d ed. Belmont, Calif.: Wadsworth, 1983.

This is written as a textbook with chapters on human population dynamics, resources, pollution, human impact on the Earth, major concepts of ecology, and economics. The concluding section, on ethics, includes a discussion of "earthmanship" and deep ecology, but Miller, perhaps unwittingly, also calls for a "balanced approach of resource use and preservation based on wise stewardship."

• Nash, Roderick. *Wilderness and the American Mind,* 3d ed. New Haven, Conn.: Yale University Press, 1982.

This is the most thorough review of changing perceptions and understandings of ecological diversity and wilderness in the context of the European invasion of North America. This edition includes chapters on the philosophy of wilderness, the irony of victory in official wilderness designation, and the international perspective. Nash does not articulate deep ecology in his chapter on philosophy, but it is there in the chapters on Muir, Thoreau and Leopold.

• Roszak, Theodore. *Where the Wasteland Ends: Politics and Transcendence in Postindustrial Society.* Garden City, N.Y.: Anchor/Doubleday, 1973.

Probably the most interesting book on the "single vision" of modern science and the uses and abuses of technology. Roszak's critique of the "citadel of expertise" is mandatory reading for those entering the professions of engineering, forestry, wildlife management, etc. He concludes with chapters on the *rhapsodic intellect* — resonance and literalism in modern intellectual circles — *the visionary commonwealth* for ecotopia, and a wonderful chapter calling for a Taoist anarchism.

• _____. *Person/Planet: The Creative Disintegration of Industrial Society.* Garden City, New York: Anchor/Doubleday, 1978.

Roszak asserts that "the needs of the person are the needs of the planet." He links the realization of personhood and saving ecological diversity to liberation from the large-scale bureaucracies which dominate our lives. He offers practical advice for home, school, work, religion, and farming. He especially addresses the responsibility of intellectuals and the politics of transformation of large-scale cities into economies of permanence.

• Sale, Kirkpatrick. *Dwellers In The Land: The Bioregional Vision.* San Francisco: Sierra Club Books, 1985.

Although Sale does not discuss one of the key elements of the bioregional vision — namely spiritual sense-of-place — he provides an excellent introduction to the politics, history and economy of the bioregional vision. The text is readable, written for a general, not just academic, audience, and the reader is invited to participate in the growth of his or her own bioregional vision.

• Shepard, Paul. *The Tender Carnivore and the Sacred Game.* New York: Scribners, 1973.

Shepard discusses the hunter/gatherer traditions and the "ten thousand year environmental crisis." His provocative essay on ritual and the "karma of adolescence" foreshadows his more theoretical treatment in *Nature and Madness.* In the concluding section Shepard proposes a "cynegetic society" as his ecotopian vision.

• _____. *Nature and Madness.* San Francisco: Sierra Club Books, 1982.

Shepard suggests we have overlooked something important in our analysis of the continuing crisis of the environment — the development of the human person. Drawing upon a diverse body of literature dealing with broad historical time frames, Shepard links the process of human development as genetically programmed with the changes in Western culture during the last ten thousand years. He interprets development literature to mean that each human must go through a certain sequence of phases during the life cycle. Some cultures facilitate this process, some do not. Contemporary Western cultures leave most people stuck in early adolescence all their lives — a phase marked by intense emotion, a "masculine" rather than "feminine" orientation and rapid alternations between regressive infantile behavior and bold, aggressive behavior that is pseudo-mature. Many environmental problems can be solved if we let people proceed through their natural ontogeny into adulthood and maturity.

263

• Snyder, Gary. *Turtle Island.* New York: New Directions, 1974.

Winner of the Pulitzer Prize for poetry, Snyder, in this collection of poems and essays, says Turtle Island is "the old/new name for the continent, based on many creation myths of the people who have been here for millennia, and reapplied by some of them to 'North America' in recent years." A tentative cross-fertilization of ecological thought with Buddhist ideas is suggested. The book concludes with Snyder's deep ecological manifesto written in 1969, "Four 'Changes.'"

• _____. *The Old Ways.* San Francisco: City Light Books, 1977.

Dedicated to the memory of Alan Watts, this slim volume contains six essays, including Snyder's statement on bioregional reinhabitation and "the incredible survival of coyote."

• _____. *The Real Work: Interviews and Talks: 1964-1979.* New York: New Directions, 1980.

A collection of talks and interviews dealing with most of the major topics of deep ecology, including the problem of ego in modern societies, bioregionalism, and right livelihood. It also discusses the influence of Native American religion and Buddhism on Snyder's work and his emerging ecological consciousness, and the "real work" of working on our selves.

• Worster, Donald. *Nature's Economy: The Roots of Ecology.* San Francisco: Sierra Club Books, 1977.

Worster traces the origin of the metaphor of ecology as "nature's economy," and discusses the thinkers who have shaped ecology as a science and how it in turn has shaped the modern perception of our place in the scheme of things. Beginning with English parson Gilbert White, he includes chapters on Darwin, Thoreau, Frederic Clements, Aldo Leopold and Eugene Odum. Worster concludes with a chapter on the relation between ecology as science and ecophilosophy.

ACKNOWLEDGEMENTS
AND CREDITS

Material for chapters in this book was drawn from papers and articles published in the following journals and texts:

George Sessions, "Ecological consciousness and Paradigm Change," *Deep Ecology: An Anthology,* edited by Michael Tobias (San Diego: Avant Books, 1985).

George Sessions, review of Henryk Skolimowski's *Eco-Philosophy* in *Environmental Ethics* 6, 2 (1984).

William Devall and George Sessions, "The Development of Natural Resources and the Integrity of Nature: Contrasting Views of Management," *Environmental Ethics* 6, 4 (Winter 1984).

George Sessions, "Ecophilosophy, Utopias and Education," *Journal of Environmental Education* 115, 1 (Fall 1983).

William Devall, "John Muir as Deep Ecologist," *Environmental Review* 6, 1 (1982).

William Devall, "Ecological Consciousness and Ecological Resisting: Guidelines for Comprehension and Research," *Humboldt Journal of Social Relations* 9, 2 (Spring 1982).

George Sessions, review of C. Bonifazi's *The Soul of the World* in *Environmental Ethics* 3, 3 (1981).

William Devall, review of Stephen Fox's *John Muir and His Legacy* in *Humboldt Journal of Social Relations* 9, 1 (Fall 1981).

George Sessions, "Shallow and Deep Ecology: A Review of the Philosophical Literature," *Ecological Consciousness: Essays from the Earth Day X Colloquium,* University of Denver, April 1980, edited by Robert C. Schultz and J. Donald Hughes (Washington, D.C.: University Press of America, 1981).

William Devall, "The Deep Ecology Movement," *Natural Resources Journal* 20, 1 (April 1980).

William Devall, "Reformist Environmentalism," *Humboldt Journal of Social Relations* 6, 2 (Spring 1979).

George Sessions, "Spinoza, Perennial Philosophy, and Deep Ecology," Reminding Conference (Unpublished, San Raphael, Ca., 1979).

George Sessions, "Spinoza and Jeffers on Man in Nature," *Inquiry* 20, 4 (Oslo, 1977).

George Sessions, "Anthropocentrism and the Environmental Crisis," *Humboldt Journal of Social Relations* 2, 1 (Fall, 1974).

George Sessions, "Panpsychism vs. Modern Materialism: Some Implications for an Ecological Ethic," Conference on the Rights of Non-Human Nature (Unpublished, Pitzer College, Claremont, Ca., 1974).

Permission to use copyright materials is hereby gratefully acknowledged:

Denise Levertov, "Candles in Babylon." Copyright © 1982 by Denise Levertov. Reprinted by permission of New Directions.

Gary Snyder, selection from *Earth House Hold*. Copyright © 1969 by Gary Snyder. Reprinted by permission of New Directions.

Gary Snyder, selections from *Turtle Island*. Copyright © 1974 by Gary Snyder. Reprinted by permission of New Directions.

Gary Snyder, selections from *Regarding Wave*. Copyright © 1976 by Gary Snyder. "Song of the Taste" was first published in *Poetry*. Reprinted by permission of New Directions.

Barry Commoner, from *The Closing Circle: Nature, Man and Technology*. Copyright © 1971 by Barry Commoner. Reprinted by permission of Alfred A. Knopf, Inc. Portions of the book originally appeared in *The New Yorker*.

Alan Watts, from *Nature, Man and Woman*. Copyright © 1958 by Pantheon Books, Inc. Reprinted by permission of the publisher.

Robinson Jeffers, "The Answer," "Oh, Lovely Rock," copyright © 1937 and renewed 1965 by Donnan Jeffers and Garth Jeffers. Reprinted from *The Selected Poetry of Robinson Jeffers,* by permission of Random House, Inc.

Vincent Rossi, "Christian Environmental Action Program." Reprinted by permission of Vincent Rossi.

Neil Evernden, "Self, Place and the Pathetic Fallacy." Copyright © 1978 by *North American Review*. Reprinted by permission of *North American Review*.

David Brower, "The Condor and a Sense of Place," from *The Condor Question*. Copyright © 1981. Reprinted by permission of Friends of the Earth.

Rainer Maria Rilke, "Letters to a Young Poet." Translated by M. D. Hester Norton; reprinted by permission of W. W. Norton and Co., Inc. Copyright © 1934 by W. W. Norton and Co., Inc. Copyright renewed © 1962 by M. D. Hester Norton. Revised Edition Copyright © 1954 by W. W. Norton and Co., Inc.

Dolores LaChapelle, "Ritual is Essential." Copyright © 1984 by Dolores LaChapelle. This essay was first published in *In Context,* No. 5, Spring, 1984, P.O. Box 215, Sequim, Wa. 98382. Reprinted by permission of Dolores LaChapelle.

Gray Brechin, "The Spirit of Mono Lake," from the *Mono Lake Handbook*. Reprinted by permission of the Mono Lake Committee, Lee Vining, California.

J. Donald Hughes, excerpts from *American Indian Ecology.* Copyright © 1983, Texas Western Press. Reprinted by permission of J. Donald Hughes.

Thomas Early, "Recovering Our Roots," "Better to Keep Your Country Small." Copyright © 1983 by Thomas Early. Reprinted by permission of Thomas Early.

Alan Gussow, "A Sense of Place," from *A Sense of Place.* Copyright © 1971 by Friends of the Earth. Reprinted by permission of Friends of the Earth.

Michael Zimmerman, "Toward a Heideggerean Ethos for Radical Environmentalism." This article first appeared in *Environmental Ethics* 5, 2, Summer, 1983. Reprinted by permission of Michael Zimmerman.

"Where You At? A Bioregional Test." This article first appeared in *CoEvolution Quarterly,* No. 32, Winter, 1981. Reprinted by permission of Jim Dodge.

Carolyn Merchant, "Feminism and Ecology." First published in *Environment* 23, 5, June, 1981. Reprinted by permission of Carolyn Merchant.

Arne Naess, selections from interview in *The Ten Directions,* Zen Center of Los Angeles, Summer, 1981. Reprinted by permission of Arne Naess.

Peter Berg, Editorial on the need for radical change. Copyright © 1984 by Planet Drum Foundation, San Francisco, California. Reprinted by permission of Planet Drum Foundation.

Tom Berry, comments on Teilhard de Chardin. First published in *Teilhardian Studies,* 1984. Reprinted by permission of Tom Berry.

Jack Forbes, "The Native American Experience in California History." Copyright © 1971 by *California Historical Quarterly.* Reprinted by permission of Jack Forbes.

Robert Aitken Roshi, "Ghandi, Dōgen and Deep Ecology." This revised version was first published in *The Mind of Clover.* Copyright © 1984 by North Point Press, Berkeley, California. Reprinted by permission.

Bob Steuding, selection from *Gary Snyder.* Copyright © 1976 and reprinted with the permission of Twayne Publishers, a division of G. K. Hall & Co., Boston.

Rachael Carson, *The Sense of Wonder* Copyright © 1956 by Rachael Carson. Reprinted by permission of Harper & Row.